岸本斉史

Oh man, it's spring! I always get sleepy in spring... I'm just sleepy... so slee... ...zzz.

—Masashi Kishimoto, 2004

Author/artist Masashi Kishimoto was born in 1974 in rural Okayama Prefecture, Japan. After spending time in art college, he won the Hop Step Award for new manga artists with his manga **Karakuri** (Mechanism). Kishimoto decided to base his next story on traditional Japanese culture. His first version of **Naruto**, drawn in 1997, was a one-shot story about fox spirits; his final version, which debuted in **Weekly Shonen Jump** in 1999, quickly became the most popular ninja manga in Japan.

NARUTO
3-in-1 Edition
Volume 8
SHONEN JUMP Manga Omnibus Edition
A compilation of the graphic novel volumes 22–24

STORY AND ART BY MASASHI KISHIMOTO

Translation & English Adaptation/Mari Morimoto, Kyoko Shapiro, HC Language Solutions, Inc., Joe Yamazaki
English Adaptation/Mari Morimoto, Ian Reid, HC Language Solutions, Noami Kokubo, Eric-Jon Rössel Waugh
Touch-up Art & Lettering/James Gaubatz, Gia Cam Luc
Design/Yvonne Cai (Original Series)
Design/Sam Elzway (Omnibus Edition)
Editor/Joel Enos (Manga Edition)
Managing Editor/Erica Yee (Omnibus Edition)

Printed in Canada

Published by VIZ Media, LLC
P.O. Box 77010
San Francisco, CA 94107

10 9 8 7 6 5
Omnibus edition first printing, May 2014
Fifth printing, April 2022

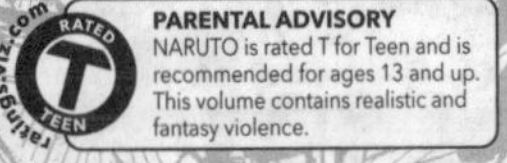

SHONEN JUMP MANGA EDITION

NARUTO

VOL. 22
COMRADES

STORY AND ART BY
MASASHI KISHIMOTO

CHARACTERS
Sasuke
サスケ
Naruto
ナルト
Sakura
サクラ
Shikamaru
奈良シカマル
Kiba &
Akamaru
犬塚キバ&赤丸
Neji
日向ネジ
Choji
秋道チョウジ
The Sound Ninja Four
音の四人衆
Sakon
左近
Jirobo
次郎坊
Tayuya
多由也
Kidomaru
鬼童丸

The Story So Far…

Twelve years ago, a destructive nine-tailed fox spirit attacked the ninja village of Konohagakure. The Hokage, or village champion, defeated the fox by sealing its soul into the body of a baby boy. Now that boy, Uzumaki Naruto, has grown up to become a ninja-in-training, learning the art of ninjutsu with his teammates Sakura and Sasuke. During the Second Chûnin Exam, Naruto and the others were attacked by Orochimaru, who left a curse mark on Sasuke and vanished…

Naruto and Sasuke proceeded to the Chûnin Exam Finals, but in the middle of the Sasuke vs. Gaara battle, Orochimaru and company launch *Operation Destroy Konoha*, which was stopped when the Third Hokage sacrificed his own life.

Sasuke, healed by Tsunade, who has become the Fifth Hokage, leaves Konoha Village with the Sound Ninja Four… The quintet of Shikamaru, Naruto, Choji, Kiba, and Neji hastily set out after them…!

NARUTO

VOL. 22
COMRADES

CONTENTS

Number 191: Comrades...!!

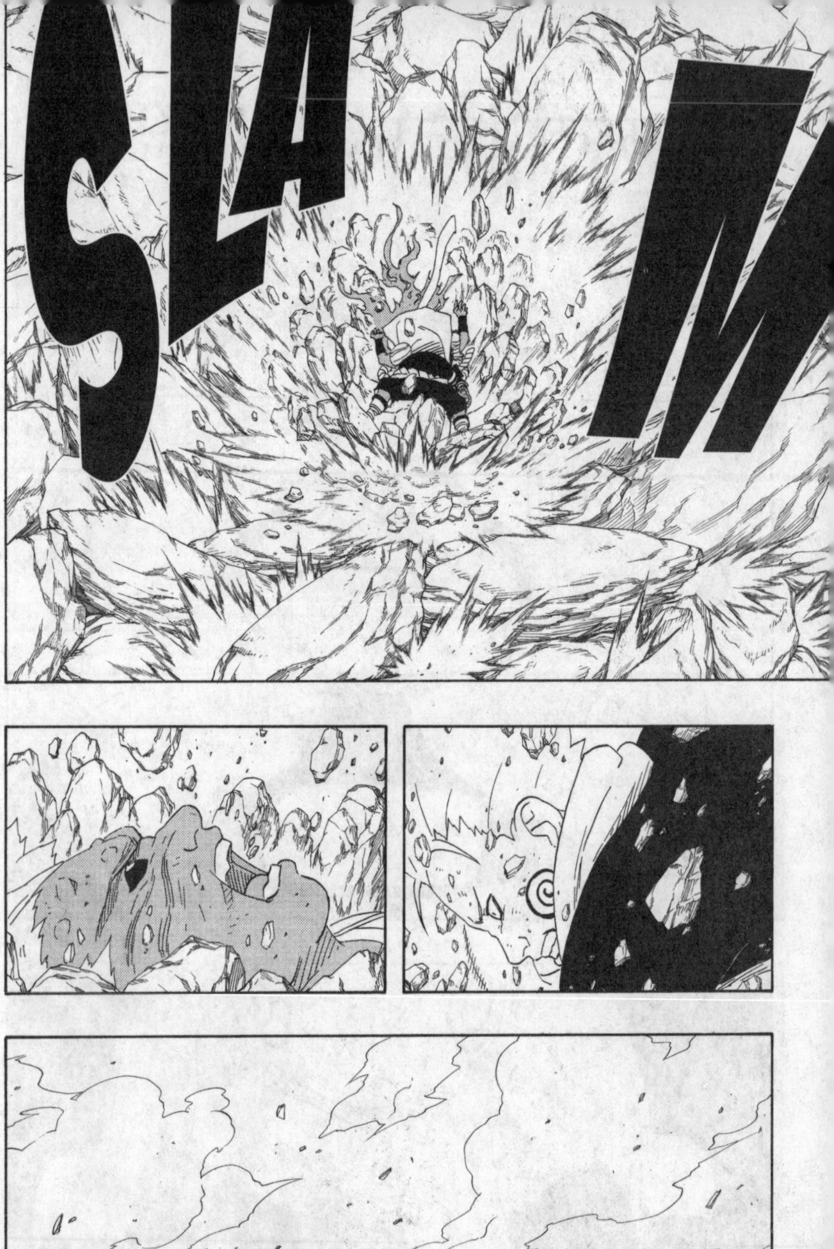

SLAM

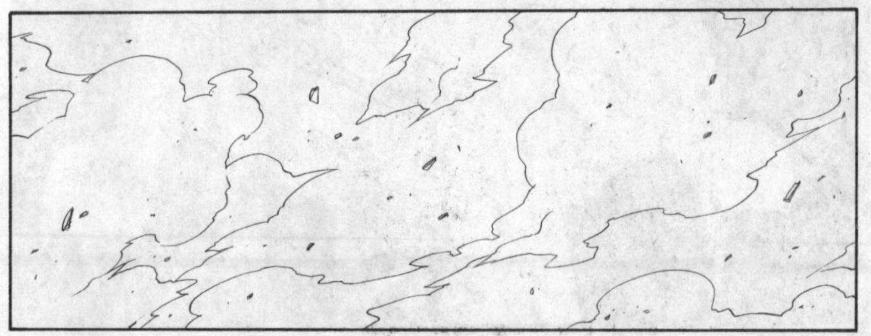

READ THIS WAY

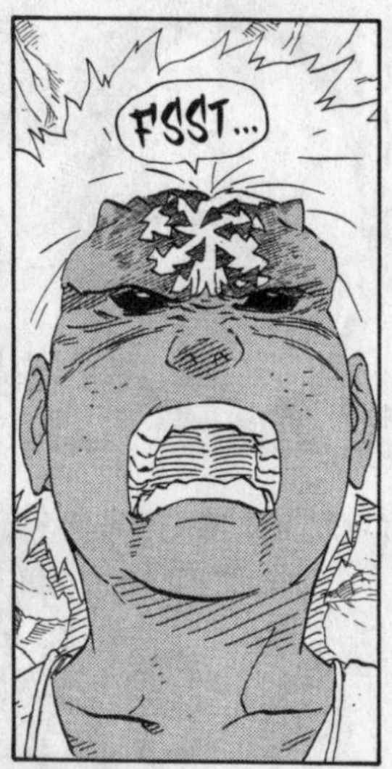

HUF
I WON...
HUF
I DID IT... I ACTUALLY WON!
HUF

UGH...!
UNNH...

HEY, YOU...
HUF
HUF
HUF HUF

HUF
HUF
HUF

...!
HUF
HUF

...

READ THIS WAY

SOONER OR LATER YOU'LL FIND A FRIEND WHO SEES THAT IN YOU.
WHEN THAT HAPPENS, YOU TREASURE THAT FRIEND.

SNIFF..

AH, CHOJI. YOU'RE A SWEET BOY. SWEETER THAN ANYBODY....

BECOME COMRADES, AND HAVE FAITH IN EACH OTHER.

PITTER...

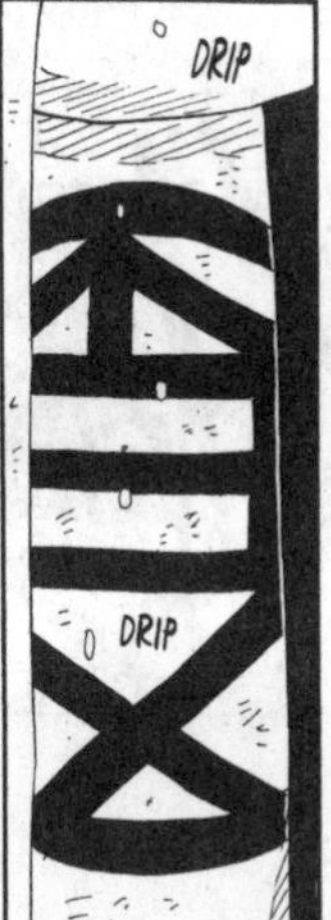
DRIP
DRIP

PA...

...

...I'VE GOT...

...LOTS OF COMRADES NOW...

READ THIS WAY

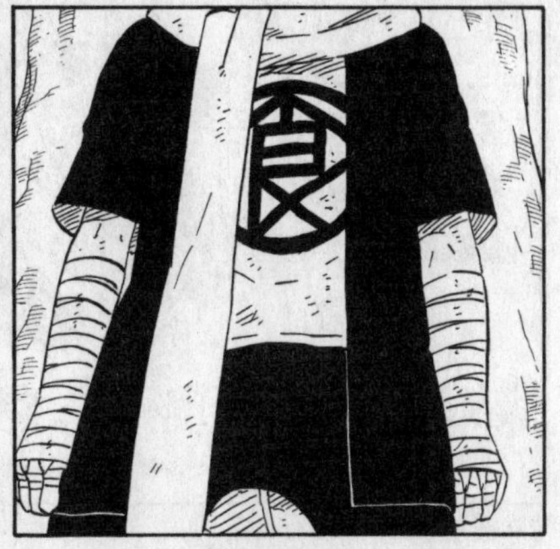

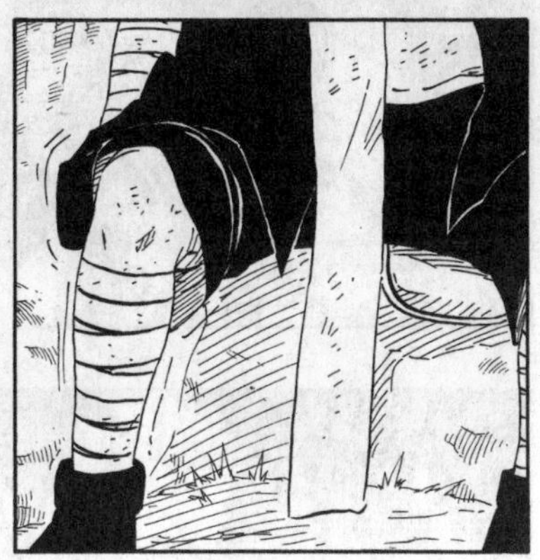

READ
THIS
WAY

!
WHAT'S UP?

...

...

NOTHING...

TOMP

WHOOSH

WE'RE CLOSE!
SNIFF SNIFF
SNIFF

THEY'VE UNDER-ESTIMATED US!

...THAT'S ODD.
THEY HAVEN'T LAID A SINGLE TRAP DOWN SINCE THEN...
SHIKA-MARU... WHAT DO YOU THINK'S GOING ON?

THEY THINK MR. HEFTY'S THE ONLY ONE WHO'S GOING TO BE CATCHING UP WITH THEM.
NO ONE LAYS TRAPS AGAINST THEIR ALLIES.

GAH!
HOW DARE THEY!!

READ THIS WAY

TOTALLY...
...THEY DON'T THINK WE CAN DO IT.
BUT... THIS GIVES US THE PERFECT CHANCE, TOO.

YUP...
...TO STRIKE!

VOOSH
WHOOSH

THAT IDIOT JIROBO... LATE AGAIN.

...NOPE... HERE HE IS...

WHOOSH

WHAT TOOK SO LONG, MAN?

FWOOSH
FWOOSH
SORRY ...
I WAS DRAINING THEM LOSERS' CHAKRA.

HEY FATSO, WE DON'T HAVE TIME TO FART AROUND!
CARRY THE CASKET!
BE USEFUL FOR ONCE!!

OK...

...
...?

READ THIS WAY

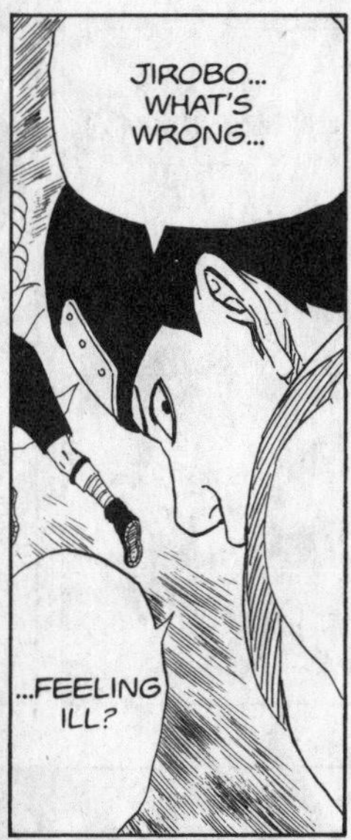

MY TURN, THIS TIME!
URGH
SAKON, TAYUYA, YOU GO ON AHEAD!

HMPH...
FAP

WHAPP

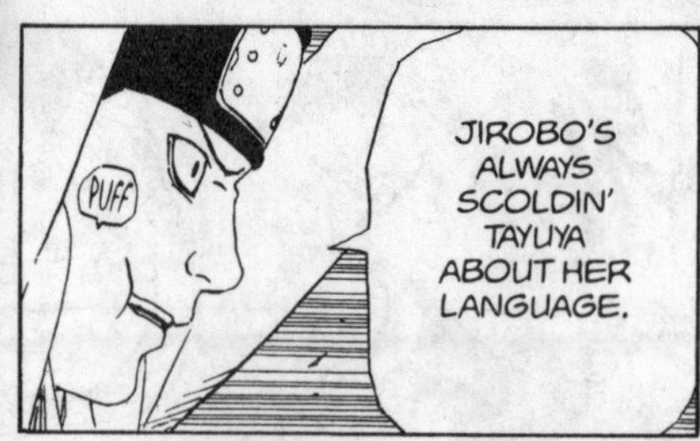
JIROBO'S ALWAYS SCOLDIN' TAYUYA ABOUT HER LANGUAGE.
PUFF

BOOF
I SEE...

NINJA ART: KUMO-SHIBARI! SPIDER WEB NET!!
SPOO
!!
SLAM
UGH!

SWISH
KONK
KONK

!!
TAK
C'MON!
PFFT

!!
WHOA!
UGH!
BOING
NOW, KIBA! AKA-MARU!
HE CAN'T DODGE YOU MIDAIR!!
TUMP
TUMP

NINJA ART: KUMO-SOKAI! SPIRAL WEB!!
FSSSH
!!
GATSUUGA! FANG OVER FANG!!

POP

SHEESH, WHAT'S FATSO UP TO?!

VWHOOOOSH

I KNEW IT WAS A MISTAKE TO LEAVE OUR WEAKEST BEHIND...

GAH!!

SHOOOOF

YOU WON'T GET AWAY!!

THAT'S MY LINE.

LOOK DOWN!

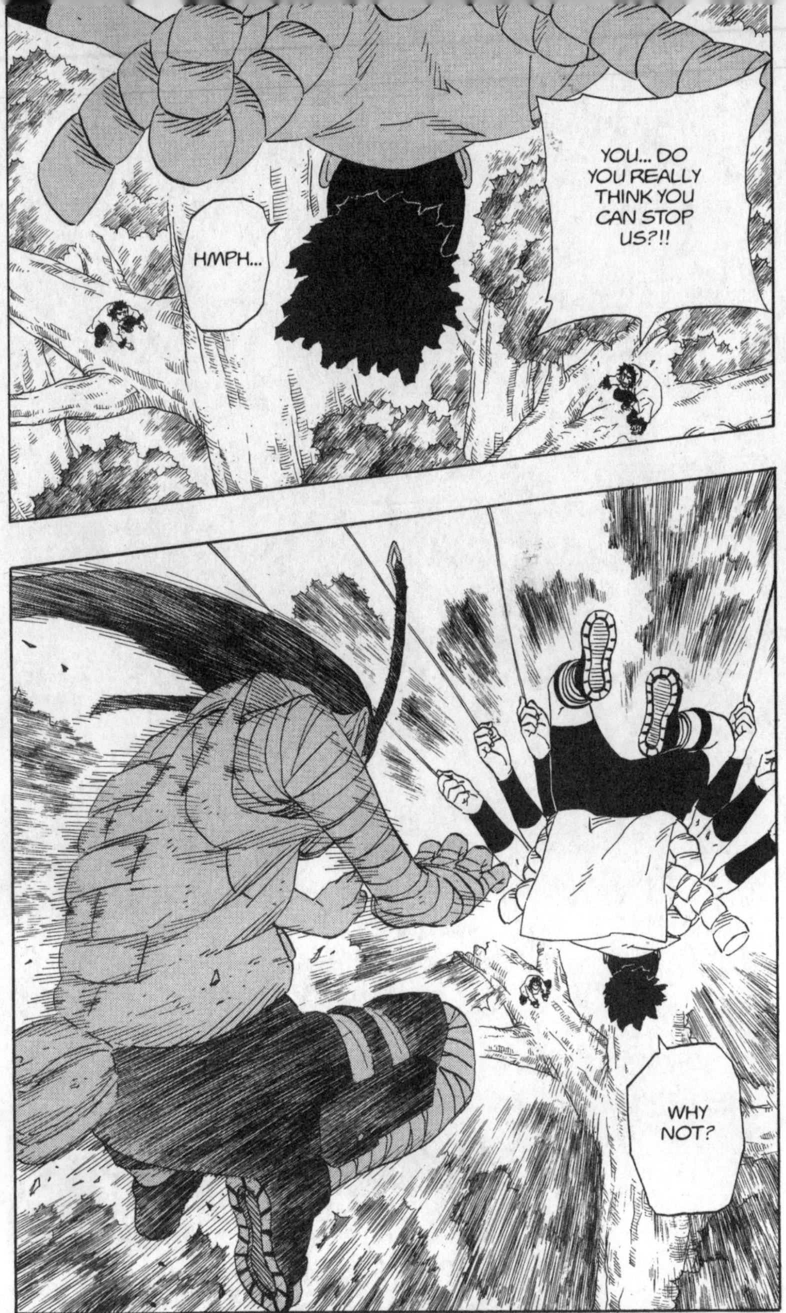
YOU... DO YOU REALLY THINK YOU CAN STOP US?!!
HMPH...
WHY NOT?

NARUTO
TM

Number 192: The Plan...!!

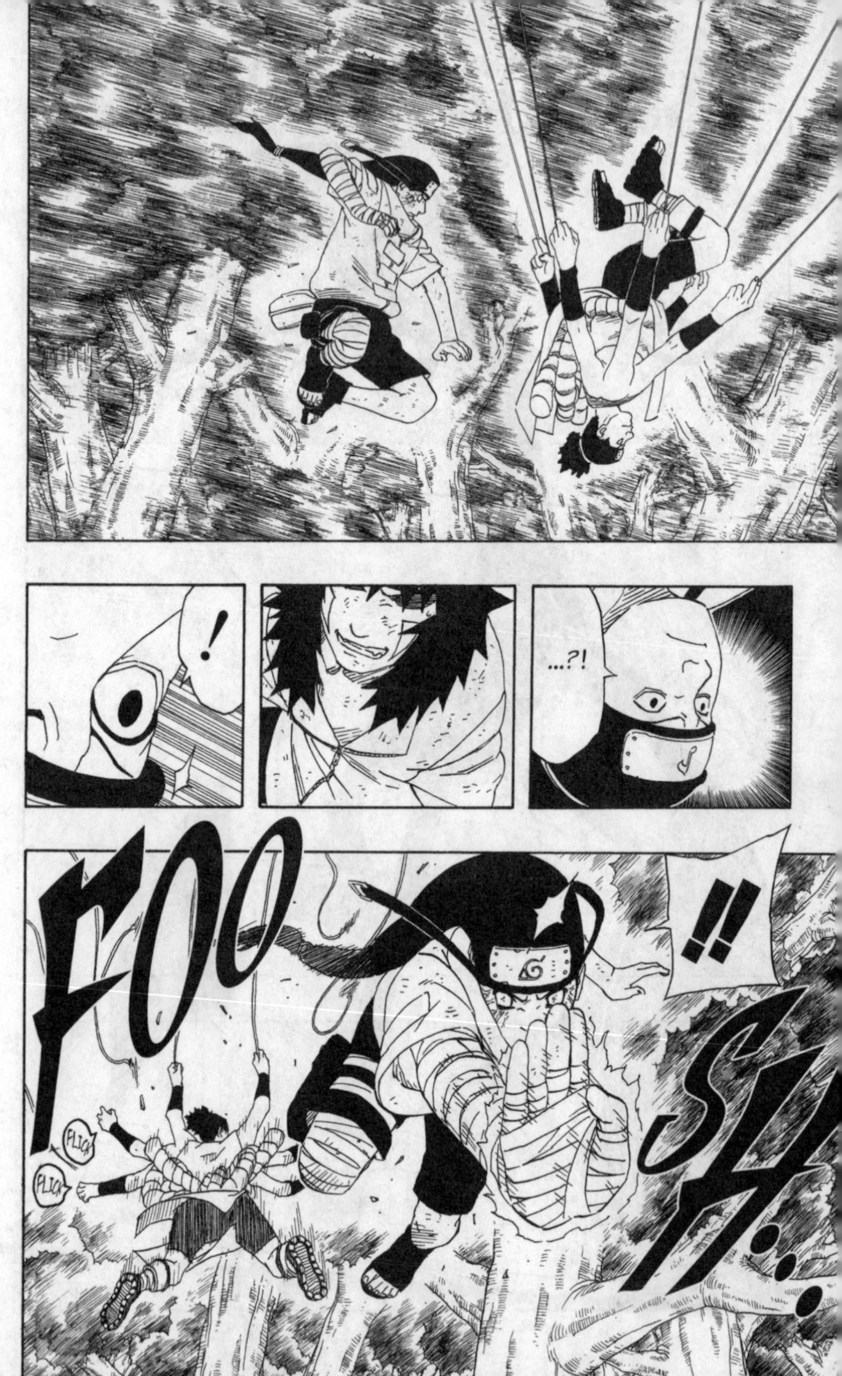

...?!
!
!!
FLICK
FLICK
FOO
SH...

READ THIS WAY

HEH...
WHIRL

!

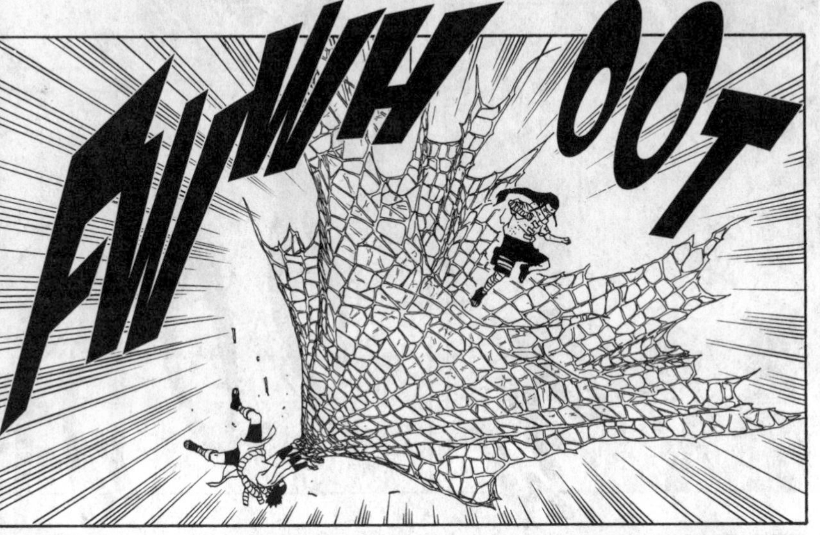
FWWHOOT

!

WHAT?!

ME, NARUTO, KIBA, NEJI...
EVEN THIS MUCH PLANNING'S NOT ENOUGH, HUH...

WHIIINE
BOOF...

SHOOOOO
UGH!
SHOOP
SHIP SHIP
ONE COCOON, COMING RIGHT UP!
TA-DAA
PLUNK
AGH!
KLAK
SCRAPE
WONG

READ THIS WAY

UGH! WHAT'S UP WITH THESE STRANDS?!
CAN'T CUT 'EM!

MY SPIDER THREADS ARE SO STRONG...
...EVEN TWO ELEPHANTS PULLING TOGETHER CAN'T SNAP 'EM.
SLITHER...

...

HUH... SHADOW DOPPEL-GANGERS, HOW INTER-ESTING.

GRR...
PUFF

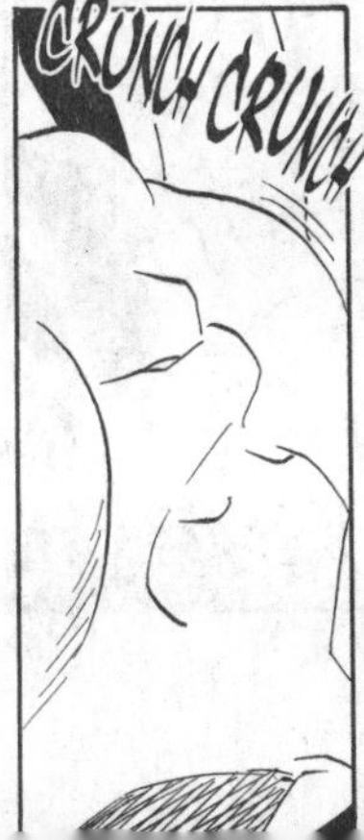
CRUNCH CRUNCH

THESE STRANDS HAVE A MIND OF THEIR OWN...
...SO STICKY... A MIX OF SPIT AND CHAKRA...

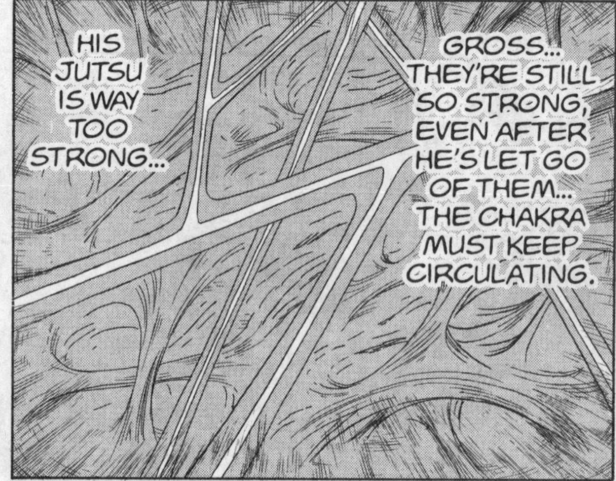
GROSS... THEY'RE STILL SO STRONG, EVEN AFTER HE'S LET GO OF THEM... THE CHAKRA MUST KEEP CIRCULATING.
HIS JUTSU IS WAY TOO STRONG...

...
HMM...

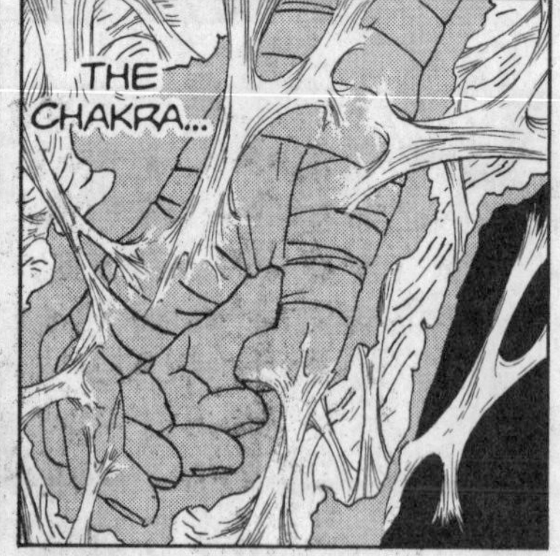
THE CHAKRA...

TAP
TAP

CHOMP
CHOMP
SNIK
SNIK
SNIK
SNIK
FSSSHT
STICKY SPIDER WEB!
SNAP
DIFFERENT COLORED STRANDS THAN BEFORE?!
WHAT ARE YOU PLANNING?
!

PLINK

!
THEY'RE STRONG!

HEH... YOU'RE THE FIRST TO GO, SO I'M GOING TO HAVE ME SOME FUN!
PLINK!

LET'S PLAY ***WHO'S THE REAL BRAT?***

UGH!
FIRST CONTESTANT, THE OUTERMOST!
FWISH
GRR...!
!
CHAK
!

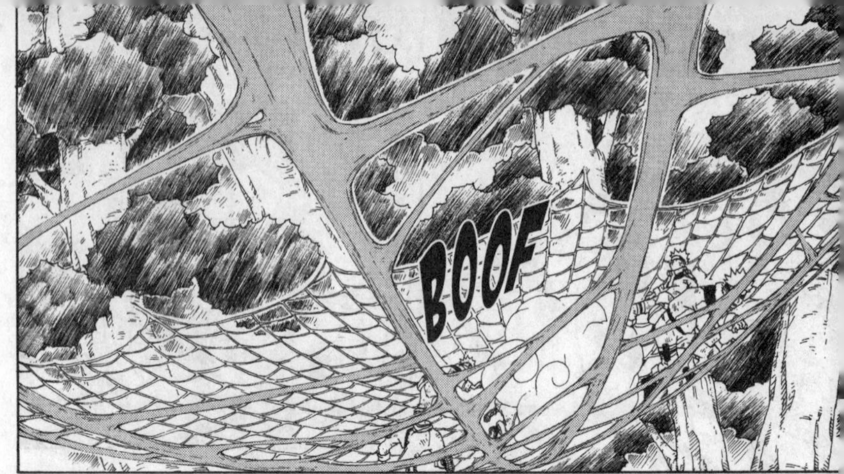
BOOF

SHUP
HUMPH... A DOPPEL-GANGER.
WELL THEN...
FWISH
HOW ABOUT THAT ONE!!
CHOK
ARGH!!
BOOF

HEH HEH...
YOU ARE
SO LUCKY.
FWISH FWISH
ALL RIGHT,
THIS TIME,
TWO AT
ONCE!
I'VE GOT
A 50
PERCENT
CHANCE!!
CHOK CHOK
BOOF BOOF
UGH...

SWISH
CHOK
ARGH!!
...!
...!!
ARF... ARF!
A-HAHAHA, WHAT LUCK!
WE'RE DOWN TO TWO!!

READ THIS WAY

CHOK

WHAT?!!

SCREECH
HUH!

FFFT
FFFT

BOOM

FWOO

TWANG

NOW I SEE... HE WAS BIDING HIS TIME WITH DOPPEL-GANGERS.

I CAN'T BELIEVE A SCUMBAG LIKE HIM PLANNED SOMETHING THIS COMPLICATED...

NOT BAD... BUT...

!

!!!

WHAT?!

THANKS FOR BUYING ME TIME, NARUTO.
FAP

TAP

THIS GUY'S JUTSU... I THINK I'M THE ONLY ONE WHO CAN HANDLE THEM.

SNAP

YOU... HOW DIDJA...?!

CHAKRA-BUILT SUBSTANCES...
...DON'T STAND A CHANCE AGAINST GENTLE FIST TECHNIQUES!
ARF!
ARF!

GO...
I'LL TAKE HIM.

NARUTO
TM

Number 193: Game Over

...
KIK
KIK

WHIIINE
HM
HM

...HE SAYS THIS GUY'S TOUGHER THAN THE BIG GUY EARLIER.
A LOT TOUGHER...

...

WE HAVE TO GO ONE-ON-ONE.
THAT'S WHAT WE DISCUSSED...
...

...YEAH.
THAT'S RIGHT.

...

BESIDES ...
...!

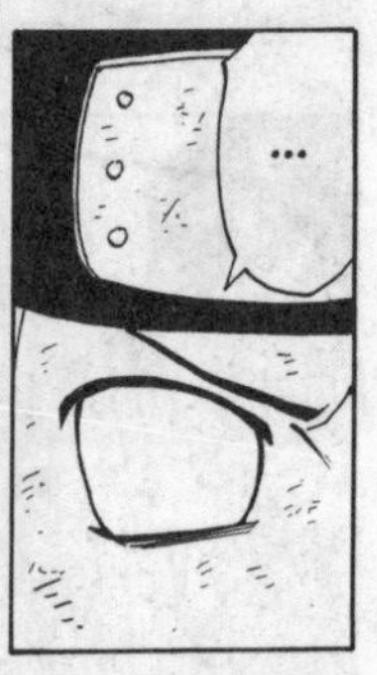

YOU'VE GOT
BETTER
SIGHT
THAN I DO.

READ THIS WAY

?

RIGHT NOW, SASUKE...
TAP

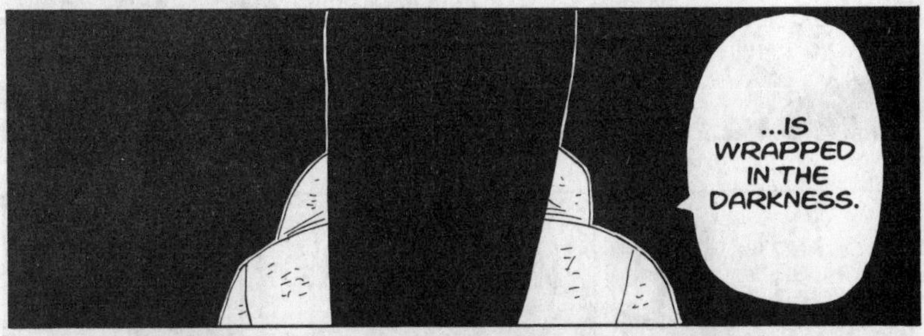
...IS WRAPPED IN THE DARKNESS.

...

NOW GO!
I'LL CATCH UP TO YOU LATER, TOO!!

YUP!

HUMPH... YOU AIN'T GETTING AWAY!
FWIP
FWSH
GRRRRR
BYAKUGAN!

WHOOOSH...
THWAP
ZIP
!
ZIP
!
BUZZ
BUZZ
!!
BA-DMP

WHAP
WHAP
WHAP
WHAP

READ THIS WAY

HEH HEH... WELL...
NEVER MIND.

SO YOU'RE THE STRONGEST...
...OF THE BUNCH, HUH.

SHEESH... YOU'RE MAKING ME WANT TO PLAY EVEN MORE.
GOTTA TAKE THE GAME SLOW, YOU KNOW.
OR ELSE IT'S NOT AS MUCH FUN...

FIRST, I NEED AT LEAST THREE MINUTES TO TOY WITH YOU BEFORE YOU DIE!

BYAKU-GAN!

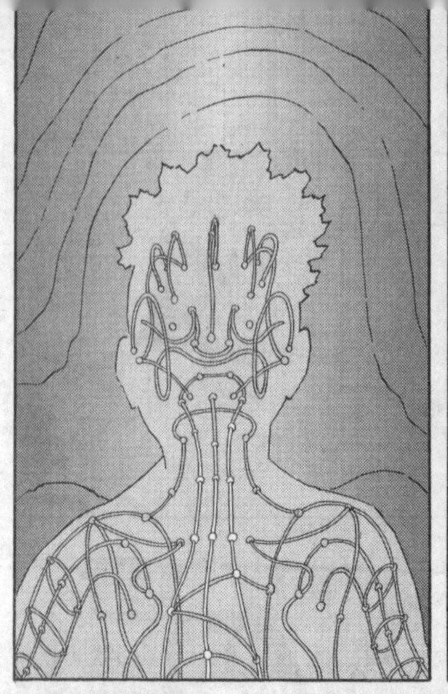
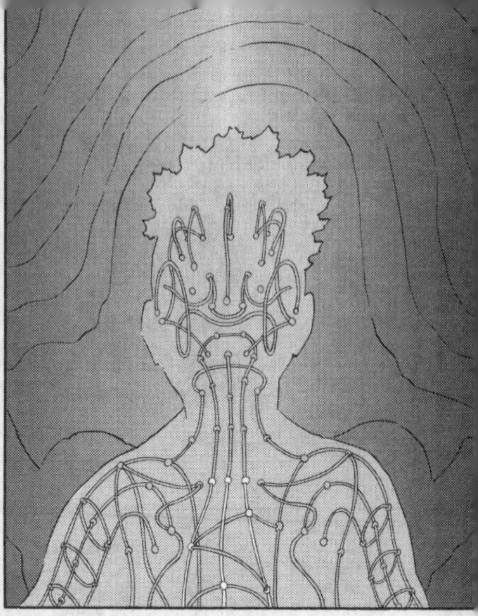

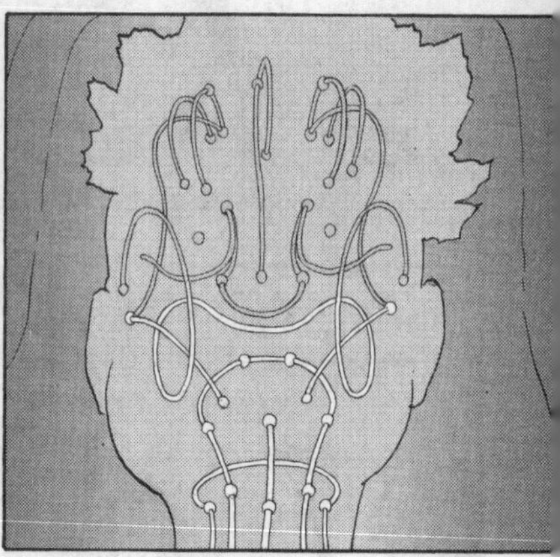

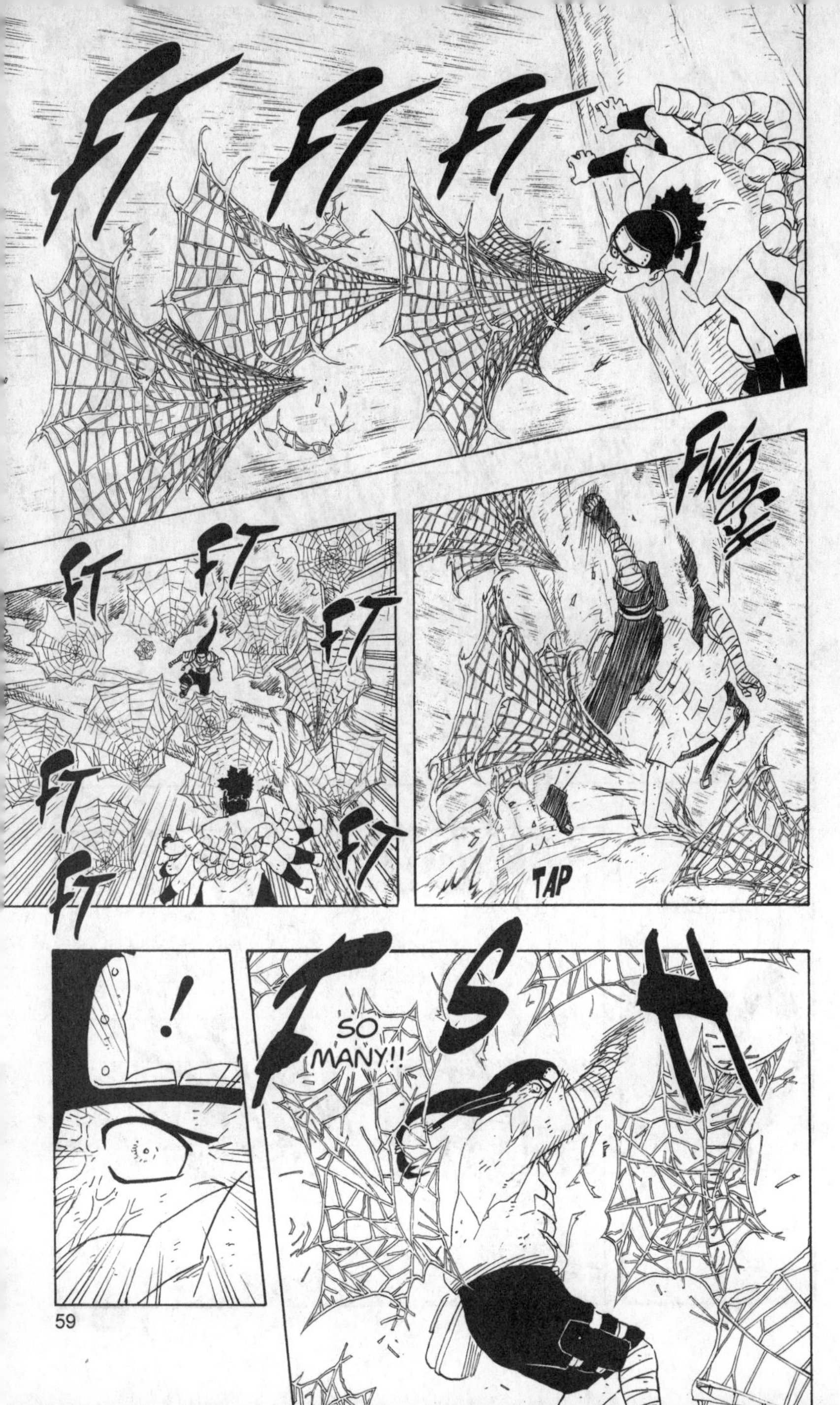
FT FT FT
FWOOSH
FT
FT
FT
FT
FT
FT
TAP
!
FTSH
SO MANY!!

!
SWHOOSH
WHAP WAP WAP WAP WAP
WHUMP
KLUNNK
KLUNNK
HUMPH... GOTCHA!

READ THIS WAY

GRRR...
UGH...

YOU'RE GOOD WITH CHAKRA.
YA GOT SHARP EYES...

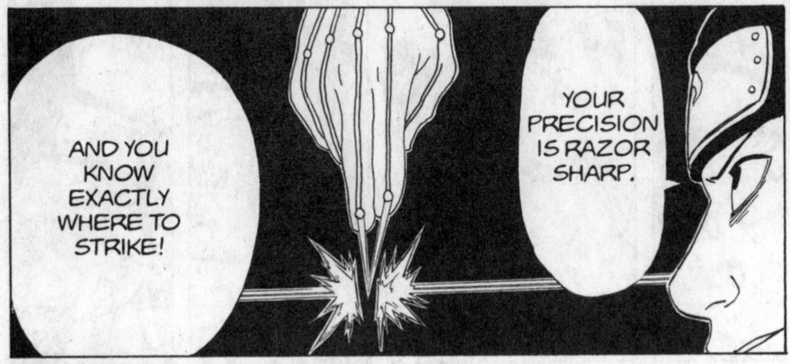
YOUR PRECISION IS RAZOR SHARP.
AND YOU KNOW EXACTLY WHERE TO STRIKE!

HUMPH...
LORD OROCHI-MARU WARNED ME.
GENTLE FIST, HUH...

IF YOU CAN'T MOVE YOUR ARMS...
...YOU WON'T SEVER MY THREADS!

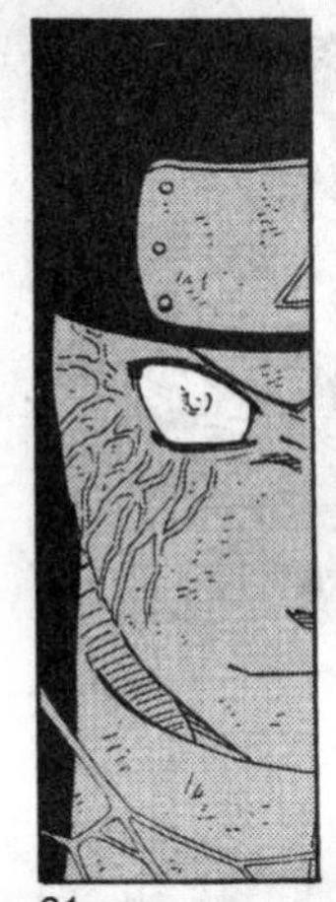

ONCE YOU FIGURE OUT THE STRATEGY BEHIND THE GAME...
...IT SUDDENLY STOPS BEING FUN...
IT'S ONLY BEEN A SINGLE MINUTE...
...BUT I'M BORED OF YOU ALREADY...
WHUMP
PUFF...
HUF
CHOMP
CHOMP
DIE!!
DFT

WOOSH
KUMO-NENKIN! GUM-STYLE SPIDER THREAD!!

PLINK

!

SNAP
CHOK
FWOOSH
WHAT?!
?!!
CHK CHK
HOW?!
!!
SWISH...

GENTLE FIST STYLE...

8 TRIGRAMS 64 PALMS!!

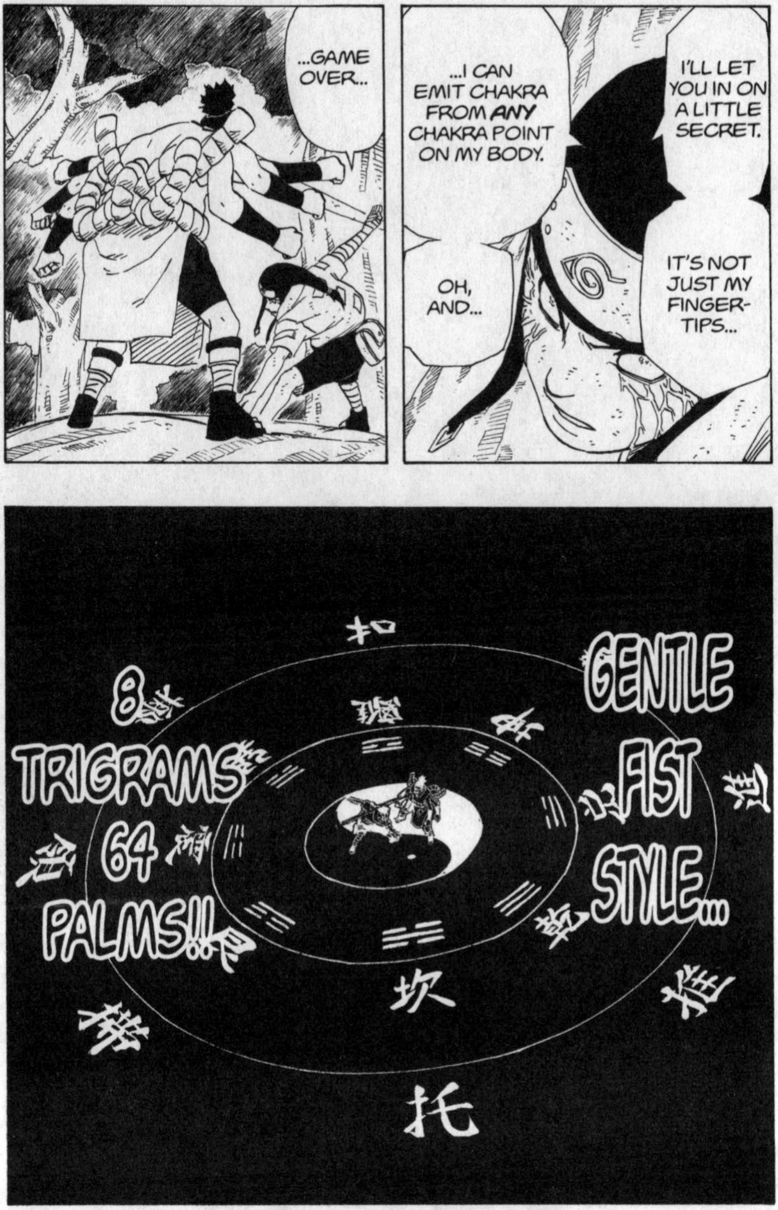

NARUTO™

Number 194: Taking Stock

SHOOT...!

SNAP

FOSH

8 TRIGRAMS 2 PALMS!!

JAB

ARGH!

JAB

4 PALMS!!
JAB
JAB
JAB
JAB
8 PALMS!!
JAB
JAB
JAB
16 PALMS!!
JAB
JAB
JAB
JAB
32 PALMS!!
JAB
JAB
JAB
JAB
JAB

64 PALMS!!!

JAB

JAB

JAB

JAB

KRAK

READ THIS WAY

KRINKLE...
KRINKLE
KRINKLE...
GOLD SKIN...?!
?!
KRINKLE
KRINKLE
KLINK
SLIP
SMAAAASH
GRR RR

(*CHAKRA NETWORK)

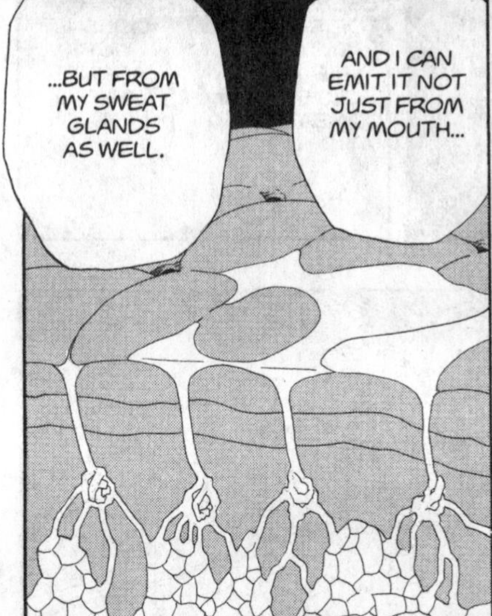

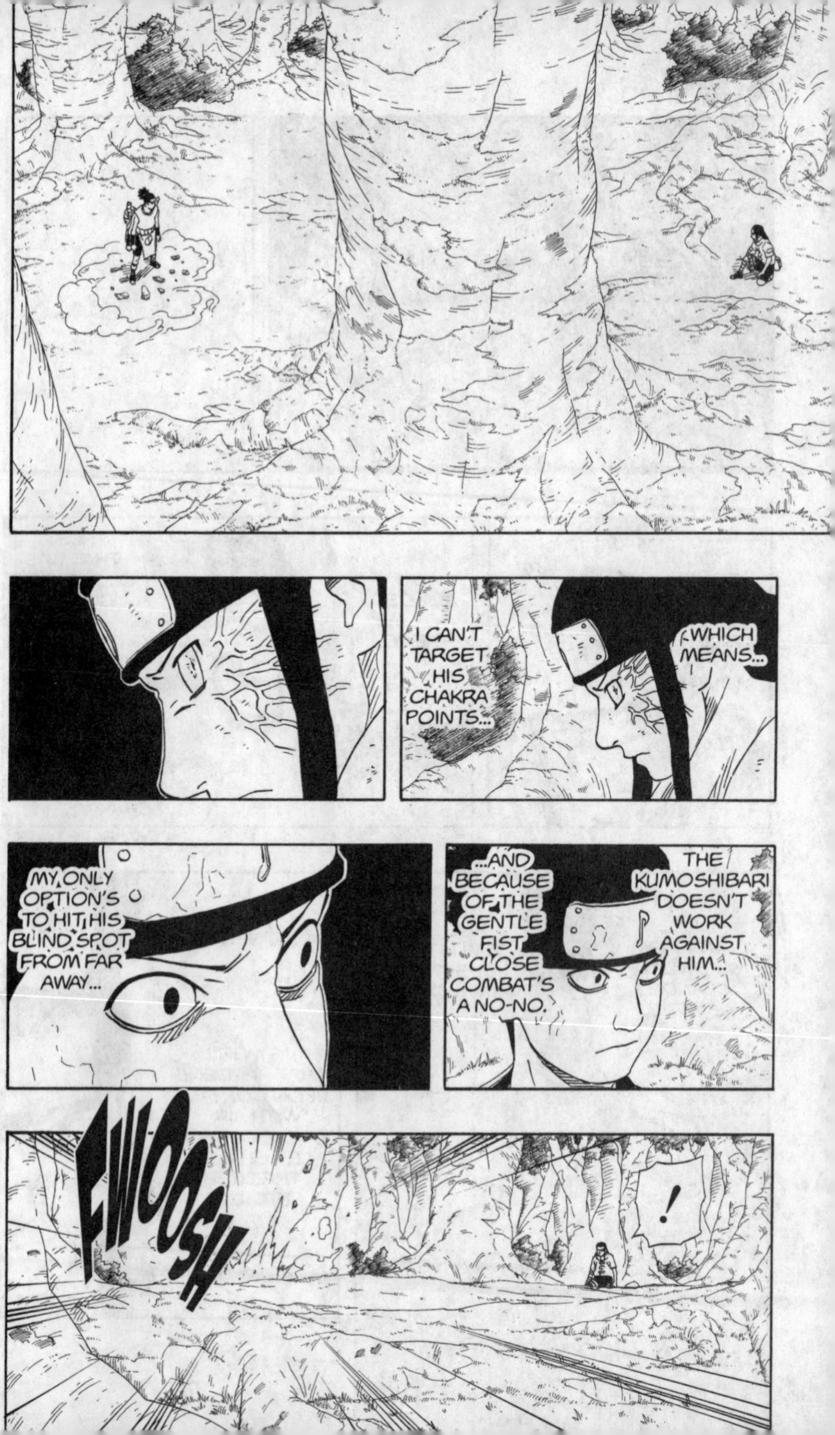

I CAN'T TARGET HIS CHAKRA POINTS...
...WHICH MEANS...

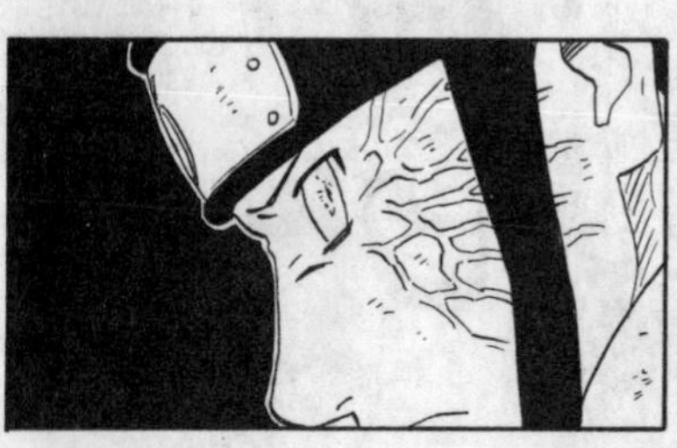

THE KUMOSHIBARI DOESN'T WORK AGAINST HIM...
...AND BECAUSE OF THE GENTLE FIST CLOSE COMBAT'S A NO-NO.

MY ONLY OPTION'S TO HIT HIS BLIND SPOT FROM FAR AWAY...

FWOOSH
!

READ THIS WAY

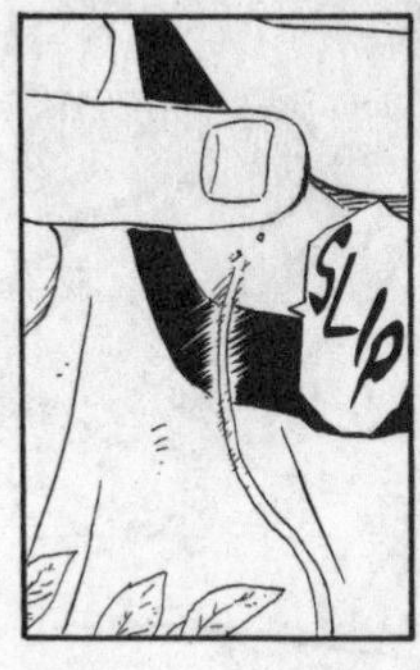

GAME OVER!
!
THAT KUNAI WAS A DECOY...!!

8 TRIGRAMS PALM ROTATION!!

WHUP

WHUP

WHUP

WHUP

WHUP

THOK
THOK
THOK
THOK
N...NO WAY...!
DOES HE HAVE EYES IN THE BACK OF HIS HEAD OR SOMETHING?!
AND THAT DEFENSIVE MOVE... HE USED CHAKRA TO DEFLECT A PHYSICAL ATTACK?!

FWISH
!

FWOOSH
PSHAW!
FWOOSH
KLUNK...
HE CAN SEE ME?!
I KNOW YOU'RE OVER THERE. COME ON OUT.
WHAT THE HECK IS HE...?!

FINE... I'LL GIVE IT TO YOU THAT THIS GAME'S GOT A HIGHER DIFFICULTY LEVEL THAN I EXPECTED!

SO FROM HERE ON OUT NO MORE MR. NICE GUY...

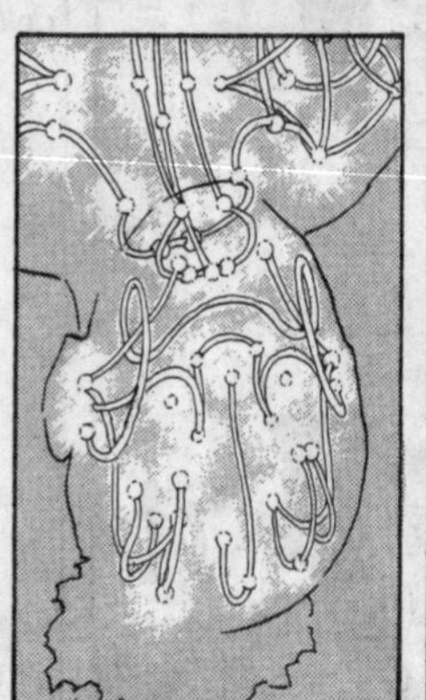

READ
THIS
WAY

THOSE MOVES... HE BLOCKED ATTACKS BEHIND HIM AND PINPOINTED WHERE I WAS HIDING...
HE'S GOT 360 DEGREE X-RAY VISION...

...AND, THAT JUTSU...

IN THAT CASE...
CHOMP

FWWT

KUCHIYOSE NO JUTSU! THE ART OF SUMMONING!!
BAM

VOMO

READ THIS WAY

!

I'M... GONNA FIGURE OUT A WAY TO TAKE YOU DOWN!

IF HE CAN BLOCK PHYSICAL ATTACKS BY EMITTING LOTS OF CHAKRA AND ROTATING...
ZURP...

ZLOO...
...ALL I NEED TO DO IS STOP THAT ROTATION!

PLINK
HACK

GO!!
FWOOSH
VOING

SHWOOOOOOM
!!

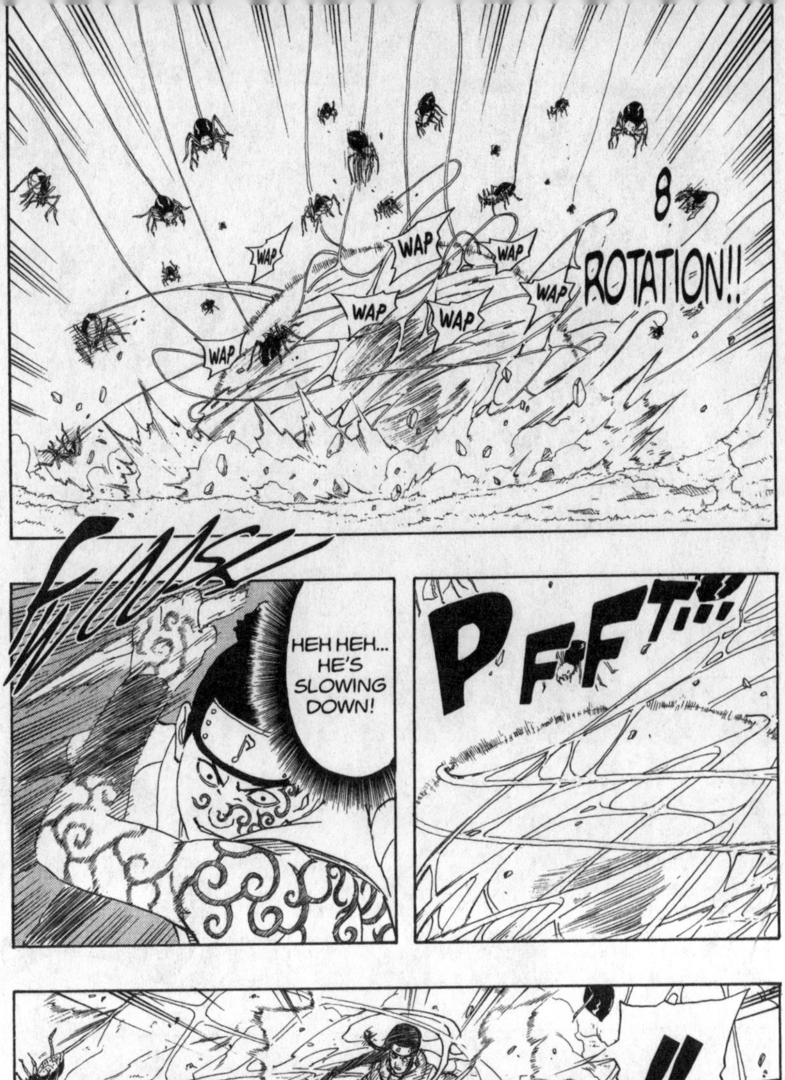

8

ROTATION!!

WAP WAP WAP WAP WAP WAP WAP

PFFT!!

HEH HEH...
HE'S
SLOWING
DOWN!

NARUTO
TM

Number 195: Capture...!!

!!
FWISH
DIE!!
GLINT

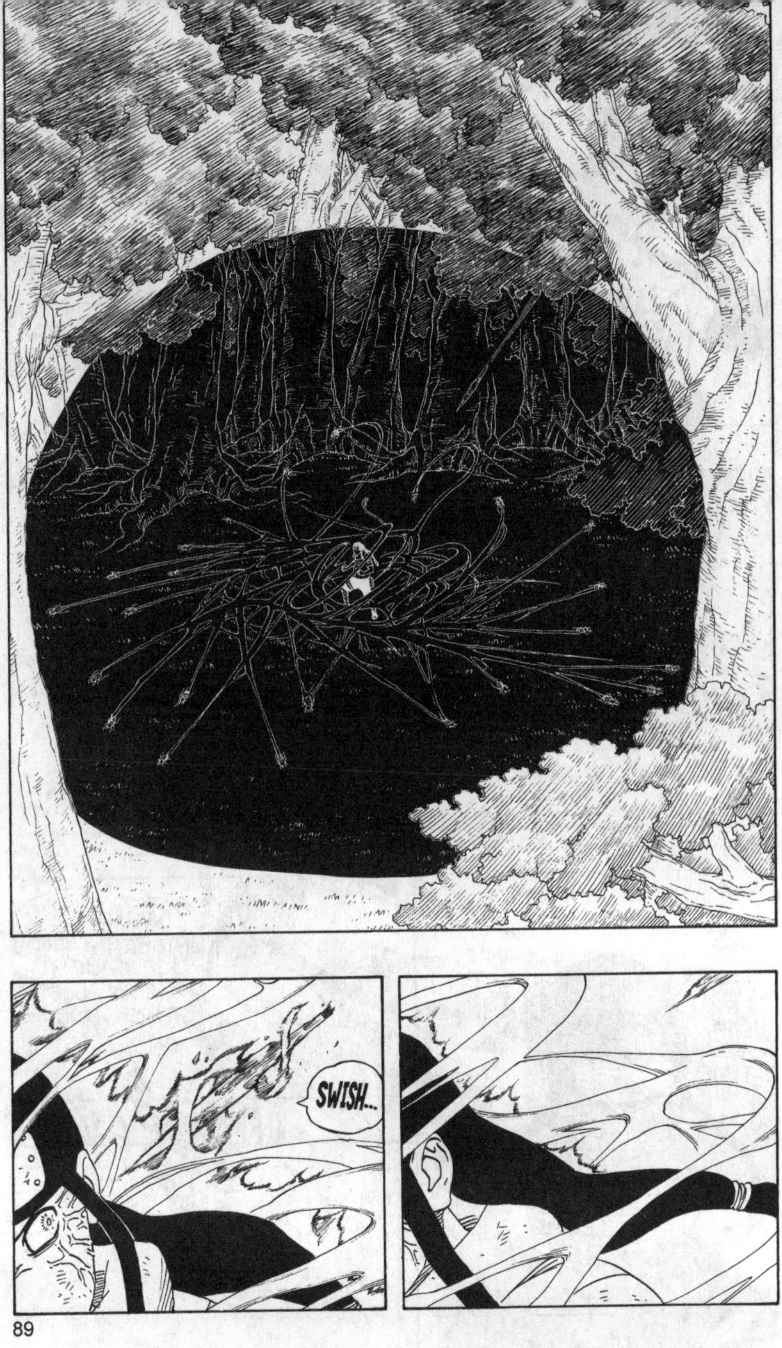

SWISH...

HE SLOWED MY DAGGER WITH CHAKRA AT THE LAST SECOND...
PSHAW ...!

THOCK

SWIRL

HUH...
WHAT? MY ROTATION GOT CAUGHT UP IN ALL THIS GUNK.

IF I CAN'T ROTATE...
...I HAVE TO BLOCK 'EM ONE-AT-A-TIME.

SNAP SNAP SNAP
ENOUGH OF THAT...

READ THIS WAY

CLOSE COMBAT TAIJUTSU...
SO AS LONG AS I STAY OUT OF REACH, I'LL BE SAFE.
RURK
RURK
RURK
SHOOM

AND THEN...
...I CAN JUST SIT BACK AND ENJOY THE SHOW... HEH HEH HEH.
SWISH

WHOOSH WHOOSH

WHOOSH WHOOSH

THUD THUD THUD THUD THUD THUD THUD THUD THUD THUD THUD
SIZZLE
HAH!
WHOOSH
SCREECH
WHIP
CLAP

SPLOOOOSH
!!
FWUT

WHAPAPAPAPAPAPAP APAP WHAP
8 TRIGRAMS 64 PALMS!!

SO MANY!!
SCREECH
TUG
CAN'T ROTATE...
UGH!

FLICKER
SWOOP
SNAP
AH!
SNAP
SNAP
SNAP
THUD
THUD
THUD
OW...!
...!

READ THIS WAY

...

IT SEEMS HE'S GOT A 360 DEGREE OCULAR RANGE. SO WITH ALL-SEEING X-RAY VISION...
...AND LONG-DISTANCE TELESCOPIC VISION, HE CAN CATCH AND REACT TO ANY ENEMY ATTACK...

...EVEN WITHOUT 360 DEGREE PERCEPTION, HIS ACTUAL FIELD OF VISION IS STILL FEARSOME.

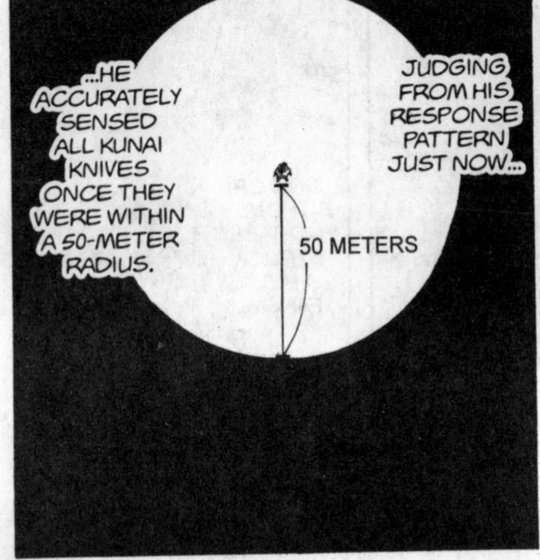
JUDGING FROM HIS RESPONSE PATTERN JUST NOW...
...HE ACCURATELY SENSED ALL KUNAI KNIVES ONCE THEY WERE WITHIN A 50-METER RADIUS.
50 METERS

(54.7 YARDS)

...AND YET... SOMEHOW HE COULDN'T AVOID ALL OF THEM.

YEESH... NEVER MIND THAT FATSO JIROBO, NOW WHAT'S KIDOMARU UP TO?!
THAT LOSER...

SHOOM
SHOOM

YOU KNOW HE LIKES TO AMUSE HIMSELF...
ONE OF THEM PROBABLY STRUCK HIS FANCY...

YEAH, BUT WHEN THAT FOOL GETS EXCITED...
...HE GOES INTO THAT STATE WAY TOO EASILY...

...

WELL... AT LEAST IF HE HITS SECOND STATE...
...HIS OPPONENT'LL BE DEAD IN NO TIME.

READ
THIS
WAY

HUF HUF
HUF

HUF
HUF

HOP
NOW... I'M FINISHED SETTING UP...

THEY'RE EVEN MORE THIS NEXT ROUND... WHATCHA GONNA DO?
SHOOSH

WHOOOOSH

WHAM WHAM WHAM WHAM WHAM
SLASH!
SLAP
JAB JAB
TWO, THIS TIME...

...HIS OCULAR NINJUTSU ISN'T PERFECT...!

HUF
HUF
HUF
HUF

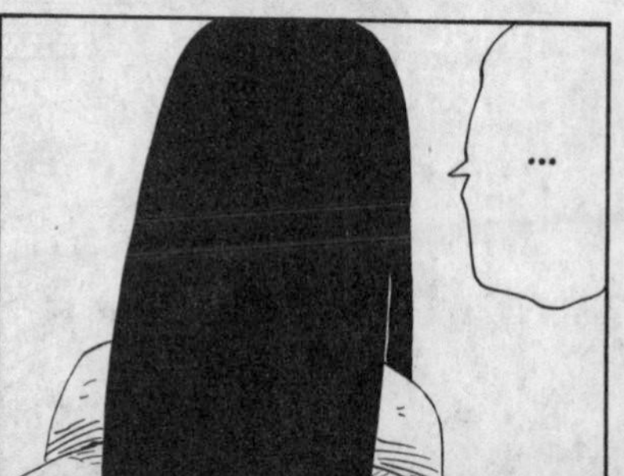

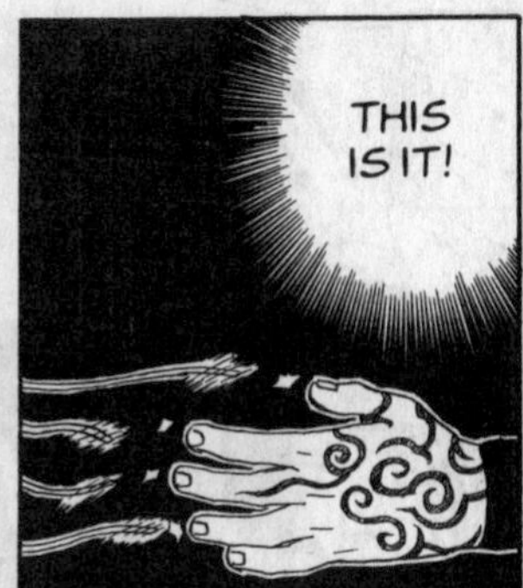

BLOP
BLOP
BLOP
BOOM
!!

!!
BO OF
SH AA AA AAA AAA
CHK
TWITCH...

READ THIS WAY

...STILL...!
...!

HEH... I SEE.
FLARE

HE JUST AVOIDED FATAL BLOWS... AND SINCE THEY'RE RELEASED FROM OVER 50 METERS AWAY, THEY DON'T RETAIN ENOUGH FORCE...
FWOOSH

WELL...
HUF
HUF
...HE DID GIVE ME MY MONEY'S WORTH.

SLIP
SO IN THANKS...
GLOOP
FAP
PLINK...
PLINK...

REEEE...

STRIKING ACCURACY: 100%.
GRRR
DESTRUCTIVE POWER: MAXIMUM!

FWIP
PCH

DIE!!

NARUTO
TM

Number 196: The Strongest Enemy!!

SWISH
VOOOOOSH
KABOOM
GAME OVER...!

READ THIS WAY

PUFF
PUFF

PUFF
PUFF

!
WHA...?!

...THAT WAS CLOSE... WAY TOO CLOSE.
URGH
HUF
BUT... I WAS ABLE TO AVOID IT JUST ENOUGH.

JUST... AS I THOUGHT...
URGH
...HE'S CAUGHT ON TO THE SECRET OF THE BYAKUGAN.
URGH

...!
WHAT'S GOING ON? HOW DID HE...?!

ZIZZLE...
HOW DID I MISS BY 15 CENTIMETERS?!
DRIP
DRIP
GRR RR!!

READ THIS WAY

AAH... IT'S CHAKRA!
HE'S... BEEN SHIELDING HIMSELF WITH CHAKRA...!

CHUNK
UGH...

...EMITTING IT IN A WIDE ARC...
NO WONDER... THAT'S HOW HE SENSED THE ARROW AND DEFLECTED ITS PATH...

SNEER
...

...HEH HEH... HE'S GOTTA BE HURTIN' FROM EXPENDING THAT MUCH CHAKRA...

BUT HE HAD TO DODGE MY ATTACKS...
FOR IF I'M RIGHT... NO MISTAKE...

...HE DIDN'T SEE THAT ARROW WITH HIS EYES!!

READ THIS WAY

...
HUMPH...

HIS VISUAL RANGE IS 360 DEGREES.
HE CAN SENSE ALL AIRBORNE ATTACKS WITHIN A 50-METER RADIUS.
HUF
AND YET, FOR SOME REASON, THERE ARE SOME KUNAI KNIVES HE CAN'T AVOID.
TWITCH

SO WHY CAN'T HE DODGE THEM?
BECAUSE HE CAN'T SEE THEM!

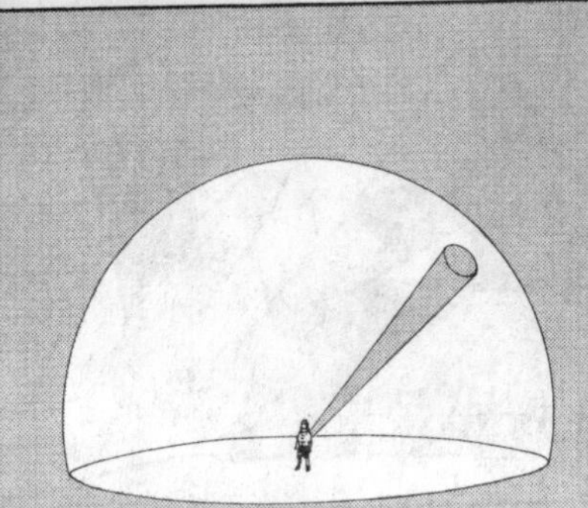
EVEN WITH HIS OCULAR NINJUTSU, HE DOES HAVE A BLIND SPOT!!

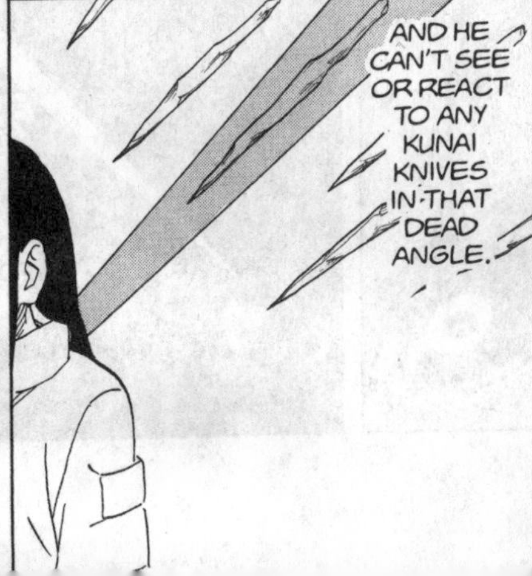
AND HE CAN'T SEE OR REACT TO ANY KUNAI KNIVES IN THAT DEAD ANGLE.

THAT'S WHY HE USES THAT ROTATION DEFENSE, TO NULLIFY THE BLIND SPOT.
WHUP

CREAK...

I'VE ANALYZED ALL MY ATTACKS, AND GLEANED ALL THERE IS TO KNOW.

HIS DEAD ANGLE STARTS AT THE LEVEL OF HIS FIRST THORACIC VERTEBRA... AND SPREADS OUTWARD AS A NARROW CONE!!

...!

READ THIS WAY

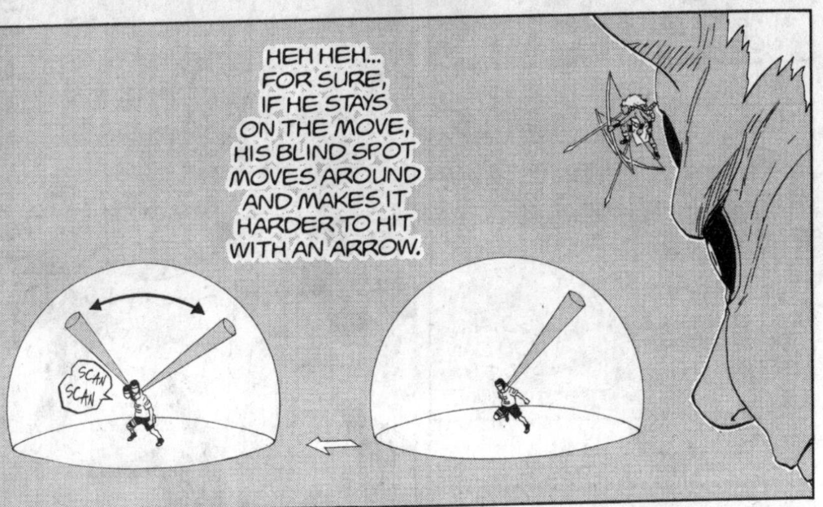

KRIK...
KRIK...

THE GENTLE FIST IS USELESS IF YOU'RE NOT RIGHT NEXT TO YOUR OPPONENT.
CREAK
AND I DON'T THINK YOU'RE IN ANY SHAPE TO GET NEAR ME NOW.

KRIK
SO ALL YOU CAN DO... IS RUN.
BUT EITHER WAY, YOU'RE GONNA DIE!

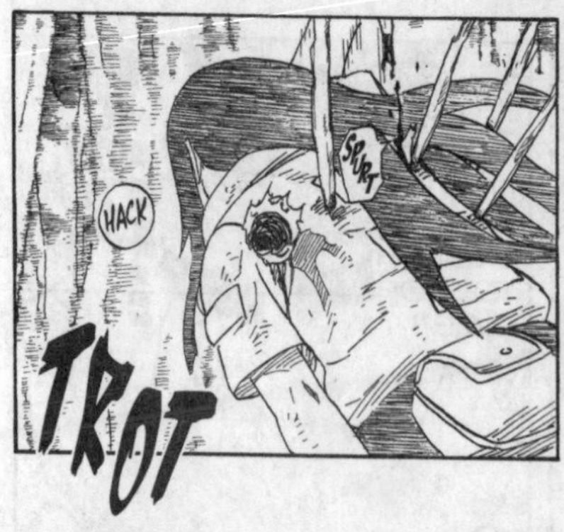
SPURT
HACK
TROT

READ THIS WAY

MINOR CHARACTERS IN A SIMPLE GAME ARE FATED TO BE KNOCKED OUT QUICKLY!
UNH
HUF

HUF
CRUNCH
UNGH
UGH!

HEH... LOOKS LIKE YOU'RE RUNNING OUT OF CHAKRA TOO.

TWANG

NEJI... YOU...
...MORE THAN ANYONE ELSE, YOU'VE BEEN BLESSED WITH THE GENIUS OF THE HYUGA CLAN...

SWISH

WOSH

ARC

WOOSH

SWA

CRACK

DRIP-DRIP

DRIP

CLATTER...

!

(THE SYMBOL PICTURED ABOVE, CALLED A MANJI, IS TRADITIONAL IN BUDDHIST IMAGERY -ED.)

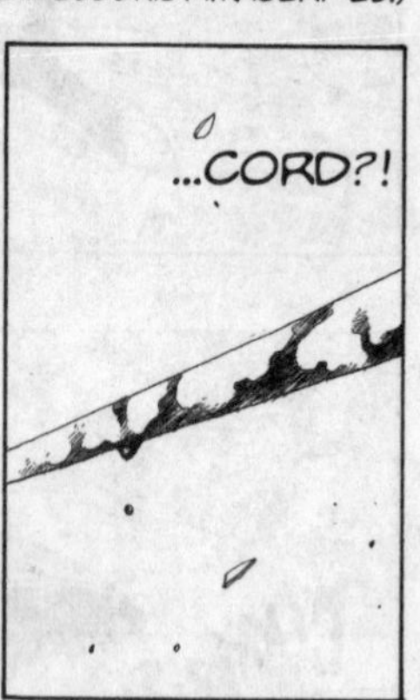

WELL THEN, NEXT...!
GLOOP...
PLINK
I'LL ADD SPIN... SO THAT EVEN IF IT HITS A TREE, IT CAN BORE THROUGH WITHOUT DEFLECTION.

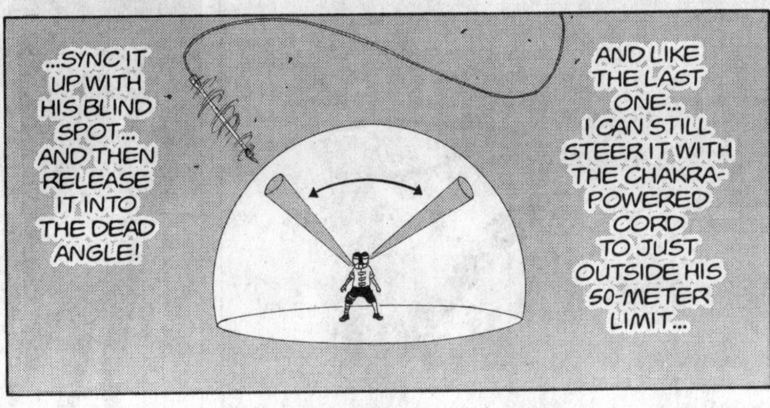
AND LIKE THE LAST ONE... I CAN STILL STEER IT WITH THE CHAKRA-POWERED CORD TO JUST OUTSIDE HIS 50-METER LIMIT...
...SYNC IT UP WITH HIS BLIND SPOT... AND THEN RELEASE IT INTO THE DEAD ANGLE!

HUF
UNH
URGH

HE'S GETTING UP...
FFT

...HE IS SO MUCH STRONGER...
HUF
HUF

I'M ALMOST OUT OF CHAKRA...
...I CAN'T DODGE ANOTHER ATTACK.

...

I VOW...
...TO WIN!!

...
NARUTO... WHAT WOULD YOU DO...?

...

READ THIS WAY

K KRAK KRAK KRAK KRA

KRA
WHIIIIRR

NARUTO
TM

Number 197: Prepared to Die!!

...GOT HIM!!

ARGH!!

SPLAT
SPLAT
SPLAT

KRAK
SLAM
SCREECH
...GOTCHA...!
SIZZLE...

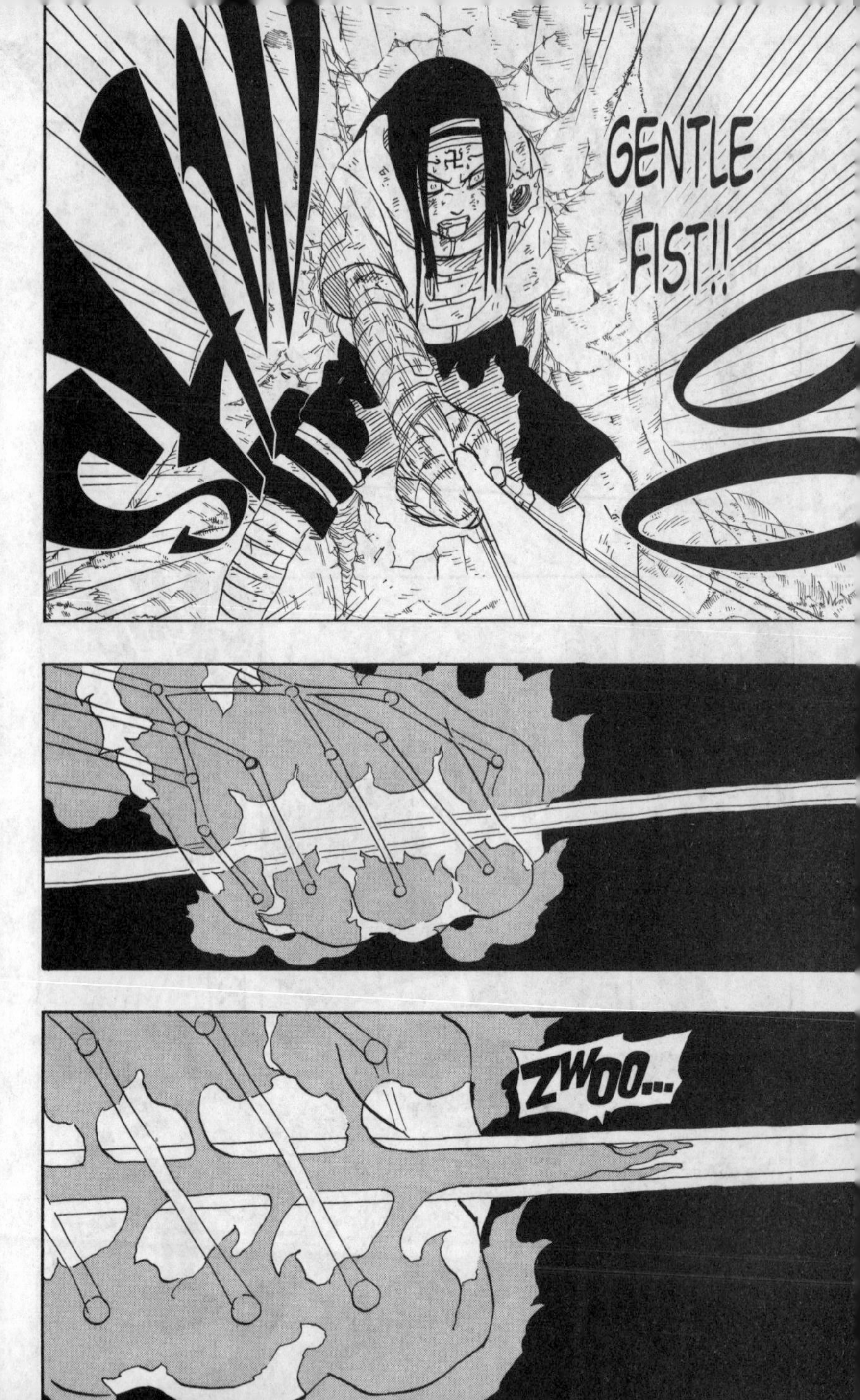
GENTLE FIST!!
ZWOO...

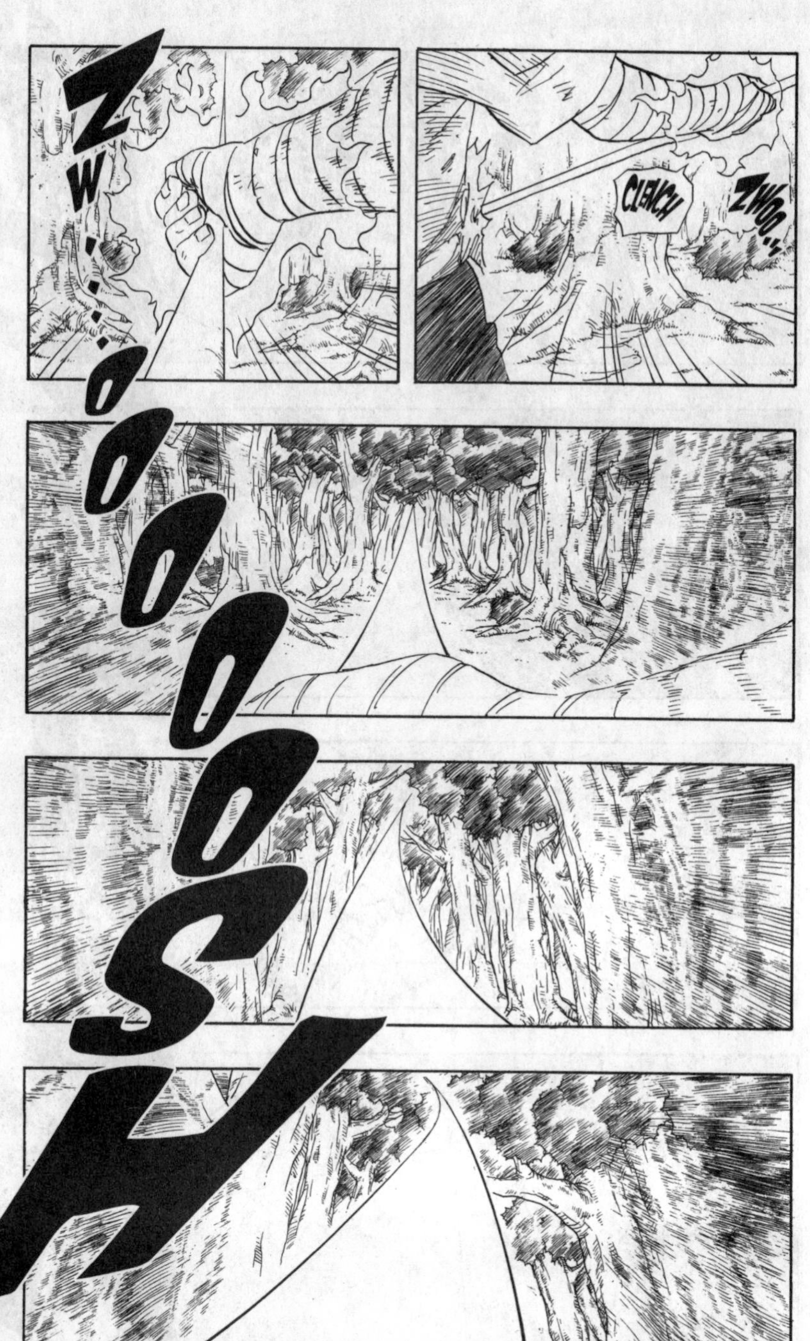
CLENCH
ZWOO...
ZW...OOOOOOSH

ZOOOSH

ZAP

?!!

...
HUNH...
WH... WHAT...
...HE'S STILL ALIVE?!

BUT... I KNOW I HIT HIM!

CHAKRA BUILT SUBSTANCES...
...DON'T STAND A CHANCE AGAINST GENTLE FIST TECHNIQUES!

...THE GENTLE FIST...
WAVER...
HUH... HE FLOODED MY CORD WITH THE LAST OF HIS CHAKRA AS HE DIED...
FLAP

ZOOM...

...EIGHT BIRDS...
...MISSED ONE AGAIN...

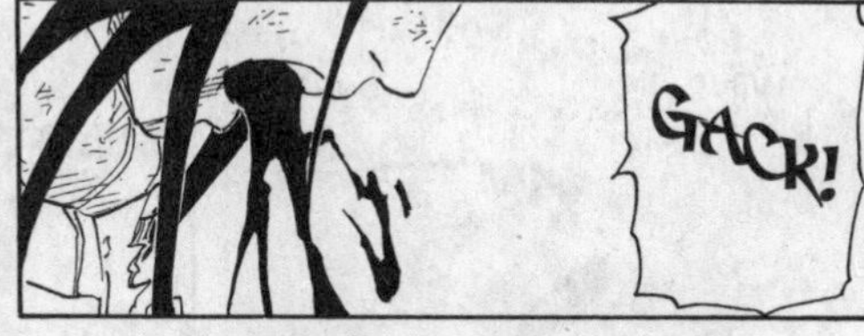
GACK!

CRASH
FWOOSH
CRASH

WHERE IS HE...?

CHOMP
VWOOOOOSH
UGH... I'M HURT...
...BUT... I CAN MOVE...

HUF
HUF
HUF

HUF
UNGH
FAILURE!
HUF

I VOW...
...TO WIN!!

...
HUF
HUF

I TOLD YOU...
...I'M A SORE LOSER...!

CAN I ASK YOU SOMETHING?
WHY DO YOU KEEP TRYING SO HARD TO DEFY YOUR DESTINY?!
HUF
HUF

READ THIS WAY

GLARE

...YOU'RE NOT A "FAILURE"!

READ THIS WAY

I CAN'T AFFORD TO LOSE...
...EVEN IF MY OPPONENT IS STRONGER...
...EVEN IF I WERE TO DIE...

I CANNOT LOSE.
CLENCH

UGH!
I SIMPLY CAN'T...!

CRASH
GAH...
I LET IT DRAG ON TOO LONG THIS TIME...
...PLAYED TOO HARD...

...!

HUH?
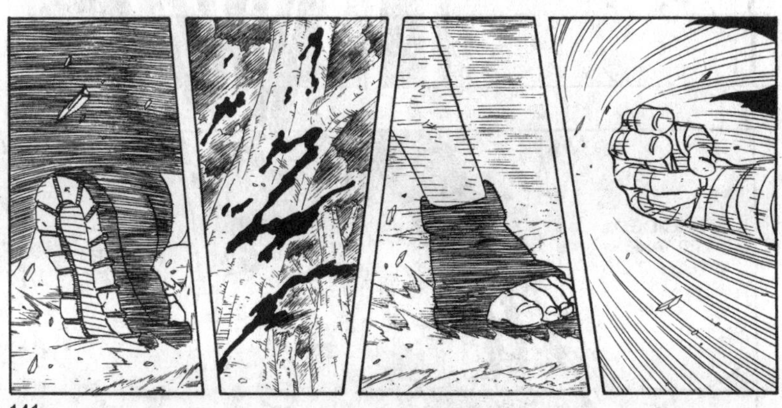

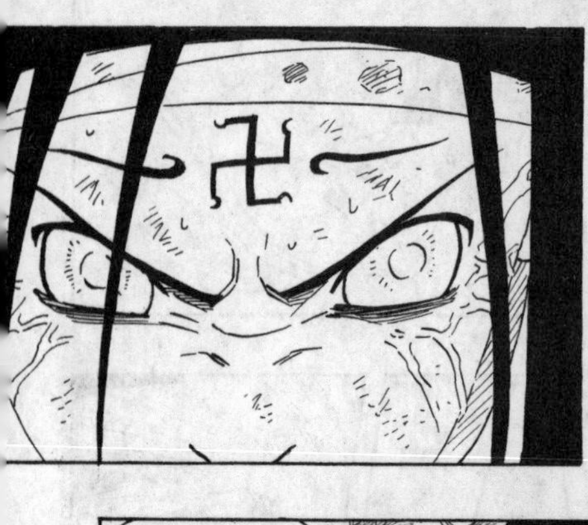

WHUMP

HUF
URGH
... COULDN'T DODGE IT ANYWAY...
...I DECIDED... TO TAKE THE HIT...

FWOOSH
HOW? YOU SHOULD BE DEAD... WHY AREN'T YOU?!

FWHOOOOOSH
CAN'T USE CHAKRA...

UGH...

I KNOW MY LIMITS BETTER THAN YOU...
FROM STICK TWO...
...SEVEN BIRDS...
...
GUESS THERE WERE EIGHT...

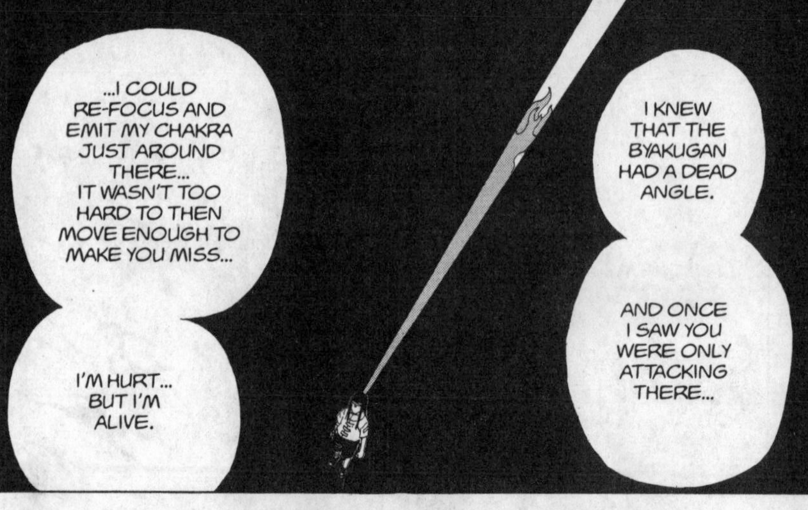
I KNEW THAT THE BYAKUGAN HAD A DEAD ANGLE.
AND ONCE I SAW YOU WERE ONLY ATTACKING THERE...
...I COULD RE-FOCUS AND EMIT MY CHAKRA JUST AROUND THERE... IT WASN'T TOO HARD TO THEN MOVE ENOUGH TO MAKE YOU MISS...
I'M HURT... BUT I'M ALIVE.

HEH HEH... YOU TOOK THE HITS...
HUF
...RISKED YOUR OWN LIFE...?
HUF
...WHY...?

HUF
YOU'RE... THE STRONGEST ENEMY I'VE EVER FOUGHT...
HUF
BUT THERE'S A REASON I CAN'T LOSE...

...ONCE, NOT SO LONG AGO, THE STRONGEST FELLOW I EVER FOUGHT SAID THIS TO ME...
"'CAUSE UNLIKE ME...

...
HACK

..."YOU'RE NOT A 'FAILURE'!"

TOO MANY PEOPLE HAVE FAITH IN ME...!

NARUTO
TM

Number 198: Transference...!!

HEH...
DIDN'T YOU SAY EARLIER...
...THAT MY FATE WAS TO GET TAKEN OUT BY SOME MINOR CHARACTER?
...

HACK!

URGH
HUF
...
HUF

LOOK WHAT HAPPENED HERE.
HUF
HUF

HUF
...!
HUF

FATE...

...ISN'T SOMETHING FOR YOU TO DECIDE.

HUF
HUF
HUF
URGH
HUF

HEH...
I WONDER...
YOU STILL LOOK DEAD TO ME...

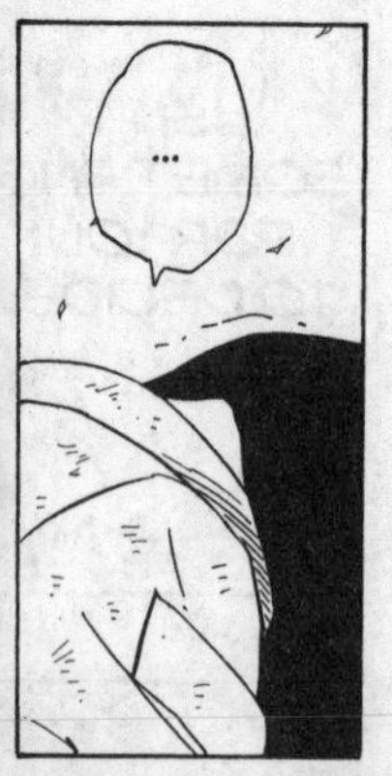
...

NEJI... YOU...
...MORE THAN ANYONE ELSE, YOU'VE BEEN BLESSED WITH THE GENIUS OF THE HYUGA CLAN...

...

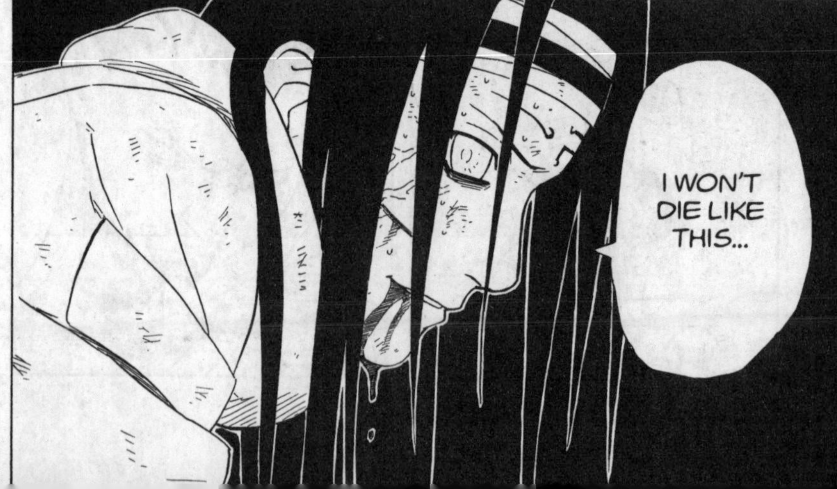
I WON'T DIE LIKE THIS...

READ THIS WAY

HUF
HUF
...TRY ALL YOU WANT, BUT YOU CAN'T STOP IT...

HUF
...

...SASUKE...
...HAS WILLINGLY JOINED THE SOUND.

RIGHT NOW, SASUKE...
...IS WRAPPED IN DARKNESS.

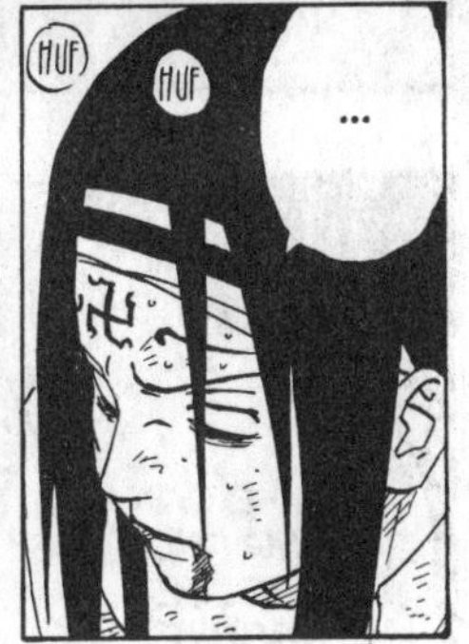
HUF
HUF
...

...

YOU'RE WRONG...
?!

NARUTO...

YOU'VE GOT BETTER SIGHT THAN I DO.

THERE IS SOMEONE...
...WHO CAN FIND AND RESCUE SASUKE FROM THE DARKNESS!

READ THIS WAY

HEH...
SASUKE BELONGS TO LORD OROCHIMARU... NO ONE CAN...
HE CAN...

HUF
?!
HUF
HUF
HUF
HUF

FOR...

...NARUTO... YOU...
CLAP
CLA
...

...SAVED ME FROM THE DARKNESS!

HUF
...!
HUF

HACK
UGH...!

SMART-
ALECK
TO, THE
END...

SHOOM

ARGH...!
...HEH,
I'M NOT
ONE TO
TALK...
SPLATTER

HE'S THE FIRST TO DRIVE ME THIS FAR SINCE KIMIMARO...
HUF
HUF
SLUMP

...UNH...

...
I'M COUNTING ON YOU... ALL MY COMRADES.
THUD...

READ THIS WAY

SHOOM SHOOM

SNIFF SNIFF

WE'RE CLOSE!

...TWO ENEMIES LEFT...
AND WE'RE THREE... THAT'S A ONE-MAN ADVANTAGE.
IF WE DO IT RIGHT, WE MIGHT GET THIS DONE WITH JUST ONE CONTACT.

ALL RIGHT! NOW WE'RE TALKING!
LET'S DO IT!!

HEY!
DON'T FORGET, IT'S FOUR-TO-TWO!

ARF!
ARF!

RIGHT, SORRY!
FOUR AGAINST TWO.

THIS TIME, WE TWO'LL TAKE CARE OF 'EM WITH OUR NEW MOVE!!
ARF!

HEY! WAIT!
I WAS THINKING ABOUT MAKING TONS OF SHADOW DOPPEL-GANGERS!

THANKS, BOTH OF YOU, BUT...

...FIRST, WE TRY MY PLAN.
ALL RIGHT?

...

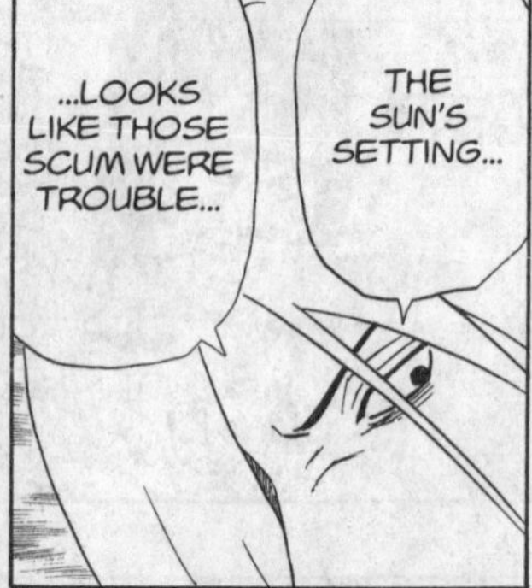
THE SUN'S SETTING...
...LOOKS LIKE THOSE SCUM WERE TROUBLE...

WHO CARES...?
I'M WORRIED ABOUT LORD OROCHIMARU.
IT'S TAKEN US HALF A DAY TO COVER ONLY A THIRD OF THE DISTANCE.

YEAH... THIS ISN'T GOOD.
WE WERE TIGHT ON TIME TO BEGIN WITH.

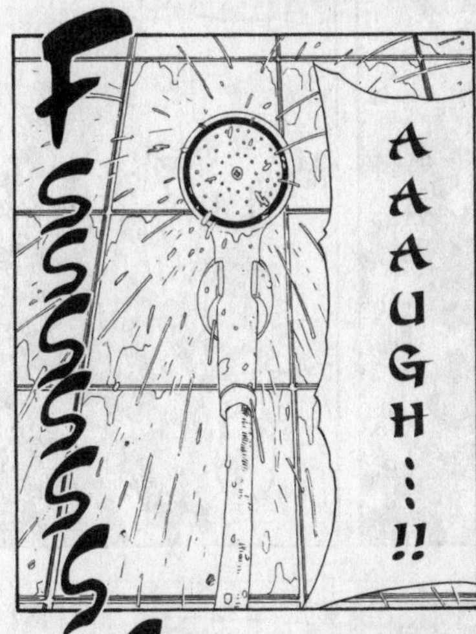
AAAUGH...!!
FSSSSSSS

SH
URGH...

UNH... UH.

FSSSSSH
RIP
RIP
UGH...

AAAAH...!
RIP
RIP
RIP

HUF
HUF
HUF
HUF

HUF
SASUKE... WHERE IS SASUKE?
HUF

...
WE'RE OUT OF TIME... THIS IS IT.

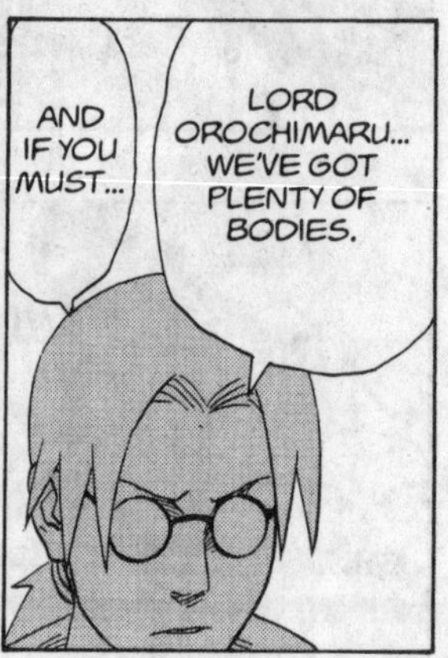
LORD OROCHIMARU... WE'VE GOT PLENTY OF BODIES.
AND IF YOU MUST...

...YOU MAY EVEN TAKE MINE.

...NO, IT MUST BE SASUKE'S...
HOW LONG DO YOU THINK I'VE WAITED FOR THIS...?!

READ THIS WAY

THIS IS AN EMERGENCY!!
THE THIRD HOKAGE'S JUTSU... IT WAS FAR MORE POWERFUL THAN ANTICIPATED.
YOU MUST TRANSFER... OR WOULD YOU RATHER LOSE EVERYTHING?!

!

AAAUGH!!
...

I'VE ALREADY ARRANGED FOR THE SELECTING.
YOU CAN ENTRUST IT TO ME... AND...

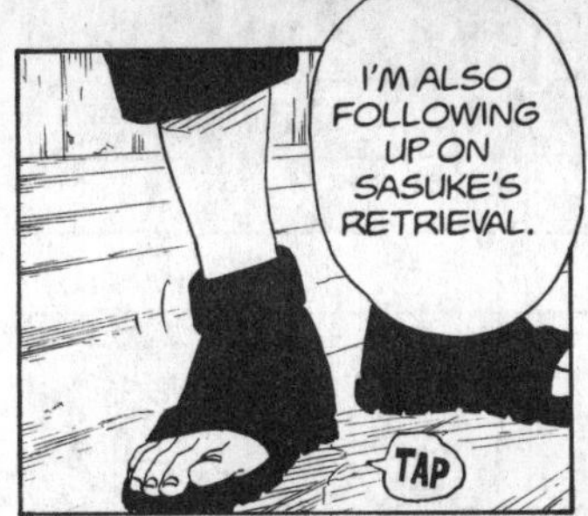
I'M ALSO FOLLOWING UP ON SASUKE'S RETRIEVAL.
TAP

WE'VE GOT TO USE KIMIMARO...!

CURSE YOU, THIRD LORD...!
RIP

SSSS
SSSSS

LISTEN CLOSELY...

BOOF

CLACK
CLACK

SSSS SSSSS

KISHIMOTO MASASHI'S REJECT MANGA SPECIAL

THE TWO-PAGE SPREAD ABOVE WAS WHAT WAS ACTUALLY PRINTED IN WEEKLY SHONEN JUMP, BUT...

...WHEN MY TWIN BROTHER SAW IT, HE PESTERED ME SO MUCH WITH "IT'S SO UNCOOL," "BORING," "DO-OVER" THAT EVEN THOUGH THERE WASN'T MUCH TIME, I DID REVISE AND REDRAW THE TWO PAGES FOR THIS GRAPHIC NOVEL EDITION.

SO, DEAR READERS, CAN YOU GUESS WHICH PAGES WERE REPLACED...?

Number 199: The Wish...!!

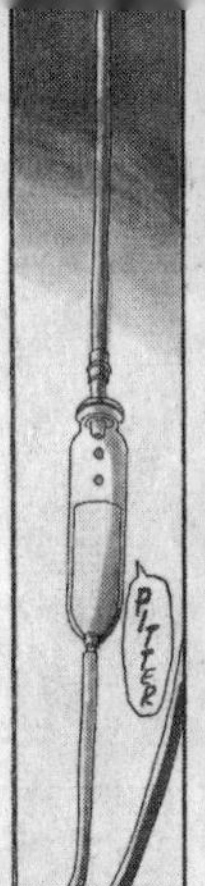

THE RESULTS OF THE FOURTH CHARACTER AND FIRST JUTSU POPULARITY SURVEY!!

CONDUCTED IN JAPAN.

SURVEY RESULTS

11TH PLACE/NINJA CENTERFOLD	1,013 VOTES
12TH PLACE/1000 YEARS OF DEATH	909 VOTES
13TH PLACE/CRESCENT MOON DANCE	864 VOTES
14TH PLACE/BARRAGE OF LIONS	700 VOTES
15TH PLACE/UZUMAKI NARUTO BARRAGE	666 VOTES
16TH PLACE/THE COFFIN OF CRUSHING SAND	641 VOTES
17TH PLACE/LOTUS	610 VOTES
18TH PLACE/TSUKUYOMI	597 VOTES
19TH PLACE/IMPLODING SAND FUNERAL	566 VOTES
20TH PLACE/THE NINJA HAREM	493 VOTES

13TH PLACE/TSUNADE	1,058 VOTES
14TH PLACE/HAKU	941 VOTES
15TH PLACE/TEMARI	930 VOTES
16TH PLACE/GEKKO HAYATE	876 VOTES
17TH PLACE/INUZUKA KIBA	599 VOTES
18TH PLACE/MIGHT GUY	567 VOTES
19TH PLACE/SHIRANUI GENMA	541 VOTES
20TH PLACE/FOURTH HOKAGE	529 VOTES
21ST PLACE/AKIMICHI CHOJI	399 VOTES
22ND PLACE/OROCHIMARU	345 VOTES
23RD PLACE/YAMANAKA INO	286 VOTES
24TH PLACE/AKAMARU	271 VOTES
25TH PLACE/ABURAME SHINO	253 VOTES
26TH PLACE/SARUTOBI ASUMA YAKUSHI KABUTO	237 VOTES
28TH PLACE/MOMOCHI ZABUZA	207 VOTES
29TH PLACE/TENTEN	135 VOTES
30TH PLACE/MITARASHI ANKO	120 VOTES

Number 199: The Wish...!!

● THE JUTSU POPULARITY

1ST PLACE/RASENGAN	5,128 VOTES
2ND PLACE/LIGHTNING BLADE	4,395 VOTES
3RD PLACE/CHIDORI	3,216 VOTES
4TH PLACE/SHADOW POSSESSION	3,160 VOTES
5TH PLACE/SUMMONING	1,897 VOTES
6TH PLACE/BYAKUGAN	1,728 VOTES
7TH PLACE/SHARINGAN	1,639 VOTES
8TH PLACE/SHADOW DOPPELGANGER	1,415 VOTES
9TH PLACE/REVERSE LOTUS	1,400 VOTES
10TH PLACE/8 TRIGRAMS 64 PALMS	1,162 VOTES

● THE REST OF THE CHARACTER POPULARITY SURVEY RESULTS ●

2ND PLACE/HATAKE KAKASHI	6,560 VOTES
3RD PLACE/UCHIHA SASUKE	4,843 VOTES
4TH PLACE/NARA SHIKAMARU	4,700 VOTES
5TH PLACE/UMINO IRUKA	3,855 VOTES
6TH PLACE/HYUGA NEJI	3,222 VOTES
7TH PLACE/ROCK LEE	2,522 VOTES
8TH PLACE/GAARA	1,868 VOTES
9TH PLACE/UCHIHA ITACHI	1,619 VOTES
10TH PLACE/HARUNO SAKURA	1,348 VOTES
11TH PLACE/JIRAIYA	1,235 VOTES
12TH PLACE/HYUGA HINATA	1,182 VOTES

NARUTO
TM

READ THIS WAY

...

I... CAN STILL...
YOUR SUCCESSOR HAS BEEN FOUND...

...

...AND...

...HE'S BEEN GRANTED THE RIVAL COUNTER-PART TO YOUR OWN EARTH CURSE MARK...

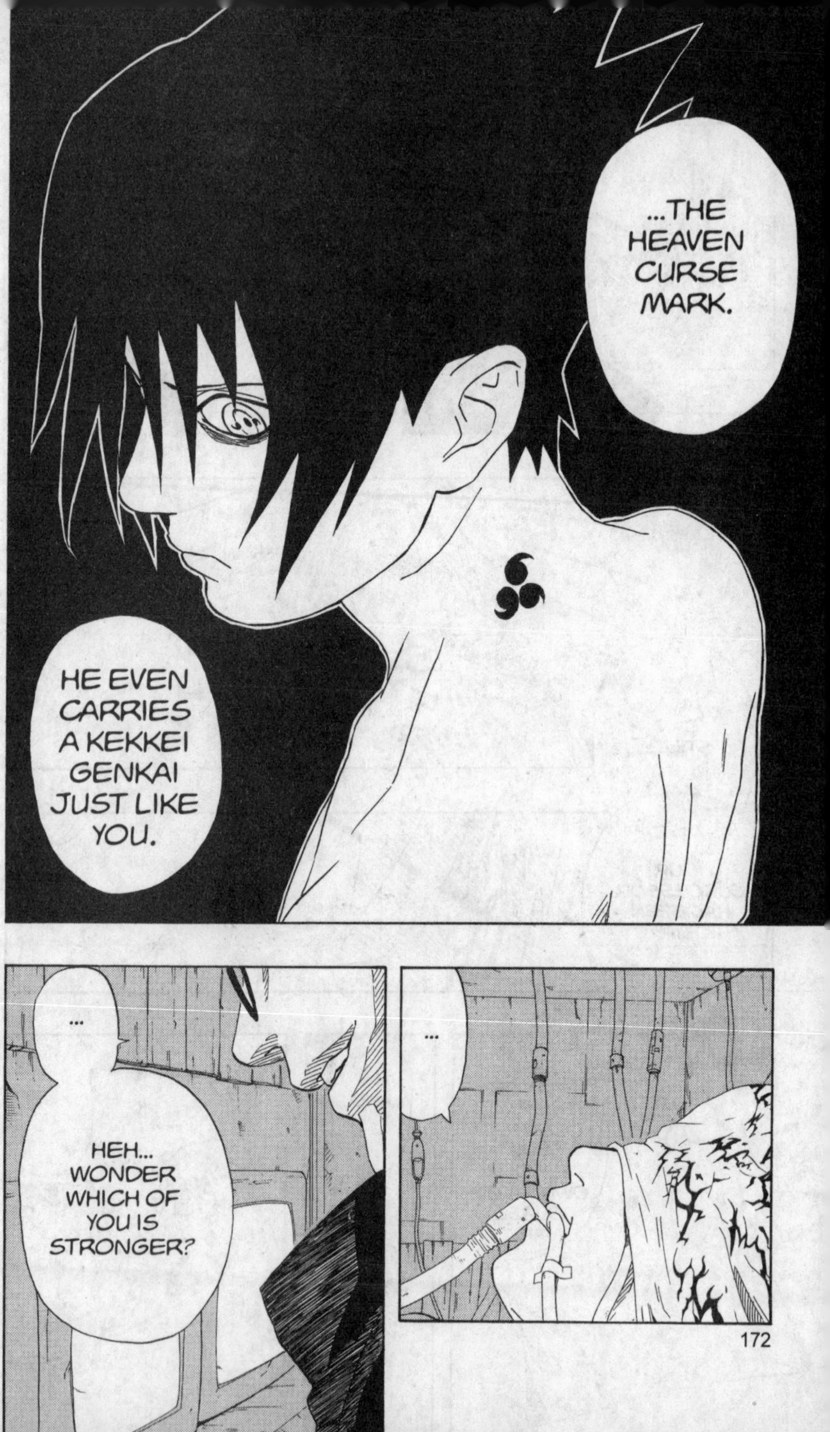

...THE HEAVEN CURSE MARK.

HE EVEN CARRIES A KEKKEI GENKAI JUST LIKE YOU.

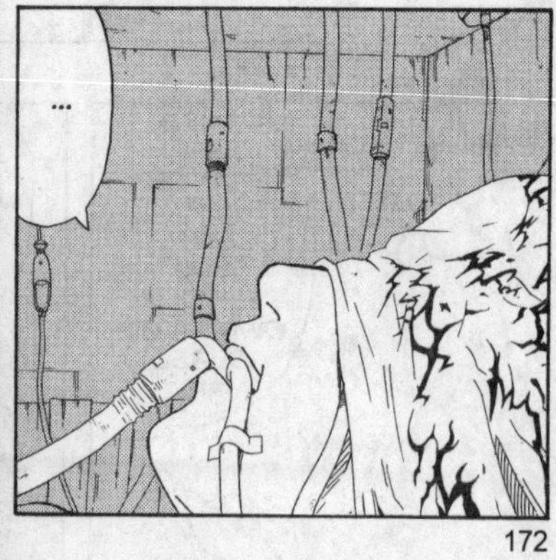

READ THIS WAY

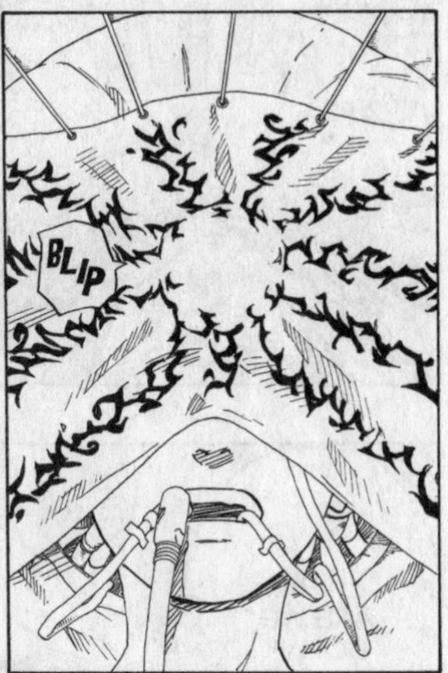
BLIP

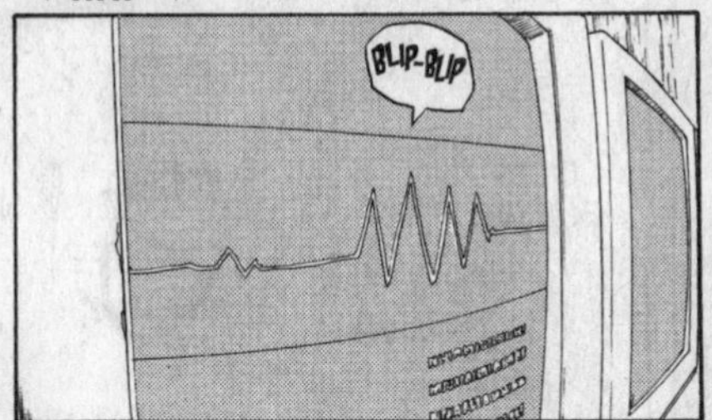
BLIP-BLIP

...WHAT'S THE MATTER?!
YOU MUSTN'T GET TOO WORKED UP.

URGH...
GAH

UNH...
DRIBBLE...

...
HOW MUCH LONGER DO I HAVE...?

...DON'T
SPEAK...
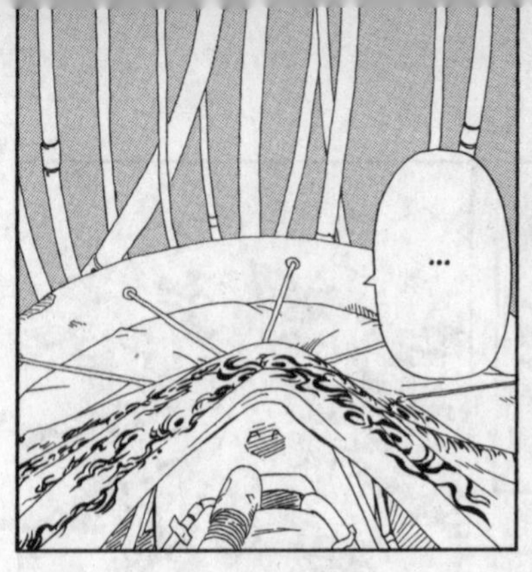
...

I
WONDER...
...WHY...
ARE WE
BORN?

DO WE
ALL CARRY
SOME
IMPORTANT
MISSION
WITHIN US...
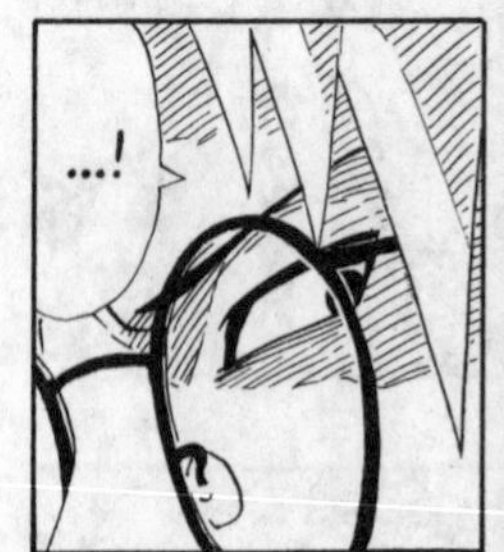
...!
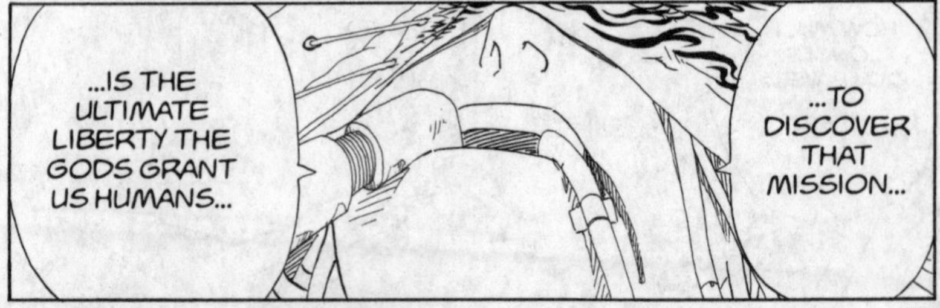
...TO
DISCOVER
THAT
MISSION...
...IS THE
ULTIMATE
LIBERTY THE
GODS GRANT
US HUMANS...

READ THIS WAY

I UNDERSTAND...
LORD OROCHIMARU IS IN A GREAT DEAL OF PAIN RIGHT NOW.
THIS IS A TRUE DILEMMA...

BUT I'M GOING TO BE BRUTALLY CLEAR...
...WHAT CAN YOU DO IN YOUR CURRENT STATE?
YOUR VALUE AS A VESSEL IS LONG LOST...

...

THERE IS A NEW VESSEL...
...ON HIS WAY NOW.

ALTHOUGH...
...HE'S TOO LATE AT THIS POINT AS WELL.

KLAK
BLEEP

READ THIS WAY

...
...

BLIP
NOW! YOU PROMISED TO LET ME OUT OF HERE!
YOU BETTER KEEP YOUR WORD!
WHAT'S GOING ON?! HURRY UP AND OPEN THE DOOR!!

BLIP
CLANG
!

BLIP
...

BLIP
SSSS SSSS

SSSS SSSS
SST

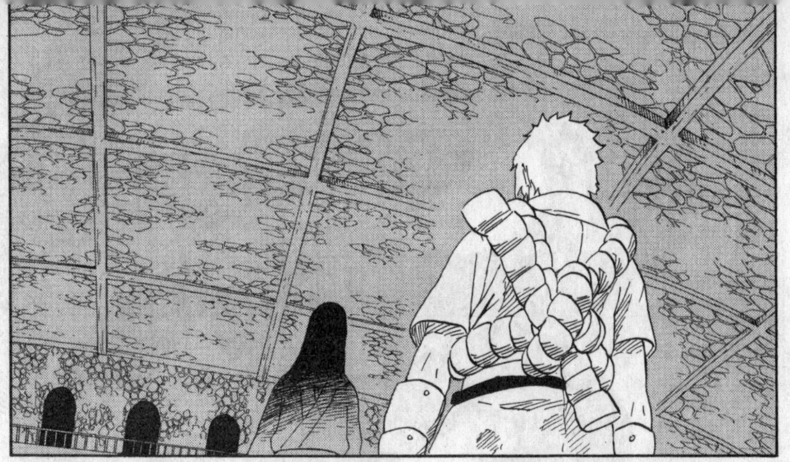

WHAT?!
THERE WAS ONE MORE OF YOU...?
FINE, LET'S...
?!!

...

SLITHER...

...OH, MAN...
...IT'S USELESS, HE'S GOING TO EAT ME...

HO HO... DON'T WORRY, I WILL LET YOU OUT OF HERE... AND I'LL GRANT YOU ONE WISH AS WELL.
WOOSH
!

READ THIS WAY

...YOU USED MY CLAN IN YOUR TESTS...
...PLEASE LET THEM GO...

...
VERY WELL... 'TIS A SIMPLE REQUEST...

...

DO NOT BE AFRAID... YOUR STRONG WILL SHALL REMAIN INSIDE ME AS A RESIDUAL AURA.
YOU WILL NOT LOSE EVERYTHING.

WELL THEN... I THANK YOU FOR YOUR BODY.

AAAAAAARRGH!!

NOW HE WON'T BE ABLE TO TRANSFER AGAIN FOR YEARS...
...BUT BY THEN... WE'LL BE READY!!

...

FOR SURE...
I MAY NO LONGER HAVE ANY VALUE AS A VESSEL FOR THE TRANSFERENCE JUTSU...
RIP
RIP

...AND IT IS DIFFICULT FOR ME TO IDENTIFY MY TRUE PURPOSE WHEN I'VE LOST EVERYTHING...
SNAP

READ
THIS
WAY

...BUT... I THINK I'VE FINALLY FIGURED IT OUT...
UNNH

?

EVEN IF IT IS NOT TO BE ME... I SHALL HELP TAKE IN THIS NEW VESSEL...
FLOP...
...EVEN AT THE COST OF MY LIFE...

IT IS... THE BEST WAY FOR ME TO REPAY LORD OROCHIMARU...

...AND THE LEAST I CAN DO...

SHOOM

!
KLUNK

HEY, HOLD UP!

ARE WE CLOSE?
SCREECH

NO... IT'S WAY TOO SOON... SOMETHING ELSE!
SCREECH

!

WHAT HAVE THOSE FOOLS JIROBO AND KIDOMARU BEEN DOING?!

...

CAUGHT UP TO YA!

FINE! HAVE IT YOUR WAY!
I'LL KILL YA ALL IN NO TIME!!
FWOOSH

岸本斉史

It's been a year since I moved into my current apartment and I just recently realized something... I can see Mt. Fuji from my porch. It took me this long to notice!

—Masashi Kishimoto, 2004

NARUTO™

SHONEN JUMP MANGA EDITION

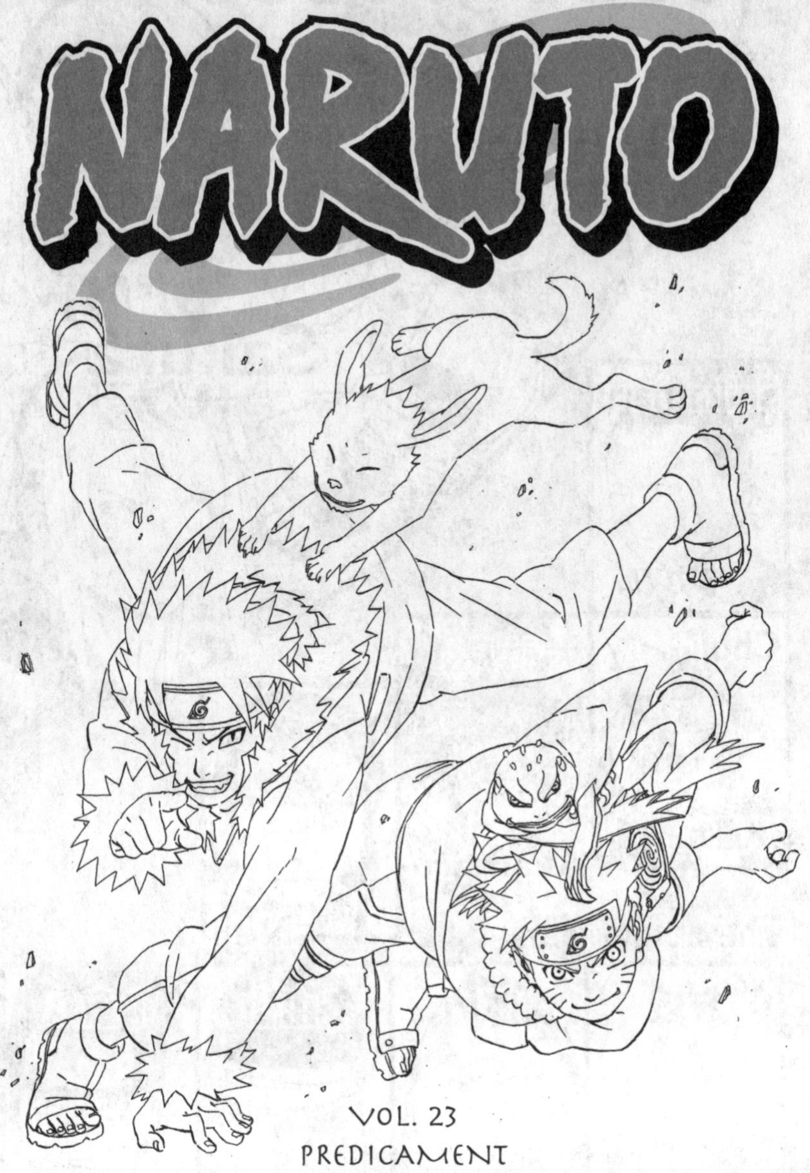

VOL. 23

PREDICAMENT

STORY AND ART BY

MASASHI KISHIMOTO

CHARACTERS
Sasuke
サスケ
Naruto
ナルト
Sakura
サクラ
Shikamaru
シカマル
Choji
秋道チョウジ
犬塚キバ&
赤丸
Kiba&
Akamaru
日向ネジ
Neji
The Sound Ninja Four
左近
Sakon
次郎坊
Jirobo
多由也
Tayuya
鬼童丸
Kidomaru

The Story So Far...

Twelve years ago a destructive nine-tailed fox spirit attacked the ninja village of Konohagakure. The *Hokage*, or village champion, defeated the fox by sealing its soul into the body of a baby boy. Now that boy, Uzumaki Naruto, has grown up to be a ninja-in-training, learning the art of ninjutsu with his cellmates Sakura and Sasuke.

Naruto and company take on the Chûnin Selection Exams but suffer a sudden attack from Orochimaru in the Forest of Death. Orochimaru leaves a curse mark on Sasuke's body and vanishes, only to return during the final round to launch *Operation Destroy Konoha!* While Naruto battles Gaara, the Third Hokage falls to Orochimaru.

After the funeral, the mysterious Tsunade becomes Fifth Hokage. Sasuke flees Konohagakure with the Sound Ninja Four. Shikamaru and a cell hurry to pursue Sasuke, but Choji and then Neji are struck down by the Sound Ninja. Can Sasuke be saved from himself?!

NARUTO

VOL. 23
PREDICAMENT

CONTENTS

Number 200: According to Plan...!!

DOESN'T WASTE ANY TIME, DOES HE?!
SHF
TAK
FWIP

READ THIS WAY
EAT THIS...
FOOSH
TARENKEN! MULTIPLE FISTS BARRAGE!!
SHOOM
FWUD
FWUD
FWUD
FAP FAP FAP FAP FAP FAP FAP

!!

GRRW

READ
THIS
WAY

SHADOW DOPPEL- GANGER TRANSFOR- MATION...?
FWIP
RASEN- GAN! SPIRAL CHAKRA SPHERE!!
GRAB
WHAT? MY HAND ...!

IT'S POINT- LESS IF I GET YOUR HAND FIRST!

UGH... KIBA, NOW!

BOOF!!

TSUUGA! TUNNELING FANG!!

WHIRRRRRK
SHF

SSH
BY LURING SAKON AND ME INTO ALIGNMENT...
THEY WERE AIMING FOR ME FROM THE START!

!

TAK
YOU THINK IT'S THAT EASY?!

SHOOOOM

GACK
?!
UNNG

KAGEMANE NO JUTSU! SHADOW POSSESSION TECHNIQUE!! SUCCESS!

A DIVERSION...
NO... HE GOT ME.

HERE IT COMES!

WHEEEEEEEEE

WOOSH
?!

!!
THAP
TAYUYA, QUIT DAY-DREAMING!
FWAP
I'M NOT ...!
CLUNK
WATCH OUT!
NO... I CAN'T DODGE.
OOF!!
THOK
SHWIP

CATCH!
SHWOO

SIGH...
SLOPPY AS ALWAYS.
TOO MUCH INDIVIDUAL SKILL CAN BE A LIABILITY TOO.

NICE JOB!
WHAK
KIBA! SHIKA-MARU!!

JUST AS PLANNED!!
WE'RE AT LEAST A STEP AHEAD OF THEM.

READ THIS WAY

YOU WON'T GET AWAY!!

AKA-MARU!!
WOOF!!
HURRY BACK AS SOON AS IT'S SET!
!
!
GRRRR

DON'T "WOOF" ME, MUTT!!

READ THIS WAY

BLAM

READ THIS WAY

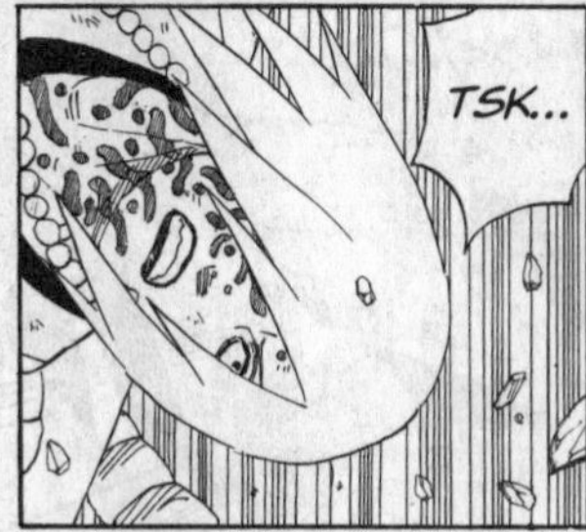
TSK...

...NO...

WHOAAAAH!!

PUNKS!!
FOOSH

NO WAY! WHAT'S WITH THEM?!
HERE COMES THE OTHER ONE!!

OH, MAN... I'LL TAKE CARE OF IT.
NARUTO, YOU GO AHEAD WITH THE COFFIN!

...
SHIKA-MARU ...

JUST GO!

!

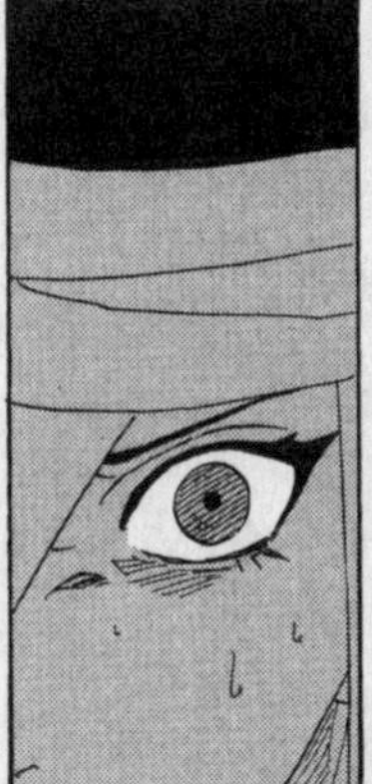

KIMIMARO.

?!

NARUTO
TM

Number 201: Miscalculation...!!

FOOSH
FOOSH
CLAK

WHOA!
RUSTLE
SHHF
RUSTLE
RUSTLE
WHAT?!
TAK

YOU'RE LATE... TAYUYA.

?!
...

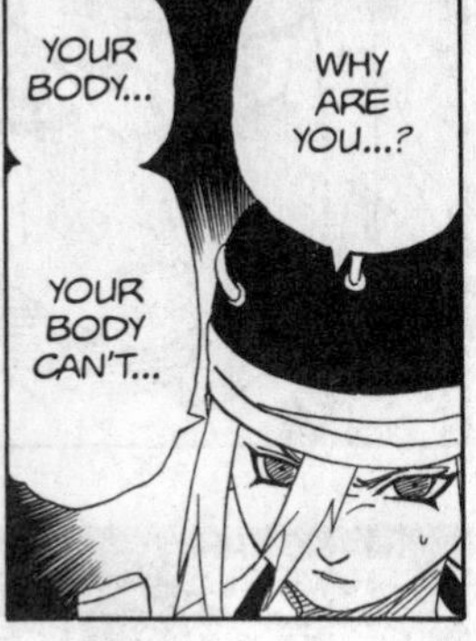
WHY ARE YOU...?
YOUR BODY...
YOUR BODY CAN'T...

I NO LONGER MOVE USING FLESH...
I USE THE POWER OF MY MIND.

HMPH.
CAN'T YOU EVEN DIE...?

I CAN FEEL IT A LITTLE NOW...
I FEEL RELEASE FROM THE PRISON OF THE FLESH...
...AS IF I CAN TOUCH JUST A SMALL PART OF LORD OROCHIMARU'S DREAM.

OROCHI-MARU...!
UGH...
GRRR

THIS IS THE DREAM VESSEL...

BUT YOU ALL WERE TOO LATE...

READ
THIS
WAY

HEY! I DON'T UNDER-STAND A WORD YOU'RE SAYING!
FOOSH
GIVE SASUKE BACK!!

!!
HEY, NARUTO ...
WAIT!!

SHF
!!

PAP
UNH...

TAYUYA...
SHWOO
TMP
TSK...

I WON'T KILL YOU...
SHF
...SO YOU CAN LIVE TO FULFILL YOUR MISSION.
!!

I'LL LEAVE THESE TWO PESTS TO YOU.

TUP

TSK...
SHF

FWIP

CALM DOWN, NARUTO!
RATS!
RATS!

...
WE MUST BRING SASUKE BACK TO KONOHA.

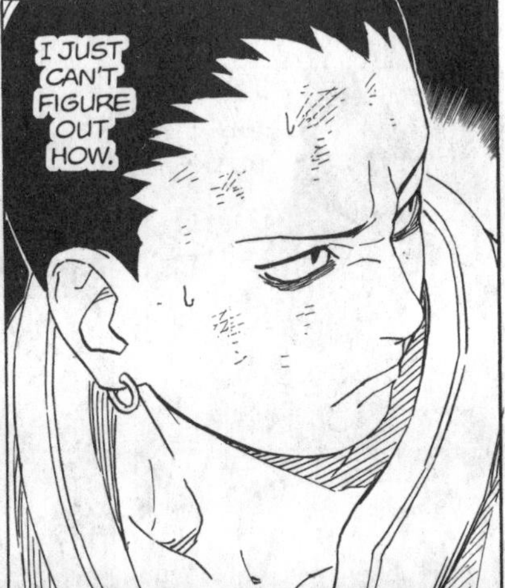
I JUST CAN'T FIGURE OUT HOW.

...

NARUTO!
DO AS I SAY!
!

THAT'S IT! TIME TO FINISH THIS!

HMPH... HE'S A TYPICAL SHORT-RANGE IDIOT ONLY GOOD AT SHADOW DOPPEL-GANGERS.
AND HE'S A MID-RANGE TYPE WHO TIES ENEMIES UP WITH HIS SHADOW ARTS... AND A SHARP-MINDED LEADER...

GOT IT...?
YEAH ...!

BRING IT, PUNKS.

ALRIGHT!!
FOOSH
LET'S GO, NARUTO!!
IT'S TWO ON ONE!!
WE CAN TAKE HER!

COME ON!!

YOU SHOULDN'T UNDER-ESTIMATE US!!
CHARGE!!

HMPH! IT DOESN'T MATTER HOW MANY OF YOU THERE ARE.

NOW!!

CLANK

YOU'RE OVER!

WHAT?! YOU TRICKED ME!

TEAM-WORK? THIS IS CHEAT-ING!

!!

SCUFF

TAK

HANG IN THERE, SHIKAMARU!

I'M COMING, SASUKE!!

MY... TO THINK HE COULD MOVE WITH HIS BODY IN SUCH A STATE...
KABUTO... YOUR ORDERS TO HIM MUST HAVE BEEN QUITE SEVERE.

NO, I GAVE NO ORDERS...
I'M NOT VERY FOND OF COERCION...
HE DID THIS ON HIS OWN...
...FOR YOU... HE WORSHIPS YOU.

KABUTO...

YOU ARE DESPICABLE...

READ THIS WAY

HIS CLAN HAS STRONG BODIES... GENUINE KEKKEI GENKAI BLOODLINE...
...OR HAD... UNTIL RECENTLY.

YES... WHENEVER I THINK OF HAVING LOST HIM MY SKIN CRAWLS...
I STILL THINK... HE WAS THE ONE I WISHED FOR IN MY HEART... THE LEAST LIKELY TO BE DESTROYED. KIMIMARO.

ALSO...
HAD HE NOT BEEN ILL, THE HOKAGE'S ASSASSI-NATION WOULD'VE GONE SMOOTHLY.
AND YOU WOULDN'T SUFFER LIKE THIS.

IN THIS WORLD... IT SEEMS THAT THINGS DON'T GO AS WE WISH THEY WOULD.

...

THAT TOO IS MERELY A MATTER OF TIME... LORD OROCHI-MARU.

SHOOM

GLANCE

TAK

SIGH.
SHF
TAYUYA... SHE CAN NO LONGER BE TOLERATED.

HEY...!
BAM
...
NOW THEN... SHALL WE MAKE THIS QUICK?
ZZZ

Number 202: Three Wishes!!

...?!

...
YOU...
THOSE EYES...

GRRR

HMM... HIS... CHAKRA IS PECULIAR.

WHAT'S OROCHI-MARU DOING?!
WHAT DOES HE WANT WITH SASUKE?!

READ
THIS
WAY

...

LORD OROCHIMARU HAS ALREADY MASTERED THE ART OF IMMORTALITY.
BUT IT TAKES TIME TO LEARN *EVERYTHING.*

WHAT'S THAT GOT TO DO WITH SASUKE?!

IMMORTALITY DOESN'T MEAN YOUR FLESH LIVES ON AS IS...
BEFORE THE BODY DECAYS, ANOTHER STRONG BODY MUST BE OBTAINED AS A VESSEL FOR THE SOUL.

THEN...

SASUKE...?!

SSH
YES...
PRECISELY
...
GRRR
I WON'T
LET THAT
HAPPEN...

READ THIS WAY

IDIOT... WHAT DO YOU THINK A TWERP LIKE YOU CAN DO?

AND... CONSIDER-ING THE TIME YOU'VE SPENT GETTING THIS FAR...
EVERY TIME YOU CATCH UP WITH US, YOU SACRIFICE ONE OF YOUR TEAMMATES IN THE PROCESS...

...

IS THIS SASUKE, OR WHATEVER HIS NAME IS, SO IMPORTANT TO YOU?

YOU'D SACRIFICE EVERYONE FOR JUST ONE TEAM-MATE...?
HEH HEH... SWEET, BUT A COMPLETELY USELESS GESTURE!

...

HAH...

THIS IS MY FIRST TIME OUT AS THE LEADER...
I WAS TOO WORRIED ABOUT LOSING SOMEONE...
I WASN'T SURE IF I'D MADE THE RIGHT DECISION.

...

AS LEADER, MY TEAMMATES' LIVES ARE IN MY HANDS...
I SHOULD'VE PLACED MORE VALUE ON THE LIVES OF MY TEAMMATES INSTEAD OF ONE PERSON ABDUCTED BY THE ENEMY.
THE RIGHT THING TO DO WOULD'VE BEEN TO ABORT THIS RECKLESS MISSION.

READ THIS WAY

THEN, WHY DIDN'T YOU?

THINGS DON'T ALWAYS WORK BY THE BOOK IN THIS WORLD.

BESIDES, ABANDONING A TEAMMATE...
...TO PROTECT YOURSELF...?
THERE'S NO ONE IN MY SQUAD LIKE THAT.

...
NOT EVEN ME.

...

ANYWAY, A LAZY DAYDREAMER LIKE ME IS A POOR EXCUSE FOR A LEADER...
ALL I CAN DO FOR MY COMRADES...

LISTEN UP...
...I DON'T THINK THEY'RE SACRIFICES.
I DON'T THINK THEY'RE DEAD...

...IS BELIEVE IN THEM...

!

FWIP

DON'T UNDER-ESTIMATE MY TEAM.
SPLASH
WHOAH!!
GRAB
GRIN
?!
WOOF WOOF!
SLOOSH

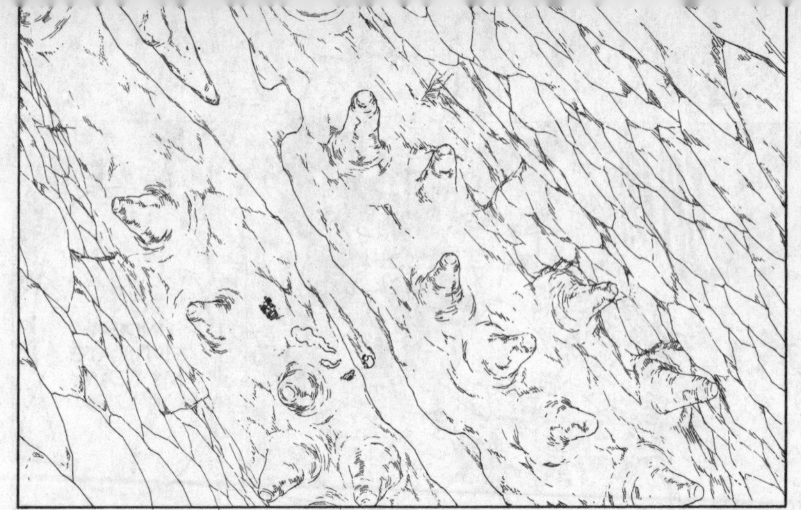

HUH ...?
WHY?!

MY ATTACK WAS DEAD ON, BUT NO EFFECT ?!
AND HOW DID HE COUNTER ?!

TSK...

LISTEN, AKAMARU. WE'LL NAIL HIM WITH GATSUUGA...
ARF ...

!

FOOSH POOF

SPLASH

SPLOSH

WHIRRRR

GATSUUGA! FANG-OVER-FANG!!

BOOM

KUCHI-YOSE NO JUTSU! THE ART OF SUMMON-ING!!
BOOF
BAMON
...
OH, NO... THIS IS BAD...

I'M GONNA PLAY A MELODY OF DEATH FOR YOU!
IT'S YOU...

...WHO SHOULDN'T UNDER-ESTIMATE US!

WHAT IS THIS GUY?!

?!

TWO ON TWO. WORKS FOR ME.
RIGHT... SAKON?

BUT... WHO WOULD'VE THOUGHT THE SOUND FOUR WOULD TAKE SO LONG...
THEY MIGHT'VE SENT PEOPLE CAPABLE OF STOPPING THEM.
OR MAYBE THEY'RE PLAYING AROUND...

HO HO...

WELL, THE ONE WHO'S SLOWING THEM DOWN IS EITHER THE PERPETUALLY HUNGRY JIROBO OR...
...THE PLAYFUL KIDOMARU.

HEH HEH... BUT SAKON'S THE MOST TROUBLE-SOME.
HE'S NOT SATISFIED UNTIL HE KILLS HIS FOE. HE COULD JUST LEAVE THEM, BUT...
HE'S THE STRONGEST OF THE SOUND FOUR. HE LIKES TO SHOW OFF.

HO HO... WELL...
TAYUYA IS NO LESS VAIN.

READ
THIS
WAY

...

WELL... IN ANY CASE, NOW THAT KIMIMARO'S THERE, WE WON'T FAIL...
HE'LL CLEAN UP WHOEVER'S BECOME USELESS TO ME...

HMM.

I WON'T GIVE UP ON SASUKE, NO MATTER WHAT...

NNG
INTERESTING.

ONN

NARUTO™

Number 203: Sakon's Secret

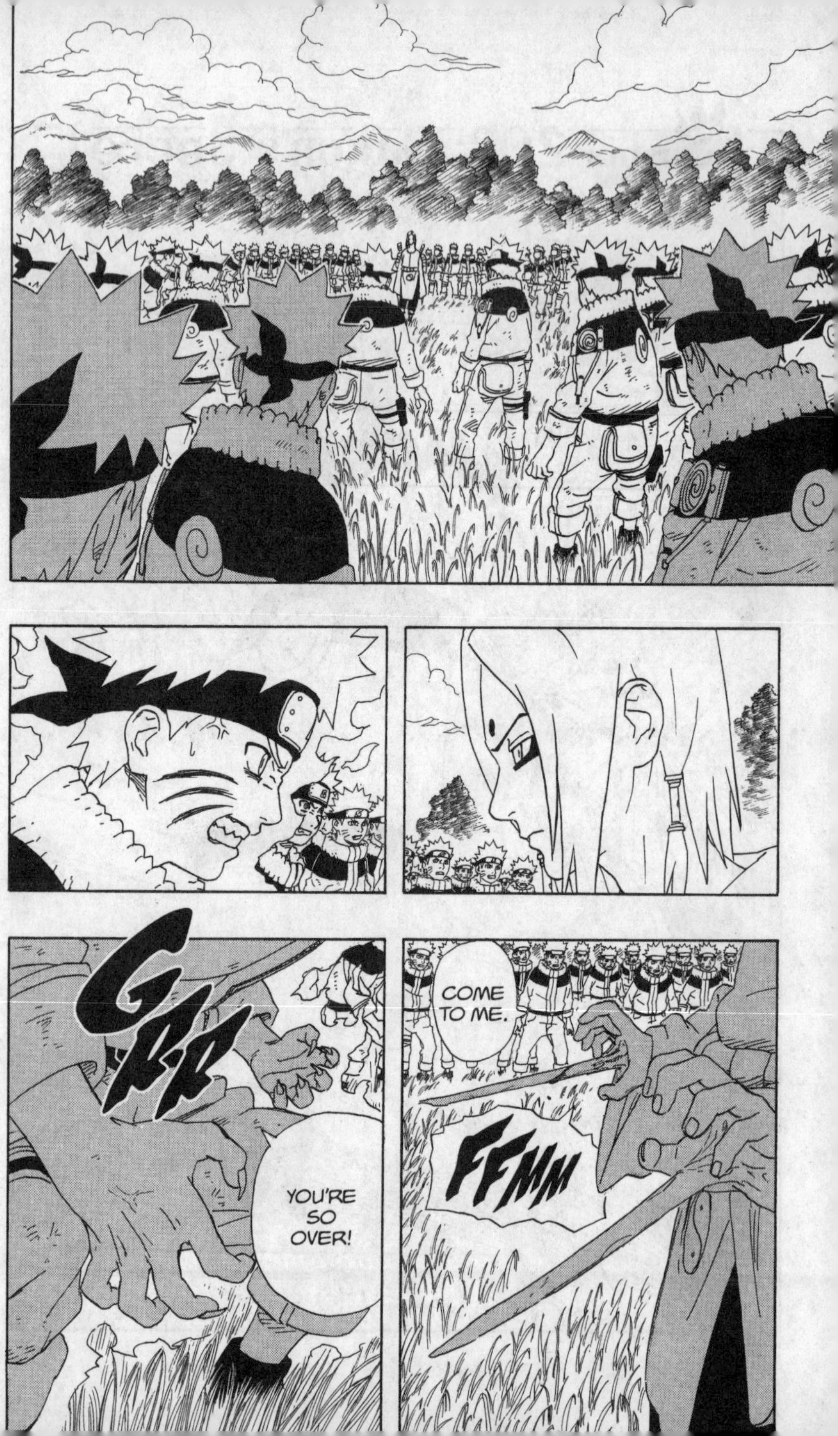

COME TO ME.
FFMM

GRR
YOU'RE SO OVER!

GAAH
GRRRRRRRRR
FOOSH

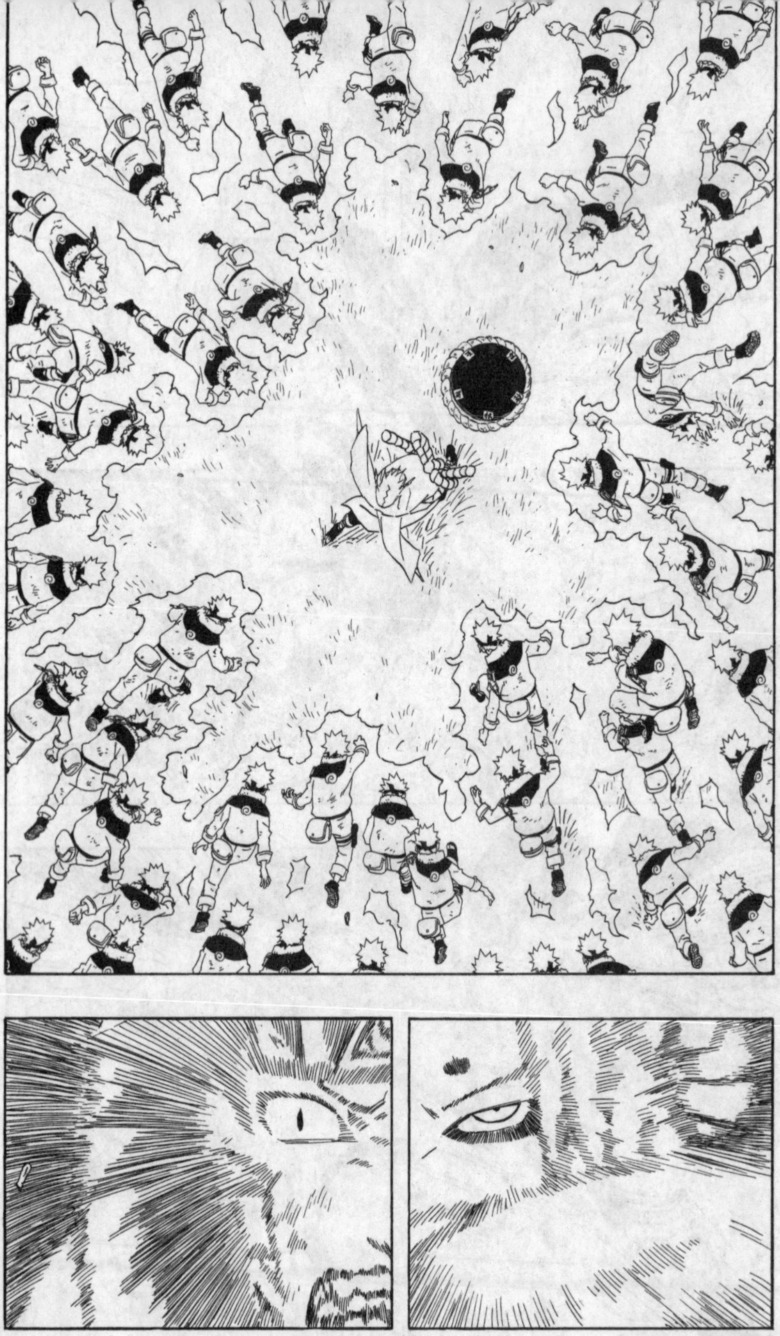

TARENKEN! MULTIPLE FISTS BARRAGE!!
SMASH!
!
HMPH...
NGH.
!

GRAB

USUALLY MY BIG BROTHER SLEEPS INSIDE ME, BUT WHEN IT COMES TO A FIGHT, HE LIKES TO HELP.
SHUU
YOU KNOW, WE'RE INSEPA-RABLE...

...SO...
SHUU
WOULD YOU LIKE TO MEET MY BROTHER, UKON?

SHUU
SHUU
SHUU

READ THIS WAY
THOK
LIKE THIS!
AGH!!
WOOF! WOOF!
FWUP
TAREN-KYAKU! MULTIPLE LEGS BARRAGE!!
WHIMPER!
AAUGH!!
A TRIPLE KICK! FEEL THE POWER? NOW...
!
THERE'S NO TIME FOR GAMES, SAKON.
WHUP
SHU

THEY ALL DIE NOW!
ACTIVATE SECOND STATE!!
SHUUU

READ THIS WAY

?!!

SHUU
YOU'RE IMPETUOUS, BIG BROTHER.

HUF HUF

WHIMPER.
SHIVR SHIVR

AKA-MARU ...
I SEE... YOU'RE SAYING THOSE HORNS AREN'T FAKE...
THE SITUATION WAS ALREADY HOPELESS WHEN THAT OTHER GUY SHOWED UP. NOW SAKON HAS TEN TIMES MORE CHAKRA...?

HOW DO YOU WANT THEM, BIG BROTHER?
IN PIECES...

WOOF WOOF!!

!!
YOU WANNA DO THAT?!

ARF!
NO WAY, AKAMARU!
IT'S TOO DANGEROUS WITHOUT OUR COMRADES.

YOU KNOW IF WE USE THAT JUTSU, BOTH OF US...
...OUR CHAKRA WILL RUN OUT AND WE WON'T BE ABLE TO MOVE ANYMORE.

IF WE MESS UP...
WE'LL DIE HERE...

OUCH ...!

READ THIS WAY

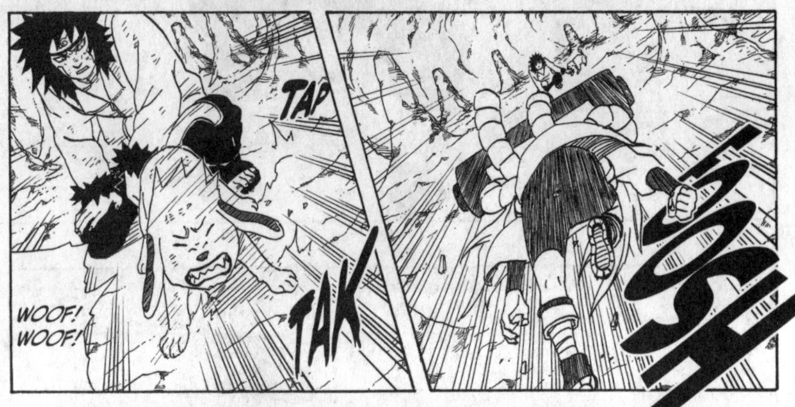

GAROGA! WOLF FANG-OVER-FANG!
SKF
ARF!!

FFMM

READ THIS WAY

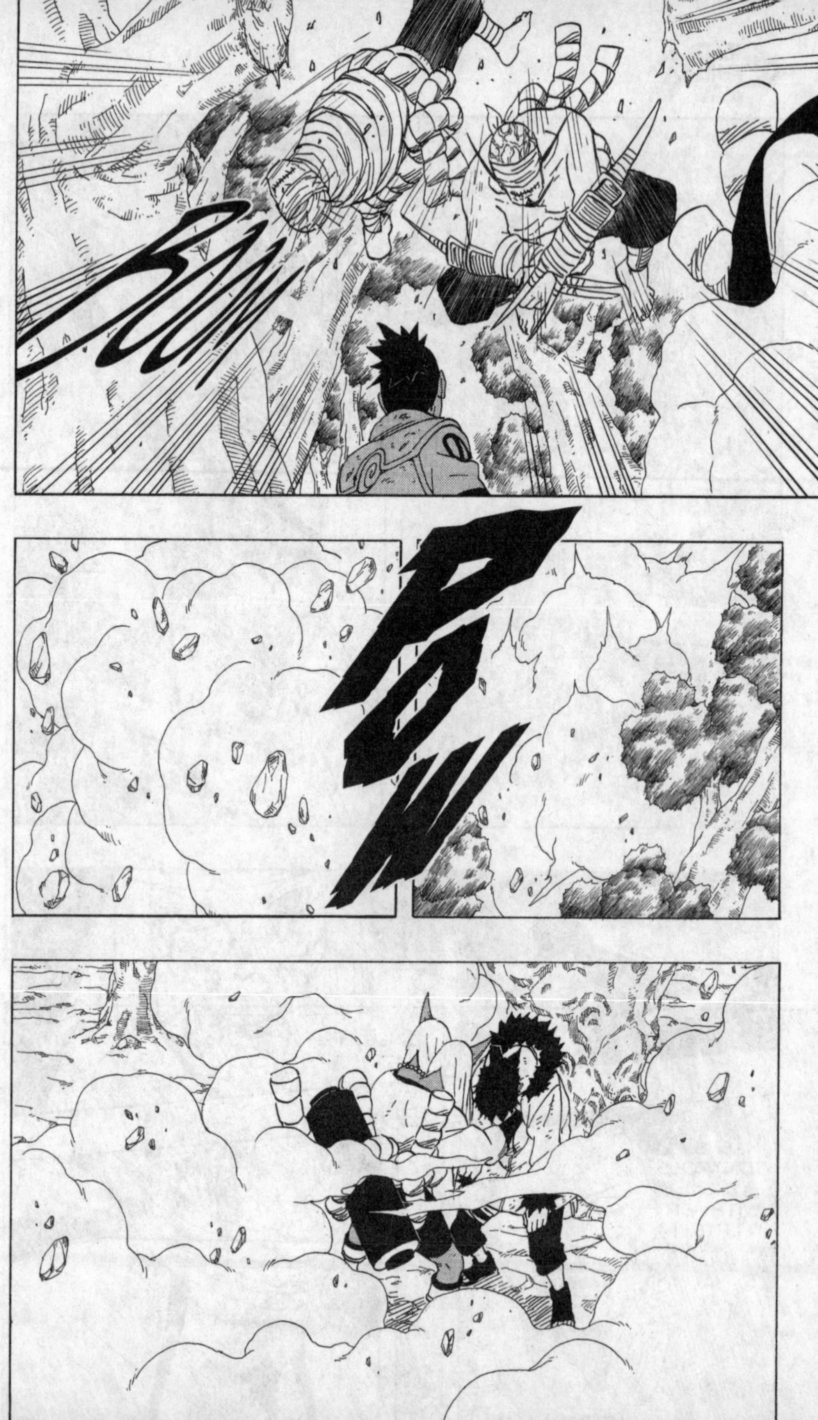
BAM
BOW

READ
THIS
WAY

SPRAAY
ARF!
DYNAMIC
MARKING!!

AKA-
MARU,
NOW!
GRAB

WHA...
DID HE
JUST
...?!
ZAP
TAK
?!

NOW
WE'RE
READY!
!!
TAP
TAP

INUZUKA
STYLE!
MAN-BEAST
TRANSFOR-
MATION
COMBO!!
TUMP
FWUP

BOOF

OMMM
GRR
NG
SOTORO! TWO-HEADED WOLF!!
DRIP DRIP

READ THIS WAY

HE-HEH HEH. AS IF IT MATTERED.
WHAT CAN A COUPLE OF DRIVELING DOGS DO...?

BAM
!

EAT THIS!!
SWIP

!

BWAFF
SHUPAAA
ZUING
ARGH!
TM
GAROGA! WOLF FANG-OVER-FANG!!

!
SLIP
DROOL ?!
SAKON, WHAT'RE YOU DOING? ON THE RIGHT!!
?!!
*@Ɛ%...
THD

NARUTO
TM

Number 204: Ukon's Prowess

OM

READ THIS WAY
THO
SHREEDD
THUD
THUD

HA... HOW'S THAT?!
GAROGA: WOLF FANG-OVER-FANG'S SPIN IS SO FAST THAT WE LOSE OUR FIELD OF VISION.
IT'S A VIOLENT ULTRA-ROTATION.

EVEN IF IT'S NOT A DIRECT HIT, YOU'RE STILL CUT DOWN...
IF YOU TAKE IT FULL BLAST, YOU GET SMASHED.

READ THIS WAY

WHATEVER... WE WERE JUST THINKING ABOUT SPLITTING UP TO FINISH YOU OFF.

CLOMP

NOW THE REAL FIGHT BEGINS.
UH-OH ...!!
WOOF!
YEAH... I KNOW, AKAMARU... WE CAN ONLY USE GAROGA ONCE MORE...
CRUNCH
SHIVR
SHIVR
THIS HAS TO END IT!!
TAK
WHREE
GAROGA! WOLF FANG-OVER-FANG!!

FSSH

WHIRRRRRR

FSSH

SHH

ZOOM

ZOOM

SHH

SWIP

NO USE HIDING!!

I TOLD YOU, WE'RE NOT FOLLOWING YOU WITH OUR EYES!

ZAP

WE'RE FOLLOWING OUR NOSES...

AND ATTACKING BY TRACKING YOUR SCENT EVER SINCE WE MARKED YOU.

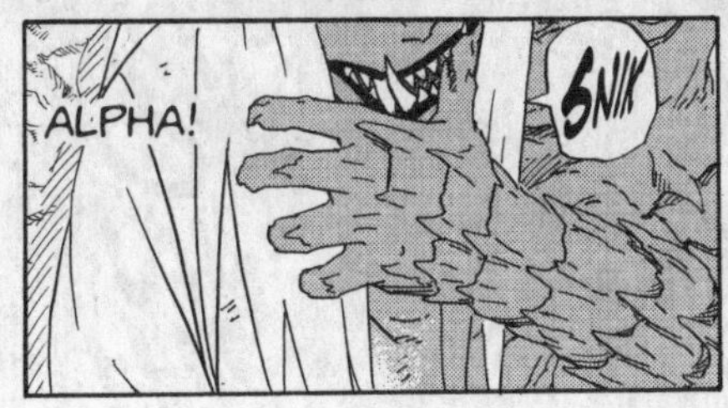

RASHOMON!!!

WHAM

!!

...
WHOMP

QUITE POWERFUL...
LORD OROCHIMARU'S RASHOMON FALTERED...
SHF

TAK

HOWEVER... HEH HEH...

TAK

GLARE
!!
WHAM
AKA-MARU!!
!!
ARGH! HE DID IT AGAIN ...!!
UNH. GAAAH... MY EYES...
NO!
TAK

THIS IS THE END!!
FWU
THUD
AKAMARU, YOU... TOOK THE BLOW FOR ME...
UGH... NGH...
?!
WHERE'S THE OTHER ONE?!

SHUU
LOOKING FOR SOMEONE?

YOU... UKON! YOU USED ME AS A SHIELD?!

ARGH...! IT BURNS... IT'S LIKE ACID IN MY EYES...

I'LL HANDLE IT FROM HERE.

RINSE YOUR EYES IN THE RIVER.

TSK...

TAK

...

SHUP

THAT'S MY SKILL... ASSASSINATION SPECIALIST.
UGH...
YOU NEED MORE THAN JUST A GOOD NOSE AND CLAWS TO DEFEAT ME.
YOU CAN'T OVERPOWER ME!
AGH...

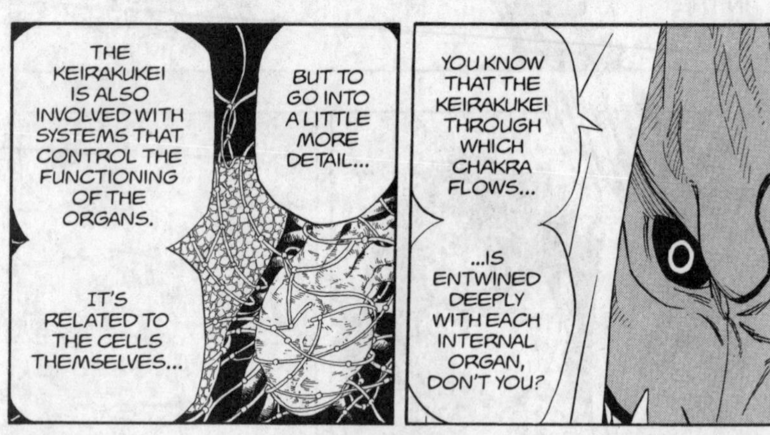
YOU KNOW THAT THE KEIRAKUKEI THROUGH WHICH CHAKRA FLOWS...
...IS ENTWINED DEEPLY WITH EACH INTERNAL ORGAN, DON'T YOU?
BUT TO GO INTO A LITTLE MORE DETAIL...
THE KEIRAKUKEI IS ALSO INVOLVED WITH SYSTEMS THAT CONTROL THE FUNCTIONING OF THE ORGANS.
IT'S RELATED TO THE CELLS THEMSELVES...

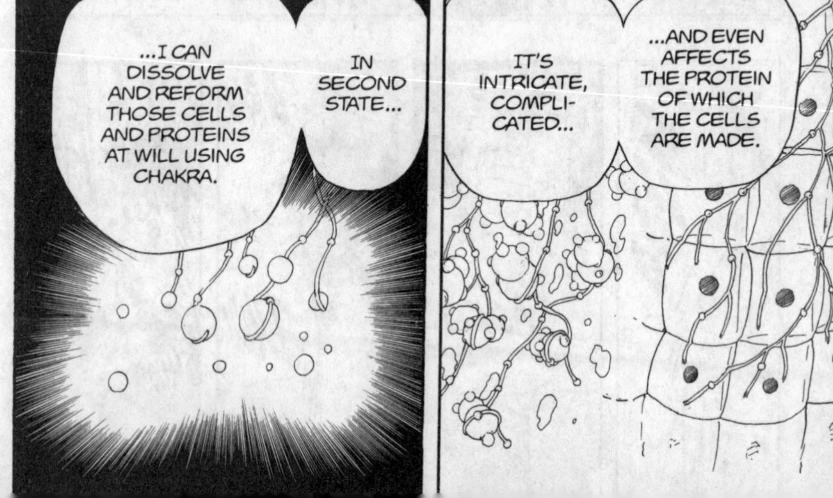
IT'S INTRICATE, COMPLICATED...
...AND EVEN AFFECTS THE PROTEIN OF WHICH THE CELLS ARE MADE.
IN SECOND STATE...
...I CAN DISSOLVE AND REFORM THOSE CELLS AND PROTEINS AT WILL USING CHAKRA.

TO PUT IT SIMPLY, I BREAK MY BODY INTO PIECES AND ENTER AN ENEMY'S BODY.
THEN I CAN RESTORE MY BODY AND COME OUT.

NOW, YOU AND I ARE IN A MERGED STATE...
WE'RE SHARING A BODY.
SHARING ?!

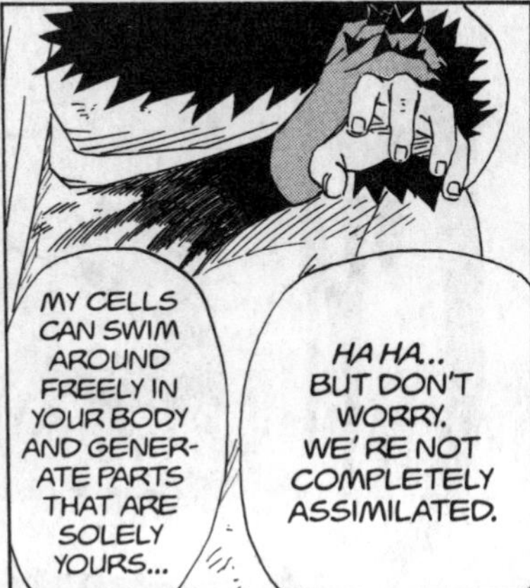
HA HA... BUT DON'T WORRY. WE'RE NOT COMPLETELY ASSIMILATED.
MY CELLS CAN SWIM AROUND FREELY IN YOUR BODY AND GENER-ATE PARTS THAT ARE SOLELY YOURS...

THEN, THERE'S THE CRUEL WAY OF KILLING YOU.
I'LL SCRAPE AWAY THE PARTS OF OUR BODY MADE OF YOUR CELLS, THE PARTS MINE HAVEN'T ENTERED.

AND THEN...

SHUP

?!

CH
AK

READ THIS WAY

ZING

UGH... URK...
HMPH... WHAT IF I... DO THIS?
WHIRL WHIRL
HE'D SACRIFICE HIMSELF ...?!
IT CAN'T BE!!

DIE WITH ME...

NARUTO
TM

Number 205: Kiba's Decision!!

SPLEK!
WHIRL
WHIRL

UGH!!
AAUGH ...!!

FOOL, WHAT ARE YOU DOING ...?!
NGH ...!
SHLUGK

HEH HEH...
YUP... JUST AS I THOUGHT ...
AFTER ALL... WE'RE SHARING A BODY, AREN'T WE?
HUF
HUF

READ THIS WAY

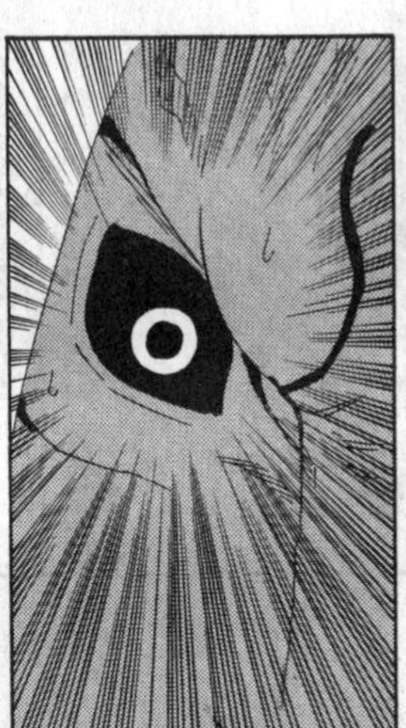

ZYUU

THUD

ARGH...!
SHAK

FWUP

!

SHF
THUNK

TSK!
GLARE

?!!

BOOF
A SMOKE BOMB?!
UGH!
!
BWAA
!
SHUP
SHUP
NO... WHERE DID HE GO...?

READ THIS WAY

HMPH... HE ABANDONED HIS MUTT AND ESCAPED.
...THAT'S THE RIGHT DECISION, BUT...
HE'S EVEN MORE HEARTLESS THAN I... HA HA...
TMP TMP

FSSSHH
TAK

?!
OH, NO...!

PUFF

BLAM

HUF
HUF
HUF

GOOD... HE'S STILL BREATHING.

UNGH...!

...
THANK GOOD-NESS...

READ
THIS
WAY

BA DUMP

AKAMARU... YOU CAME THROUGH...
HUF
HUF
THANKS TO YOU, WE SLOWED 'EM DOWN PRETTY GOOD... EVEN WOUNDED THEM...

THAT'S ENOUGH... YOU'VE DONE ENOUGH...
...IT'S MY TURN TO PROTECT YOU...

PLIP
PLIP

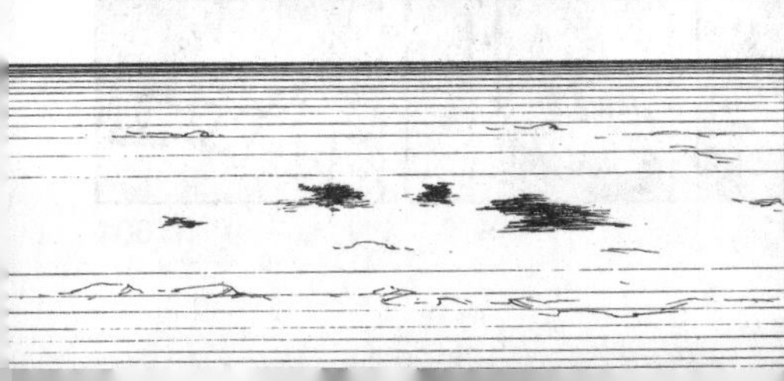

SNEAKY RATS...
THEY SET A TRAP...

ZING
!!

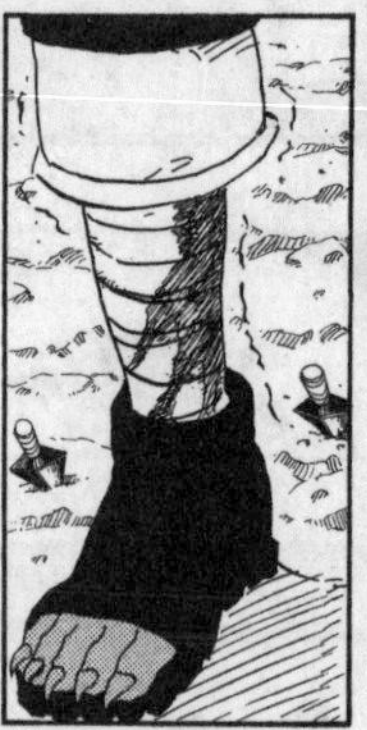

...
GRRR
THEY'RE DEAD!!
HEY! SAKON! WHERE ARE YOU?!
SAKON!!
CLOMP
!
SPLOSH
WHAT'RE YOU MAKING SUCH A FUSS ABOUT?
YOUR VOICE IS SO LOUD IT EVEN HURTS MY EYES...
!!

THEY STILL MUST DIE...

BUT IT'S TIME FOR MY REST...

CLOMP

CLOMP

KEEP THEM ALIVE!!

I'LL FINISH THEM OFF WHEN I AWAKEN!

GOT THAT? TAKE THEM ALIVE, SAKON!!

SHUU

READ
THIS
WAY

BOOF

BEHOLD! YANAGI NO MAI! WILLOW DANCE!!
TAK

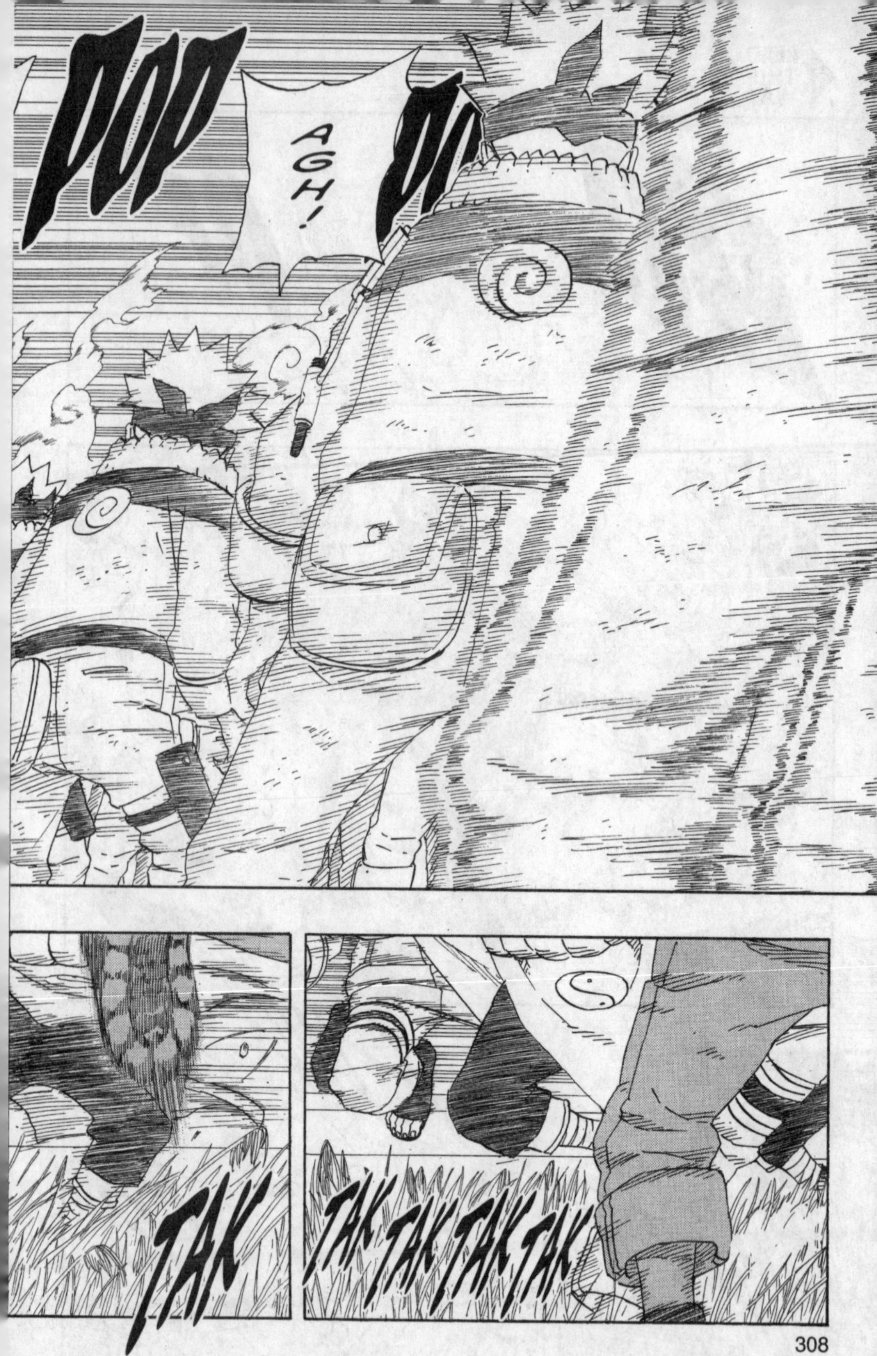
POP
AGH!
POP
TAK
TAK TAK TAK TAK

AAUGH!

UGH!

THAK
THAK
POP 
POP

READ THIS WAY

YAAAAAH!!
BAM

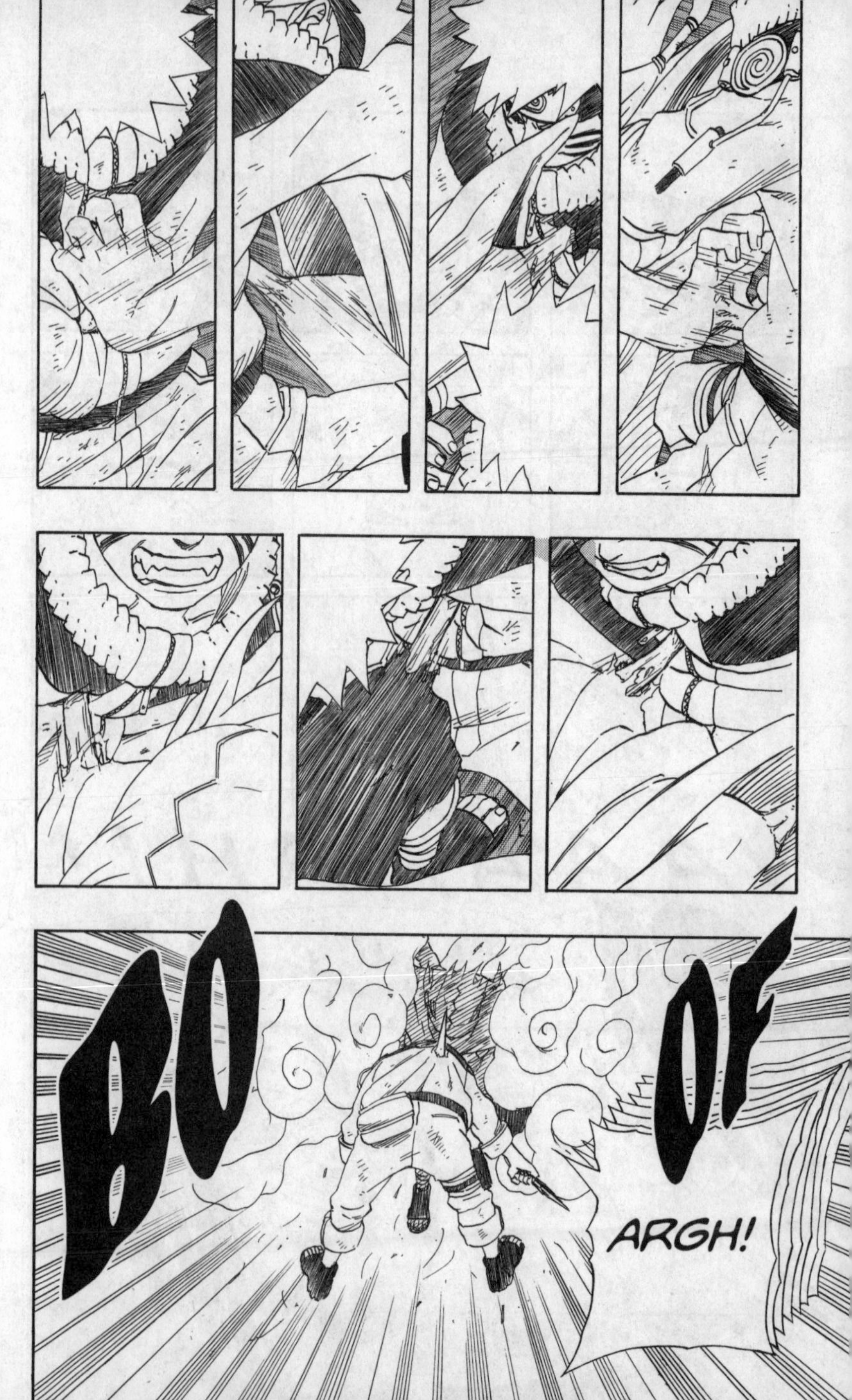

BOOF
ARGH!

A BONE ...?!

Number 206: Predicament...!!

WHAT IS THIS GUY?! HE YANKED THOSE BONES OUT OF HIS OWN BODY?!

READ
THIS
WAY

SHUU

SHUP

SHUU

SHUP

SKF

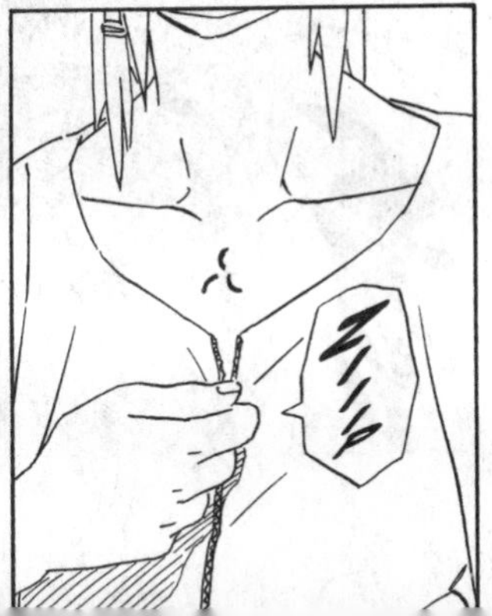

?!

CRACK
SHF

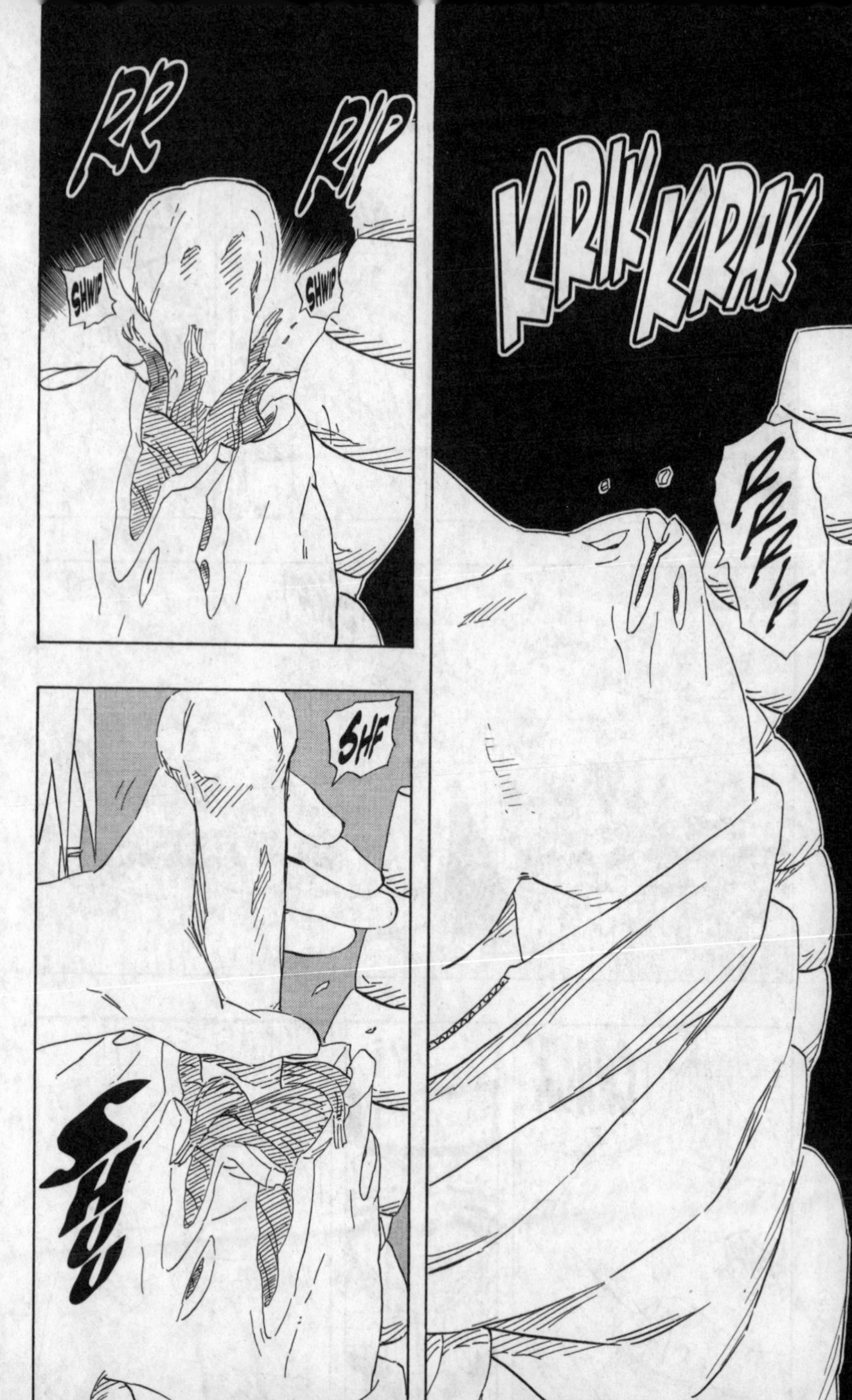
KRIK KRAK
RIP
SHWIP
RIP
SHWIP
SHF
SHUU

READ THIS WAY

SHUK

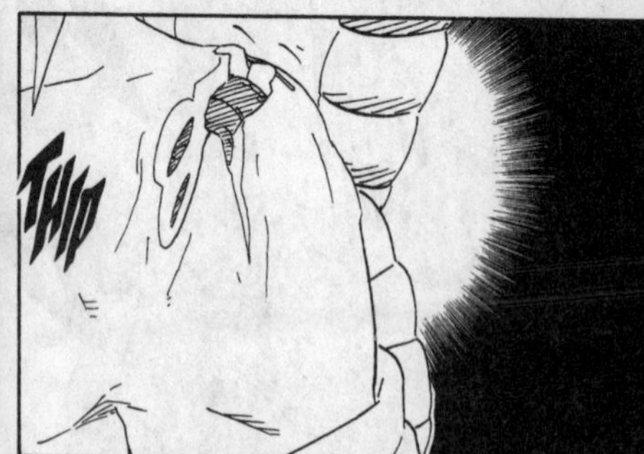

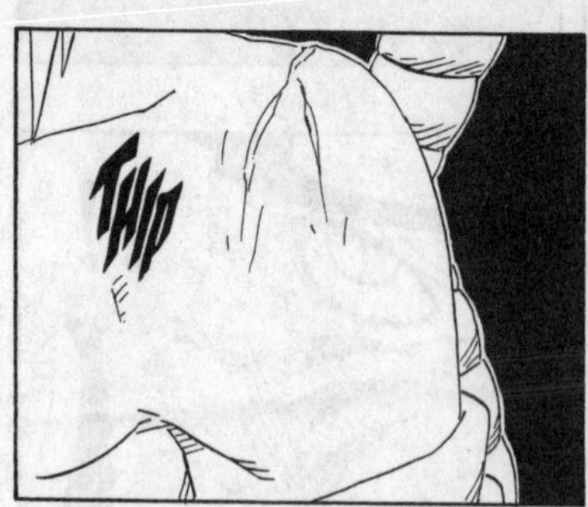

A BONE FOR A SWORD ...?

HIS WOUNDS HEALED...

SHFF

CLINK

CHING

CHING

?!

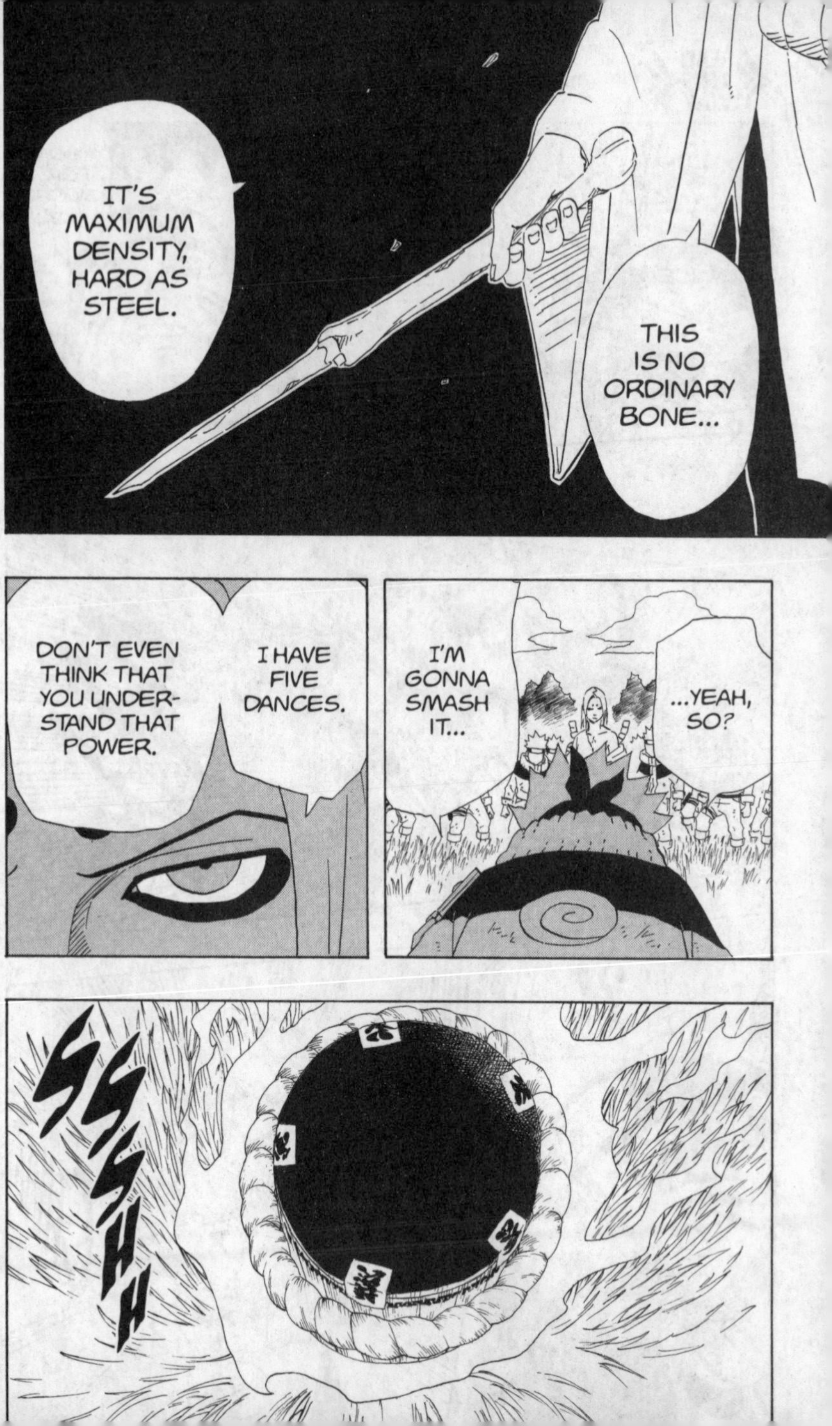

THIS IS NO ORDINARY BONE...

IT'S MAXIMUM DENSITY, HARD AS STEEL.

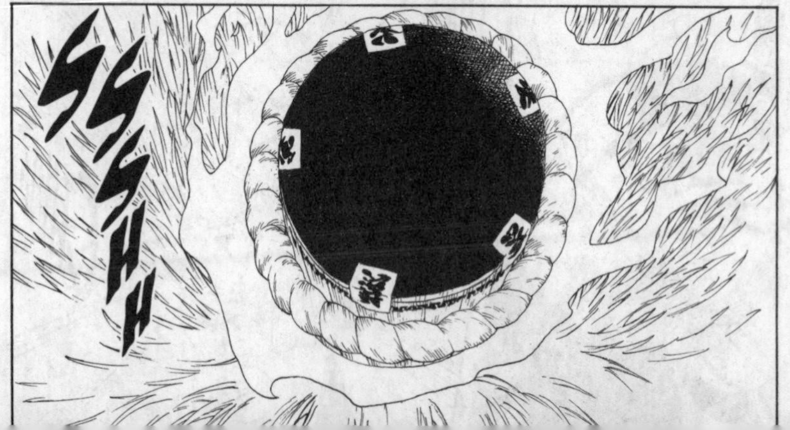

PARTI-CULARLY, THE NEXT ONE...

I'LL SHOW YOU TSUBAKI NO MAI! CAMELLIA DANCE!!

I'M GONNA CRUSH YOU!!

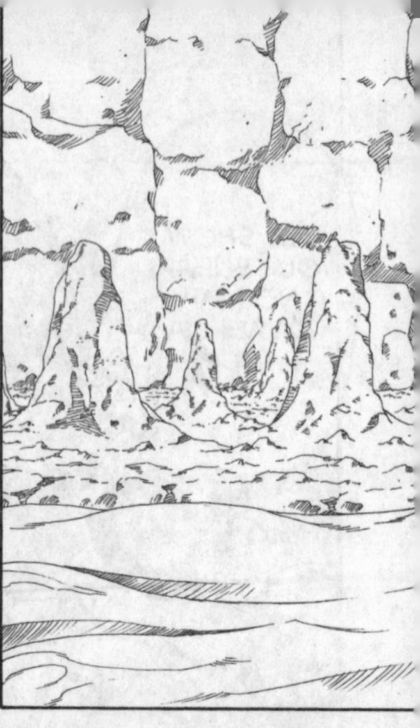

LITTLE BY LITTLE, THEY'RE GETTING CLOSER...

UH-OH... BLOOD-STAINS...
PLIT PLIT

...

READ THIS WAY

SHAAA
RATS... I RESCUED AKAMARU, BUT...

I MIGHT'VE PUSHED IT A LITTLE TOO MUCH... HEH HEH...
OW...

SIGH...

?!!

SNIF
SNIF

THAT SMELL... WHAT'S GOING ON?!
WHY...? WHY ARE THEY COMING THIS WAY...?!

MAN... IT DOESN'T MAKE SENSE...
SKF
ANYWAY, I GOTTA GET OUT OF HERE...

!!
ZING
UGH...

...
FWUMP

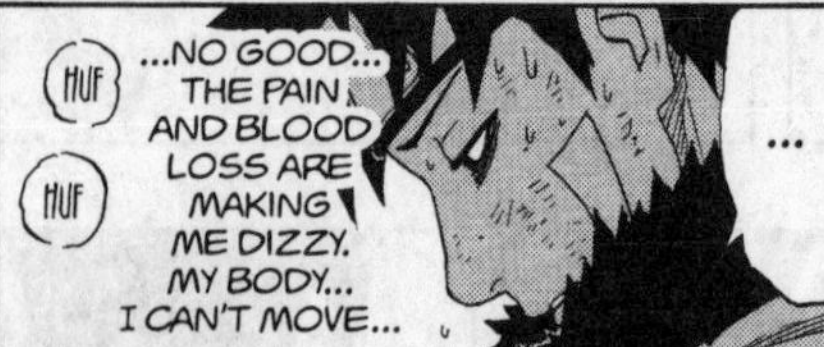
...NO GOOD... THE PAIN AND BLOOD LOSS ARE MAKING ME DIZZY. MY BODY... I CAN'T MOVE...
HUF
HUF

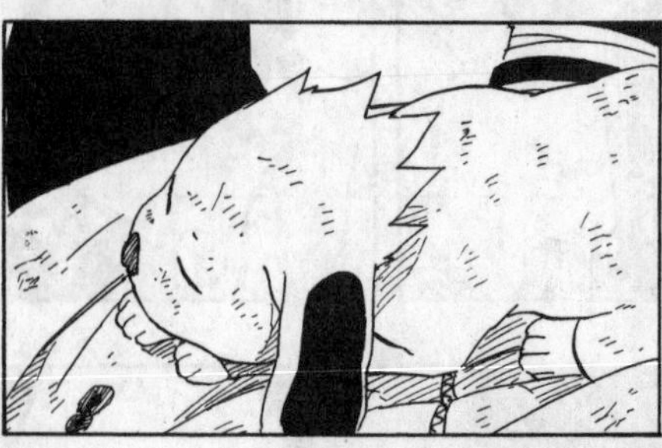

...AKAMARU...

READ THIS WAY

CLOMP

GRIN

KRIK
FOO
SH

!!
...
TSK...
TOK
...MUST'VE GOT AWAY DOWN THE RIVER...

READ
THIS
WAY

SNEAKY
RATS!!

BOOM

HUF
HUF

TMP

WELL... GOT YOU CORNERED, PUNK!

NOT BAD.
YOU TIMED THOSE ATTACKS WELL...
SO WELL THAT I HAD NO CHANCE TO USE JUTSU...
YOU MUST'VE PRACTICED HARD, HUH?

...

THAT'S A PRETTY COMPLICATED MELODY.

HMM... YOU FIGURED OUT THAT I CONTROL THEM WITH MY FLUTE.
AND THE DIFFICULTY OF THE MELODY... NOT BAD, FOR A LITTLE PUNK.
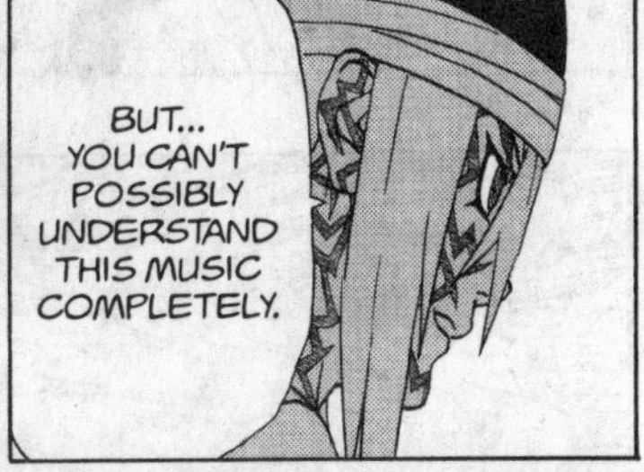
BUT... YOU CAN'T POSSIBLY UNDERSTAND THIS MUSIC COMPLETELY.

TRUE...
ART ISN'T REALLY MY STRONG SUIT...
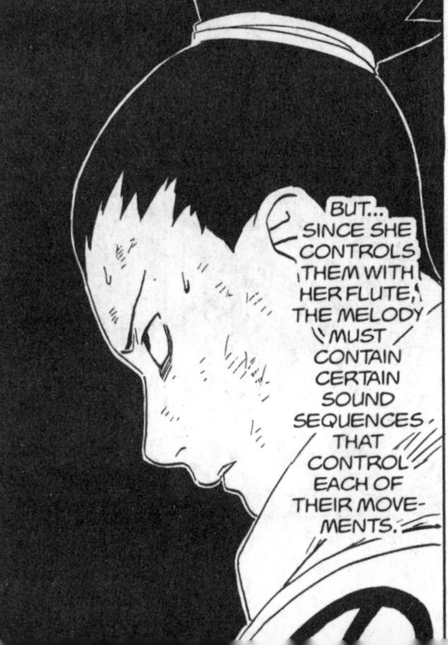
BUT... SINCE SHE CONTROLS THEM WITH HER FLUTE, THE MELODY MUST CONTAIN CERTAIN SOUND SEQUENCES THAT CONTROL EACH OF THEIR MOVEMENTS.

IF IT WERE JUST A MATTER OF ANALYTICAL ABILITY I'D BE FINE, BUT...
...THIS TIME, I MIGHT BE IN BIG TROUBLE... BECAUSE...

HEH HEH...
SHF

I STINK AT MUSIC!

NO ONE SURVIVES THIS PIECE!
FINALE! NINTH PASSAGE ...!!
MAKYO NO RAN! DEMON REVOLUTION!!

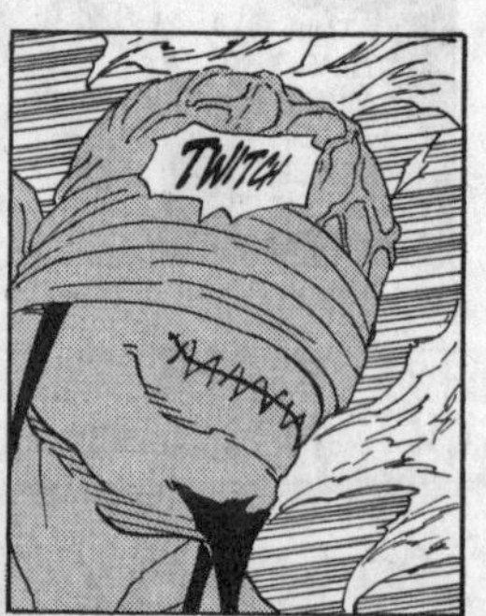
TWITCH

TWITCH

TWITCH

TAK

SOME-THING'S COMING!!

THE WORLD OF KISHIMOTO MASASHI
MY PERSONAL HISTORY: A STORY TOO EMBARRASSING TO WRITE DOWN, PART I

IT'S ABOUT TIME I ENDED WRITING MY PERSONAL HISTORY, BUT I'VE GOT NOTHING TO FILL OUT THIS BLANK PAGE WITH, SO I DECIDED TO CONTINUE WRITING A LITTLE BIT MORE. IT SEEMS THE MORE I WRITE, THE MORE I EMBARRASS MYSELF... BUT, I'M GOING TO WRITE AGAIN ANYWAY, AGAINST MY BETTER JUDGMENT. FIRST OF ALL, THIS STORY IS SO POINTLESS AND SILLY THAT I'VE AVOIDED WRITING IT UNTIL NOW, AND I'M NOT REALLY GUNG-HO ON WRITING IT NOW EITHER. BUT, AGAINST... MY...BETTER...JUDGMENT...

I THINK IT WAS WHEN I WAS IN THE FIRST GRADE. I WAS SO INTO THIS ONE SENTAI, SFX ACTION/ADVENTURE HERO SERIES. THE ONE I PLAYED MOST OFTEN AT THAT AGE WAS *TAIYO SENTAI SAN BARUKAN* (SOLAR SQUADRON SUN VULCAN). I USED TO PLAY SUN VULCAN FIGHTERS WITH MY FRIEND AND MY TWIN BROTHER A LOT. SUN VULCAN WAS A BIT DIFFERENT FROM THE OTHER SENTAI SERIES. WHILE MOST SENTAI SERIES HEROES WERE MADE UP OF A CELL OF FIVE, SUN VULCAN WAS BRAVE ENOUGH TO SAVE THE EARTH WITH A CELL OF THREE. THE CELL CONSISTED OF VULEAGLE, VULSHARK AND VULPANTHER.

I'VE NEVER LIKED BEING THE LEADER, EVER SINCE I WAS A KID. SO I DECIDED TO PLAY THE ROLES OF EITHER VULSHARK OR VULPANTHER, THE SECOND OR THIRD RANKED GUYS. BUT, BECAUSE VULSHARK'S POSE LOOKED LAME TO ME, EVEN AT THAT AGE, I DECIDED TO GO WITH VULPANTHER. ...ANYWAY... WELL... *UMM*... I REALLY GOT INTO THE VULPANTHER CHARACTER. OR, IT WAS MORE LIKE... I ALREADY WAS VULPANTHER. BASICALLY, I WAS INTOXICATED WITH VULPANTHER. HOW MUCH SO...? TO BE CONTINUED...

P.S. THE TRUTH SHALL BE REVEALED!

Number 207: Deadlocked

SMASH
ZOOM
SOME-THING'S COMING!
SKRITCH SKRITCH
SKRITCH SKRITCH
SKRITCH SKRITCH

READ THIS WAY

ARGH!

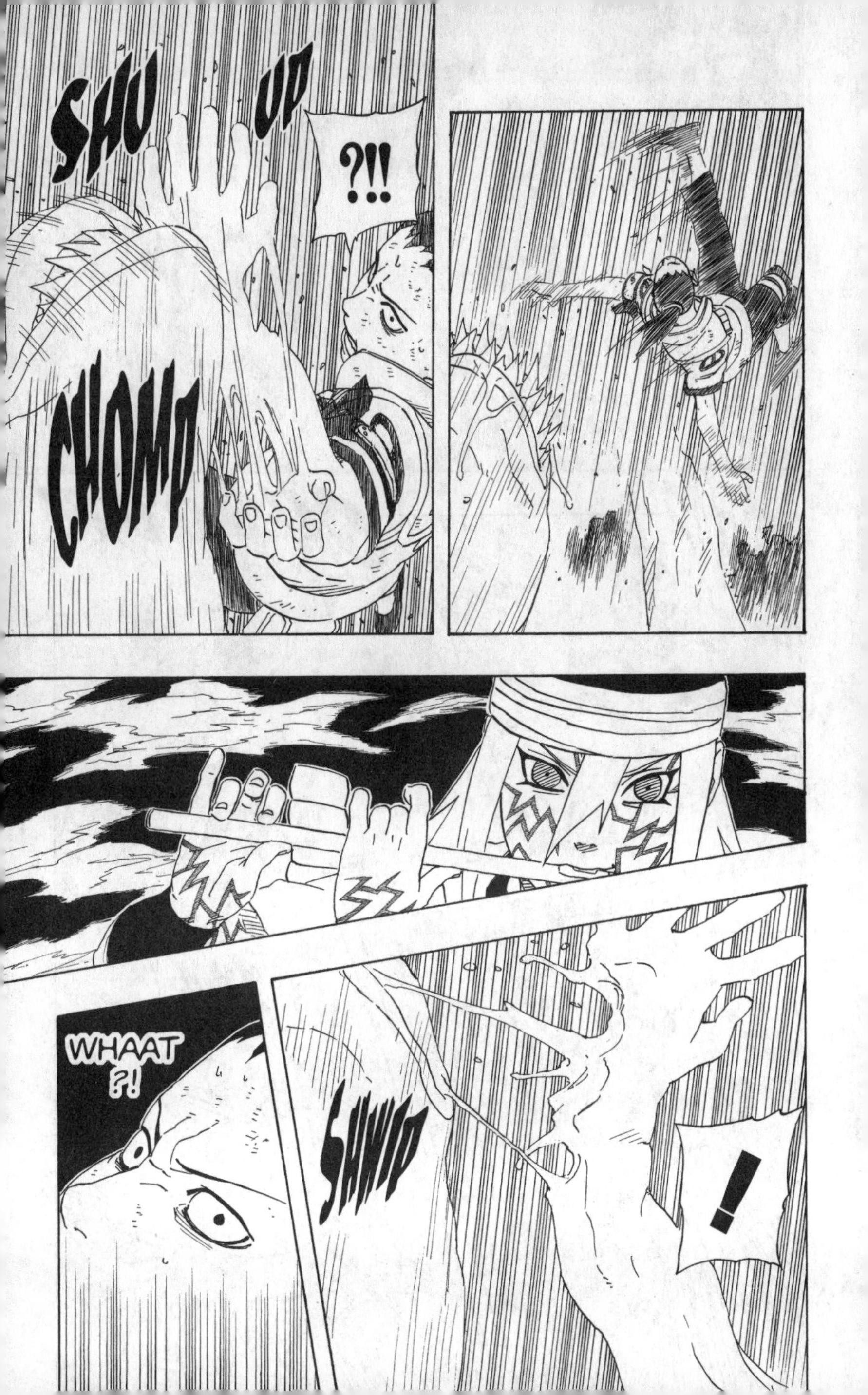

!
SHWIP
WHAAT ?!

TAK
FWIP
GUOOOH
TSK!!
CLINK
THEY'RE...
ZWIP

TAP

BOOF

HE BOLTED ONCE HE REALIZED THE ENORMOUS POWER OF THE SPIRITS...HE'S SMARTER THAN I THOUGHT... BUT...

SHU
UP
?!!
THAT WHITE THING...
IT BIT OFF MY PHYSICAL ENERGY...
CHOMP

HUF
HUF

FROM THE LOOKS OF WHERE MY SHURIKEN WENT IN, THEY MUST BE...
...SEMI-SUBSTANCES.
JUST CHAKRA WITH AN APPETITE.

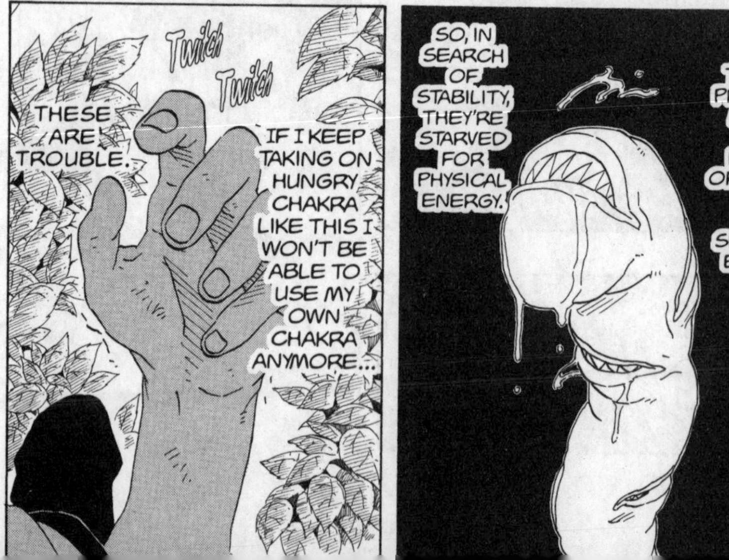
THEY'RE PROBABLY MAINLY COM-PRISED OF CHAKRA MADE FROM SPIRITUAL ENERGY.
SO, IN SEARCH OF STABILITY, THEY'RE STARVED FOR PHYSICAL ENERGY.
Twitch
Twitch
IF I KEEP TAKING ON HUNGRY CHAKRA LIKE THIS I WON'T BE ABLE TO USE MY OWN CHAKRA ANYMORE...
THESE ARE TROUBLE.

A SHINOBI THAT MAKES SPECIAL CHAKRA LIKE ME... NO DOUBT IT'S A SECRET TECHNIQUE.
I HAVE TO IGNORE THE WHITE THINGS AND AIM FOR THE MAIN BODIES.

THE QUICKEST WAY IS TO SILENCE THAT FLUTE, THOUGH.
BUT UNDER THESE CIRCUMSTANCES IT'S IMPOSSIBLE TO GET NEAR HER.

ANOTHER WAY IS TO CAPTURE THE BODIES OF THOSE THREE ALL AT ONCE WITH SHADOW POSSESSION TECHNIQUE...
BUT IT'LL BE DIFFICULT TO PULL OFF WHILE BEING ATTACKED BY EACH OF THEM INDIVIDUALLY...

IF I MISS EVEN ONE, I'LL GET ATTACKED FULL BLAST AND IT'S GAME OVER.

SHE... LEAVES NO OPENINGS, OFFENSIVELY OR DEFENSIVELY.
I BET SHE'S A CHESS-WHIZ.

...
ALL THE NINJA TOOLS I HAVE LEFT ARE 12 KUNAI KNIVES, NINE SHURIKEN, 12 METERS OF WIRE, ONE FLASH BOMB AND ONE LETTER BOMB...

MAN... I FEEL LIKE I'M PLAYING WITHOUT A ROOK OR A BISHOP.

SHF

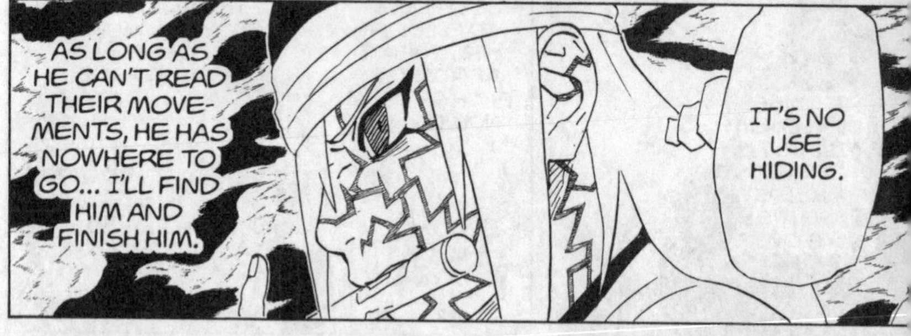

READ
THIS
WAY

SHOOP
TAK

OKAY. ALL SET...
ALL I GOTTA DO NOW IS GO FOR IT.
CHINK

I HAVE NINE ATTACKS...
THE TIME BETWEEN ATTACKS WILL MAKE OR BREAK THIS!

!
THUNK
HOP

BOOM

GIVE IT UP! THE JUTSU CONTROLLED WITH THIS MELODY IS UNBEATABLE... NOTHING CAN WORK.
SHWIP

TWITCH

FWOOM

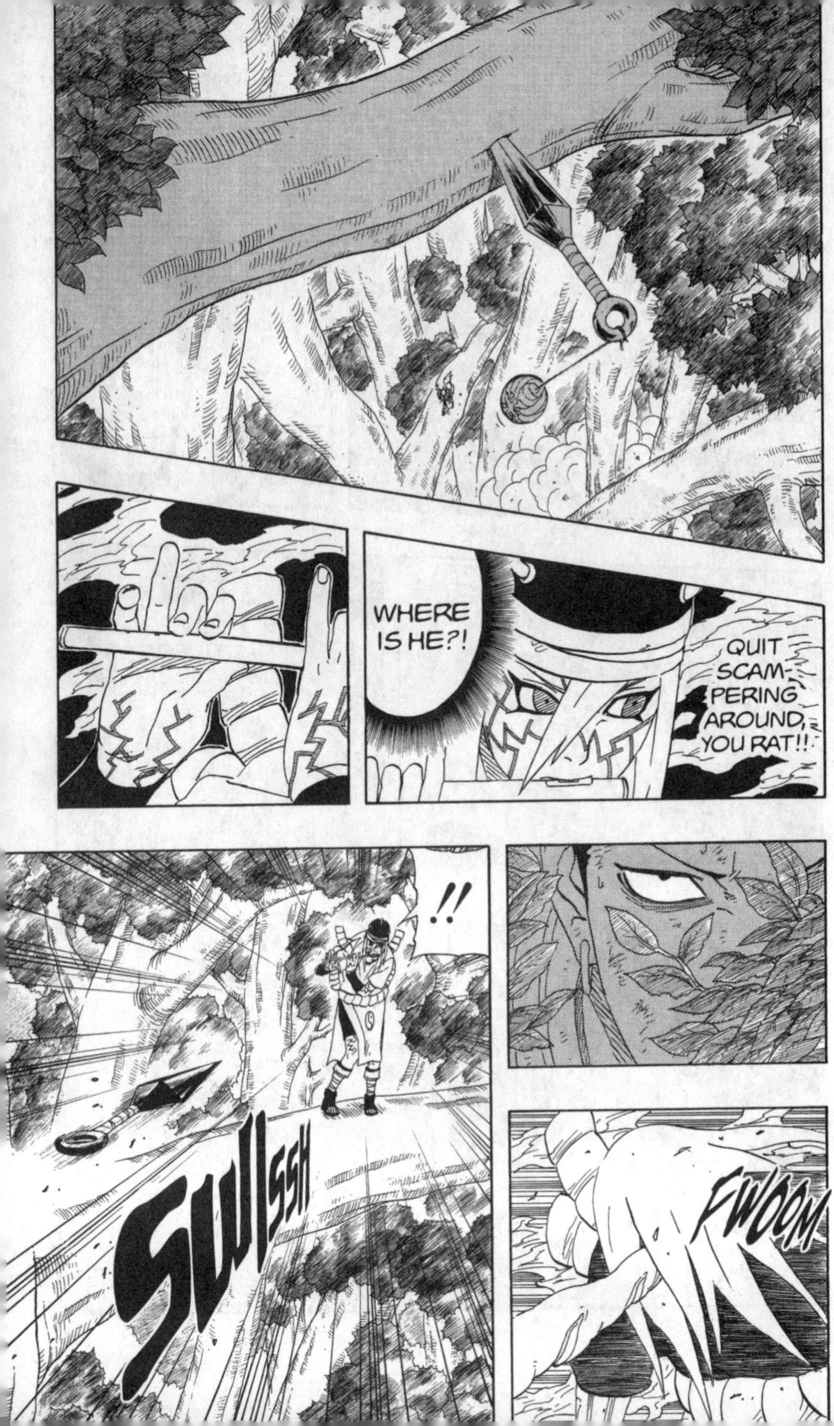

WHERE IS HE?!

QUIT SCAMPERING AROUND, YOU RAT!!

SHOOM
THUNK

OVER THERE!

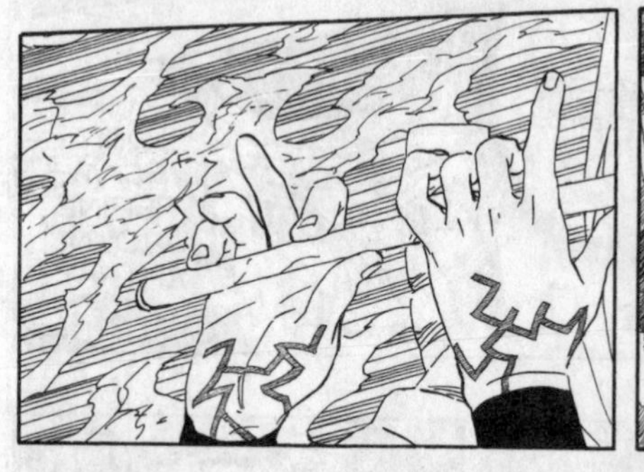

FWAA

TAK

READ THIS WAY

SHUNG
SPING
TSK!
THUNK
A PLOY TO CONCEAL HIS LOCATION...?!
STOP MESSING AROUND!!
SHF
SWISH
SWISH
SWISH
SWISH

SCURRYING LIKE THAT...
WHAT'S HE UP TO?!

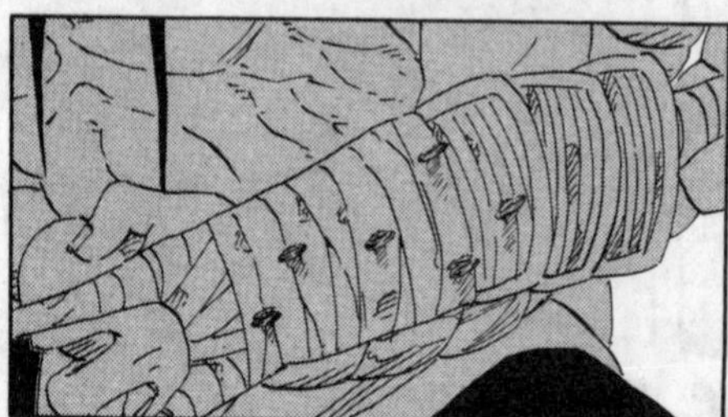

FWIP

SHUK
THE MOST INTERESTING RULE IN CHESS IS...
TAK

!!

YOOSH
SWPT
...ONCE YOU GET YOUR OPPONENT'S PAWNS, THEY BECOME YOURS TO COMMAND.
SSH
...FLASH?!
?!
OH, NO! HE'S USING THE LIGHT FROM THE FLASH TO EXTEND SHADOWS...

KAGEMANE NO JUTSU! SHADOW POSSESSION TECHNIQUE!!

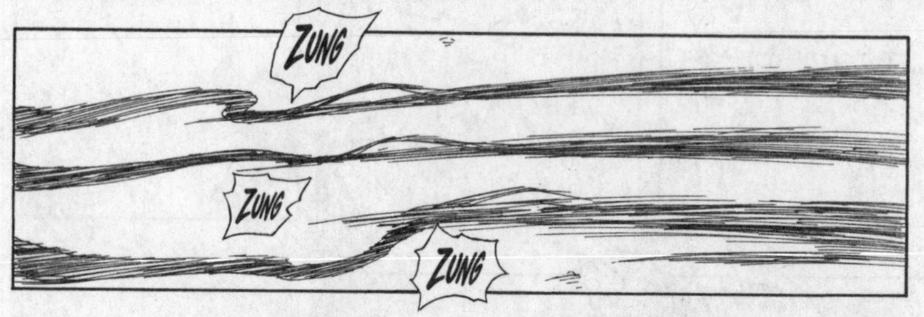

YOUR FINGERS.

THE WORLD OF KISHIMOTO MASASHI
MY PERSONAL HISTORY: A STORY TOO EMBARRASSING TO WRITE DOWN, PART 2

FOR THE ALMOST ONE YEAR I DECIDED TO IDENTIFY MYSELF WITH VULPANTHER, I ENCOUNTERED MANY DIFFICULTIES. VULPANTHER IS YELLOW. BOTTOM LINE, HE'S SYMBOLIZED BY THE COLOR YELLOW! SO, WHENEVER I HAD TO CHOOSE A COLOR, I CHOSE YELLOW! ANYTHING AND EVERYTHING HAD TO BE YELLOW!

VULPANTHER WORE A YELLOW JACKET SO, OF COURSE, I WORE YELLOW CLOTHES. BUT... THE YELLOW CLOTHES LOOKED WORSE THAN I THOUGHT.

VULPANTHER IS [SYMBOLIZED BY] CURRY. BOTTOM LINE, HE LOVES CURRY AND RICE! SO, EVERY TIME SOMEONE ASKED ME, "WHAT'S YOUR FAVORITE FOOD?" OF COURSE I ANSWERED "CURRY AND RICE!" ... FOR SOME REASON, IN THIS KIND OF SENTAI SERIES, MANY CHARACTERS WHOSE SYMBOLIC COLOR WAS YELLOW LIKED CURRY AND RICE. THE YELLOW RANGER OF THE GO RANGERS (MIGHTY MORPHIN POWER RANGERS IN ENGLISH) WAS NO EXCEPTION.

VULPANTHER IS A CHARACTER THAT EATS TONS OF CURRY AND RICE AND ALWAYS ASKS FOR SECONDS. HE PILES UP PLATES ONE AFTER ANOTHER, EATING AS FAST AS WANKO SOBA SPEED-EATERS. AS FAR AS I CAN REMEMBER, HE WOULD PILE UP ABOUT 20 PLATES. BASICALLY, ONE LOOK AT HIM REVEALED CLEARLY THAT HE LOVED CURRY AND RICE.

SO YOU CAN IMAGINE HOW EXCITED I GOT ON DAYS WHEN CURRY AND RICE WAS SERVED FOR DINNER!! A WANNABE VULPANTHER DEFINITELY HAD TO ASK FOR SECONDS NO MATTER WHAT, EVEN WHEN HE FELT LIKE THROWING UP OR THAT HIS STOMACH WAS GOING TO BURST. THEN I WOULD SAY TO MY MOTHER, "SECONDS, PLEASE! NEXT PLATE!" MY MOTHER WOULD SAY, "...? WHAT ARE YOU TALKING ABOUT?! IF YOU WANT SECONDS, PUT IT ON THE SAME PLATE YOU HAVE NOW!! NO NEED TO DIRTY ANOTHER PLATE!!" I THOUGHT, "...CAN'T ARGUE WITH THAT..."

VULPANTHER ALSO CLIMBS WALLS. HE HAS SHARP CLAWS AND CAN CLIMB NO MATTER WHAT, EVEN IF THE WALL IS PERPENDICULAR TO THE GROUND! OF COURSE, I HAD TO CLIMB ANY PERPENDICULAR WALL I SAW WHEN PLAYING SUN VULCAN. ...EVEN I, AS A FIRST GRADER, KNEW THAT NO ONE COULD CLIMB A PERPENDICULAR WALL. BUT, IN FRONT OF VULEAGLE AND VULSHARK, I HAD NO CHOICE BUT TO GO FOR IT. AS I RAN TOWARD THE WALL, I THOUGHT, "...HONESTLY, PLAYING VULPANTHER IS TOUGH..." JUMP!! AND SPLAT, I FLATTENED MYSELF AGAINST THAT WALL! SCRATCH! "OUCH!!" ...MY FINGERNAILS GOT TORN OFF. ...FROM THAT DAY FORWARD, I QUIT PLAYING VULPANTHER.

Number 208: Fake-Out!!

IT CAN'T BE!!

HE READ THEIR MOVES... BY MEMORIZING MY FINGER MOVE-MENTS...?

IMPOSSI-BLE!

YOUR RIGHT INDEX FINGER AND RING FINGER...

TWITCH
!

READ
THIS
WAY

AND YOUR LEFT MIDDLE FINGER AND PINKY. WITH THE MELODY THOSE FINGERS PLAY...
...THE GUY IN THE MIDDLE BENDS FORWARD.

WHILE YOU WERE BUSY DODGING MY ATTACK AND SEARCHING FOR ME...
...I CAREFULLY EXAMINED THE MOVEMENTS OF EACH OF YOUR FINGERS AND THOSE THREE...
THAT'S HOW I WAS ABLE TO ANALYZE AND MEMORIZE THEM.

UGH.

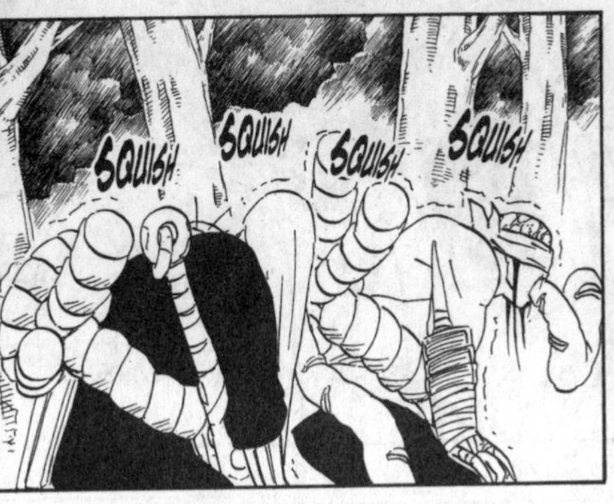
SQUISH
SQUISH
SQUISH
SQUISH

IT'S USE-LESS.
THEY'RE BOUND WITH MY SHADOW POSSESSION TECHNIQUE.

...TSK...

...
SHUF
NOW FOR SOME HARD-CORE CHESS.
SNIK

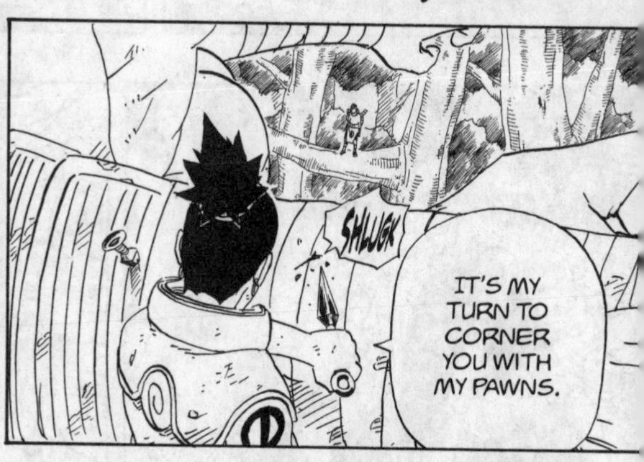
SHLUGK
IT'S MY TURN TO CORNER YOU WITH MY PAWNS.

HMPH.

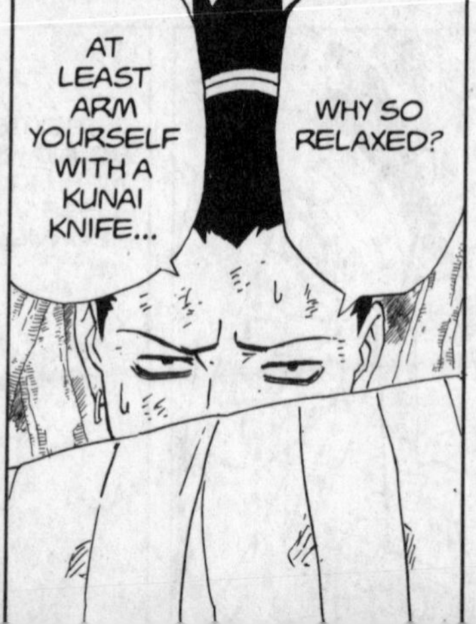
WHY SO RELAXED?
AT LEAST ARM YOURSELF WITH A KUNAI KNIFE...

THE FLUTE IS MY ONLY WEAPON!
I TOLD YOU NO ONE'S EVER SURVIVED HEARING MY FLUTE, STUPID!!

READ THIS WAY

PRETTY CONFI-DENT, HUH?
SKF
FOOSH
TAI! DISPEL!!

BOOF BOOF BOO

!

SKREE

TOO BAD YOU DIDN'T GET TO USE YOUR PAWNS!

READ THIS WAY

GAH
?!

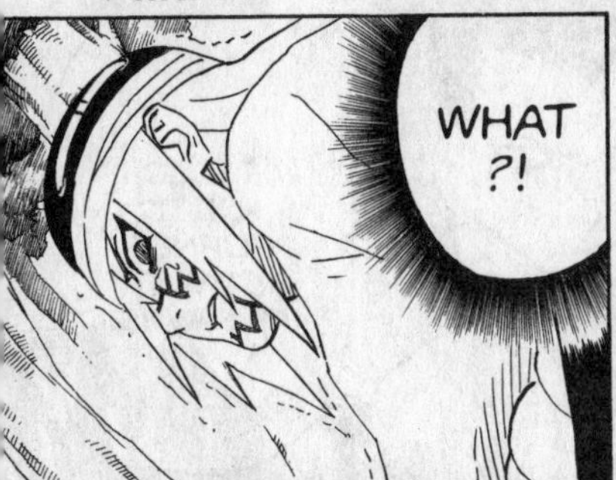
WHAT ?!

SHADOW POSSES-SION! SUCCESS!!

I TOLD YOU I'D CORNER YOU WITH MY PAWNS.

THEY WERE ONLY DECOYS.

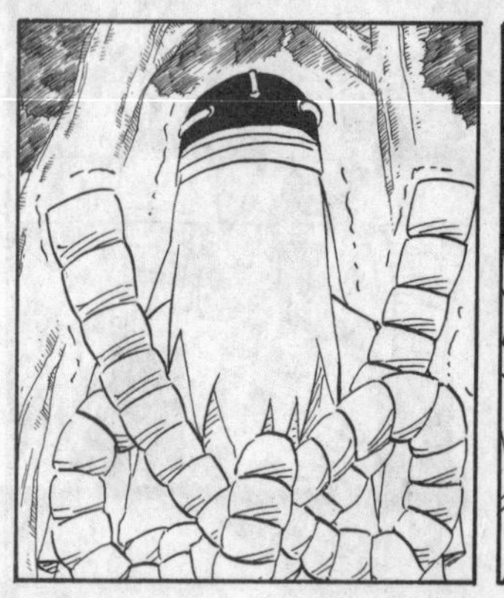

I... GOTTA TAKE HIM DOWN BY FORCE.
FFM
MM
NEVER THOUGHT I'D USE SECOND STATE HERE.

FFF
MM

I HATE TO ADMIT IT... BUT I GOTTA HAND IT TO HIM...
FUMP
...THIS LITTLE PUNK IS GOOD.

SHOOOO

READ THIS WAY

...
WHAT... IS SHE ...?!

YOU'RE SMART, BUT...
FROM HERE ON, THINGS WILL NOT GO ACCORDING TO YOUR PLAN!
SHIVER
TWITCH
TWITCH

?!
GULP

WHAAT?!
GRRMM
SHE GOT OUT OF MY SHADOW POSSESSION... WHAT'S THAT INCREDIBLE CHAKRA?!

SHE BROKE MY TECH-NIQUE.
SHE CAN'T GET AWAY...! NO MORE CONSERV-ING CHAKRA ...!!
TOK

FWIP
SWIP
HAVE TO USE THAT TECH-NIQUE ...!

KAGE KUBISHIBARI NO JUTSU! ART OF SUFFOCATING DARKNESS!!

?!!
SHOOOOOO
GRRR

THIS ISN'T THE SAME JUTSU!
THE SHADOW'S PUTTING PRESSURE ON ME DIRECTLY... IT FEELS LIKE REAL HANDS... BUT...
SHF

READ THIS WAY

ACK... WHAT STRENGTH!!
AT THIS DISTANCE... THIS FORCE WILL BREAK MY JUTSU.
SHLUGK

TAKE THIS...
WHT

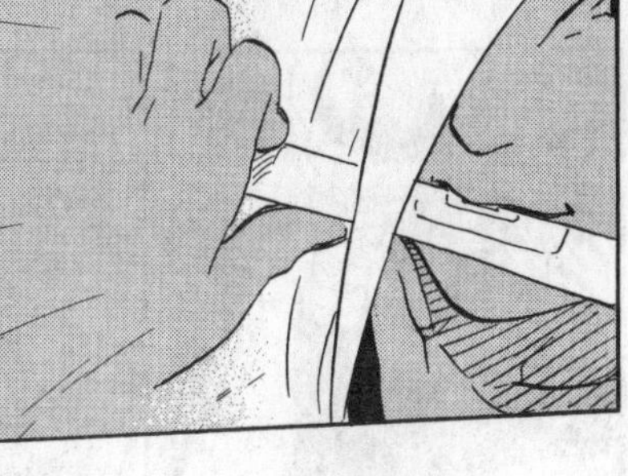
MUSICAL GENJUTSU! CHAINS OF FANTASIA!!

!!
WHOA! IS THIS...
TWITCH

GENJUTSU?!

...
GLARE

TWITCH
SHWIP

UGH...
THUNK

TWITCH
...

HMPH... WHAT'RE YOU AIMING FOR?
SHOOO

SWHOO
SHWIP

UGH... I CAN'T MOVE...
TWITCH
TWITCH

!

?!

SHLIP

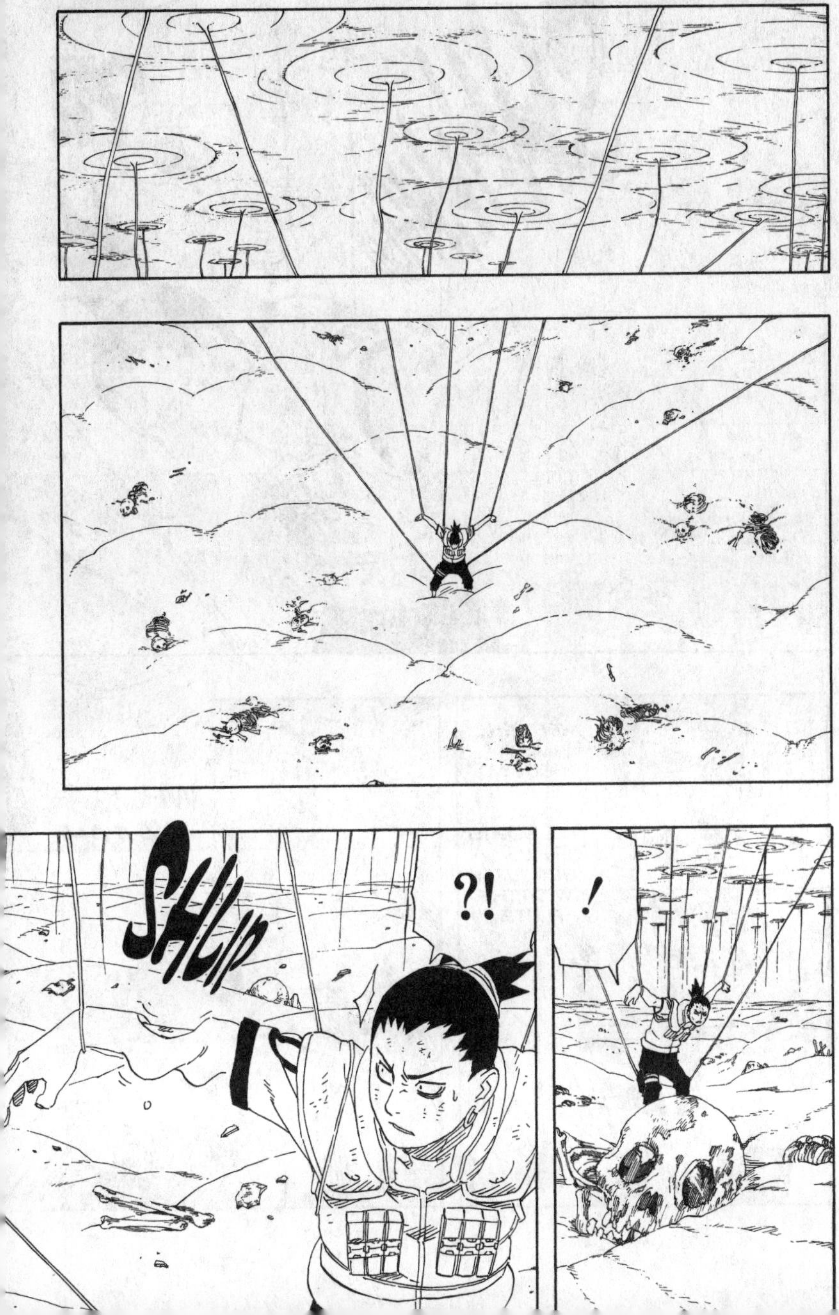

?!!

SHHHHHP

WHOAA-AAAAH ...!!

HEH HEH... AS A SECOND STATE I CAN DO ALL SORTS OF MUSICAL GENJUTSU WITH THIS FLUTE...
BUT OF EVERYTHING THIS SUITS THE TWERP BEST...

READ THIS WAY

GAH... AAUGH!!
THIS GENJUTSU STOPS ITS PREY'S PHYSICAL MOVEMENTS AND BINDS IT!

!

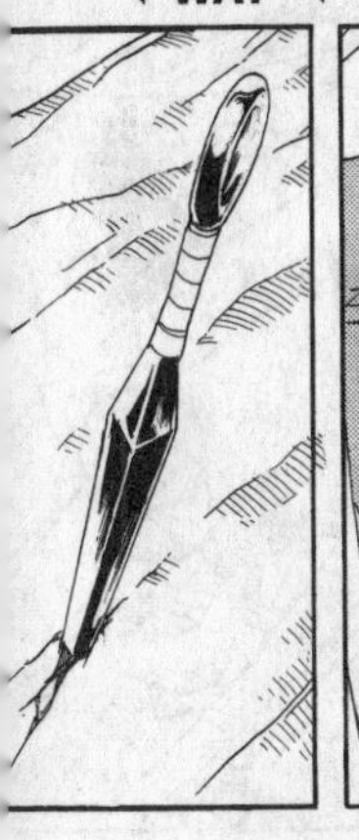

TELL ME... HOW DOES IT FEEL TO BE THE ONE TIED UP?
UNNH...

TAK
SHF

DIE, YOU RAT.
TUMP

FWUP

THWAP
?!!
HUH ...?!

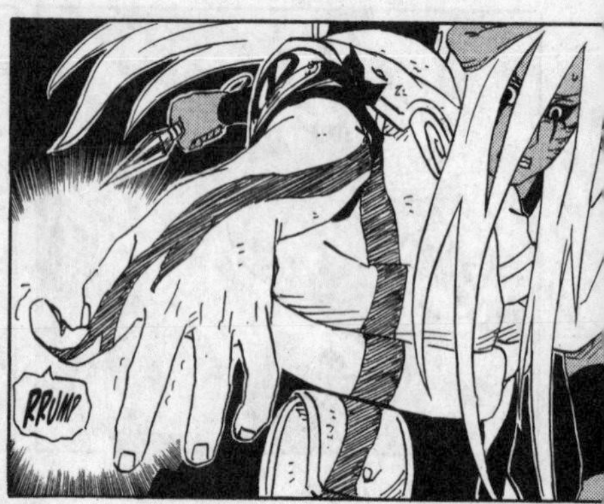
RRUMP

SSHH
HE'S USING HIS OWN SHADOW TO MOVE HIS FINGERS ...!
HE BROKE MY GENJUTSU WITH SELF-INFLICTED PAIN?!

ARGH!
HE WAS JUST PRETENDING TO BE TRAPPED...
FWIP

TOLD YOU, THE FIRST MOVE IS A FAKE-OUT...
AND THE SECOND MOVE HITS THE TARGET. BASIC STRATEGY, REMEMBER?

BUT THIS SECOND MOVE... IT'S DIFFERENT FROM THE ONE I JUST USED.
WITH THE ART OF SUFFOCATING DARKNESS, THE CLOSER THE TARGET IS, THE MORE TIGHTLY I CAN BIND IT.
...NO ...
...I MOVED IN TOO CARE-LESSLY...

NO... NOT EXACTLY. THE MOST CARELESS MISTAKE YOU MADE WAS SAYING THAT THE FLUTE'S YOUR ONLY WEAPON.
TWITCH
TWITCH
SHWOOO...

?!
!!

CAN'T BE...!
...THAT'S RIGHT... I THREW THAT KNIFE DOWN IN FRONT OF ME AS THOUGH I MISSED...
...JUST SO YOU'D PICK IT UP AND COME AT ME WITH IT...
SCUFF

NARUTO
TM

岸本斉史

Naruto' s already at volume 24! In volume 24 of *Dragon Ball**, Goku was about to fight Ginyu. It was so awesome, I was way too hyper reading it... I gotta make *Naruto* more exciting!!

—*Masashi Kishimoto, 2004*

(* Vol. 24 of *Dragon Ball* was released as Vol. 8 of *Dragon Ball Z* in the U.S. - Ed.)

NARUTO
TM

VOL. 24
UNORTHODOX

STORY AND ART BY
MASASHI KISHIMOTO

CHARACTERS
Sasuke
サスケ
Naruto
ナルト
Sakura
サクラ
Shikamaru
シカマル
Kiba &
Akamaru
キバ&
赤丸
Neji ネジ
Rock Lee
ロック・リー
Choji
チョウジ
The Sound Ninja Four
音の四人衆
Sakon
左近
Ukon
右近
Jirobo
次郎坊
Tayuya
多由也
Kidomaru
鬼童丸

The Story So Far…

Naruto was once the bane of the Konohagakure Ninja Academy. Despite the rough start, he and his friends Sasuke and Sakura successfully join the ranks of the ninja. But during the final tournament of the Third Chunin Exam, the nefarious Orochimaru launches *Operation Destroy Konoha*, during which the Third Hokage sacrifices his own life.

In the aftermath, Tsunade steps up to become the Fifth Hokage. Charmed by the power of Orochimaru, Sasuke joins up with the Sound Ninja Four. During a battle with the Sound Four, Choji and Neji both fall, but Naruto, Shikamaru and Kiba are still standing…

NARUTO

VOL. 24

UNORTHODOX

CONTENTS

Number 209: Help Arrives!!

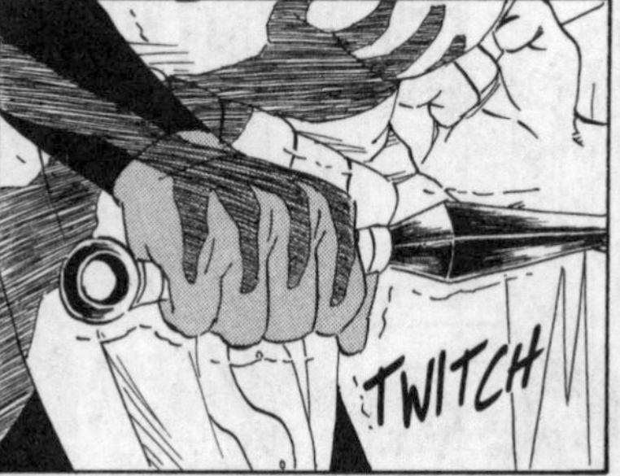
TWITCH

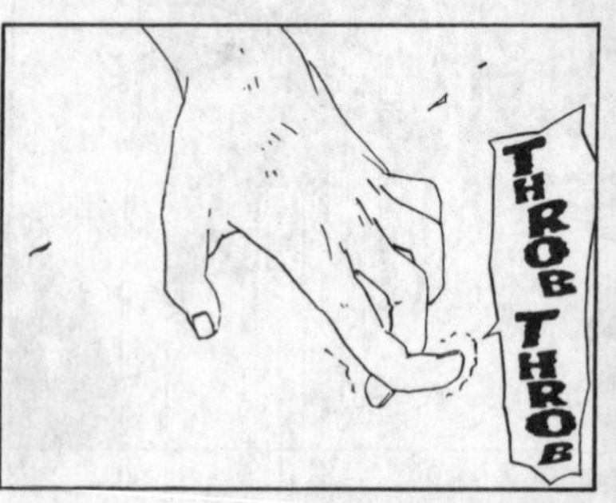
THROB THROB

HMPH... I GOTTA GIVE IT TO YOU...
YOU MAY BE STUPID... BUT YOU'RE BRAVE.

READ
THIS
WAY

...

AND I'M SUCH A NICE GUY.

SEE, IT'S AGAINST MY CODE TO STRIKE A LADY.
THEN AGAIN, DO YOU REALLY FIT THE DEFINITION...? NAH, GUESS NOT.
SHF

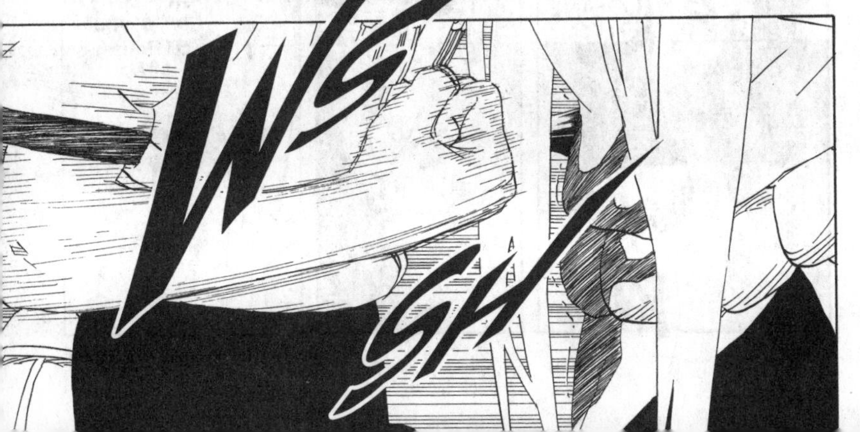
WSSH

BAM

!!

GRR

SO YOU BLOCKED MY GENJUTSU. DON'T LET IT GO TO YOUR STINKING HEAD!

I CAN'T SUBDUE HER COMPLETELY. NOT JUST YET.
NUTS...

BUT I AM NOT LOSING THIS...
SKRRT
RRG

READ THIS WAY

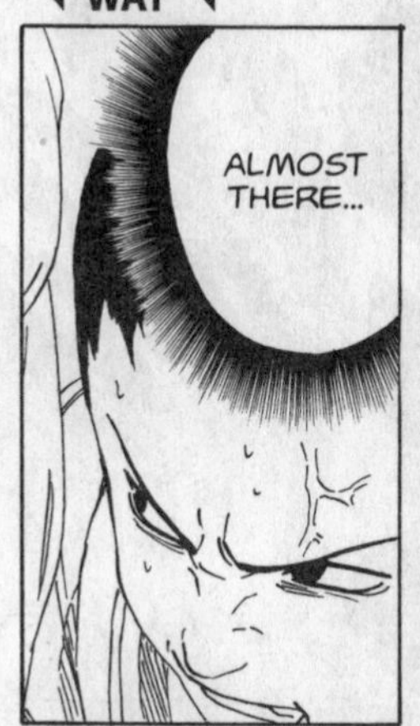

GAA

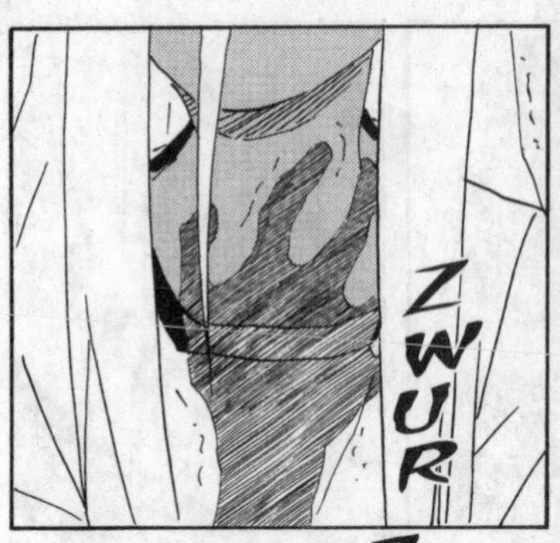
ZWUR

ZWURR

WHAT'S UP WITH HER CHAKRA...
I GOT HER THIS CLOSE, BUT STILL SHE KEEPS PUSHING BACK!

...

THIS SHADOW PARALYSIS EATS UP WAY TOO MUCH CHAKRA.
BUT IF I LET GO, I'M DEAD.
MMF
CRAK

I'VE GOTTA FINISH HER OFF.
GRR... RRUH...
MMP
URK...

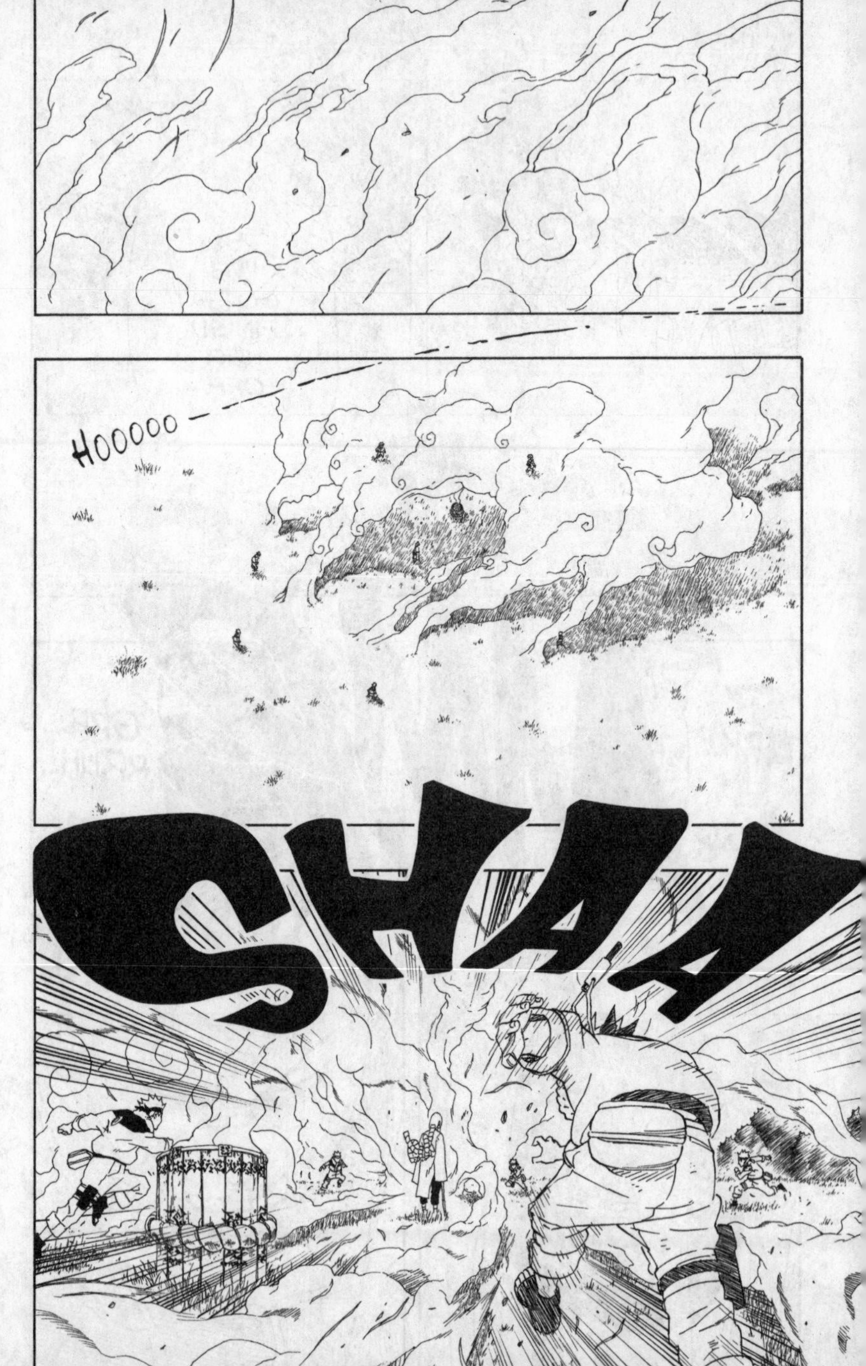
HOOOOO
SHAA

WHOA!!!

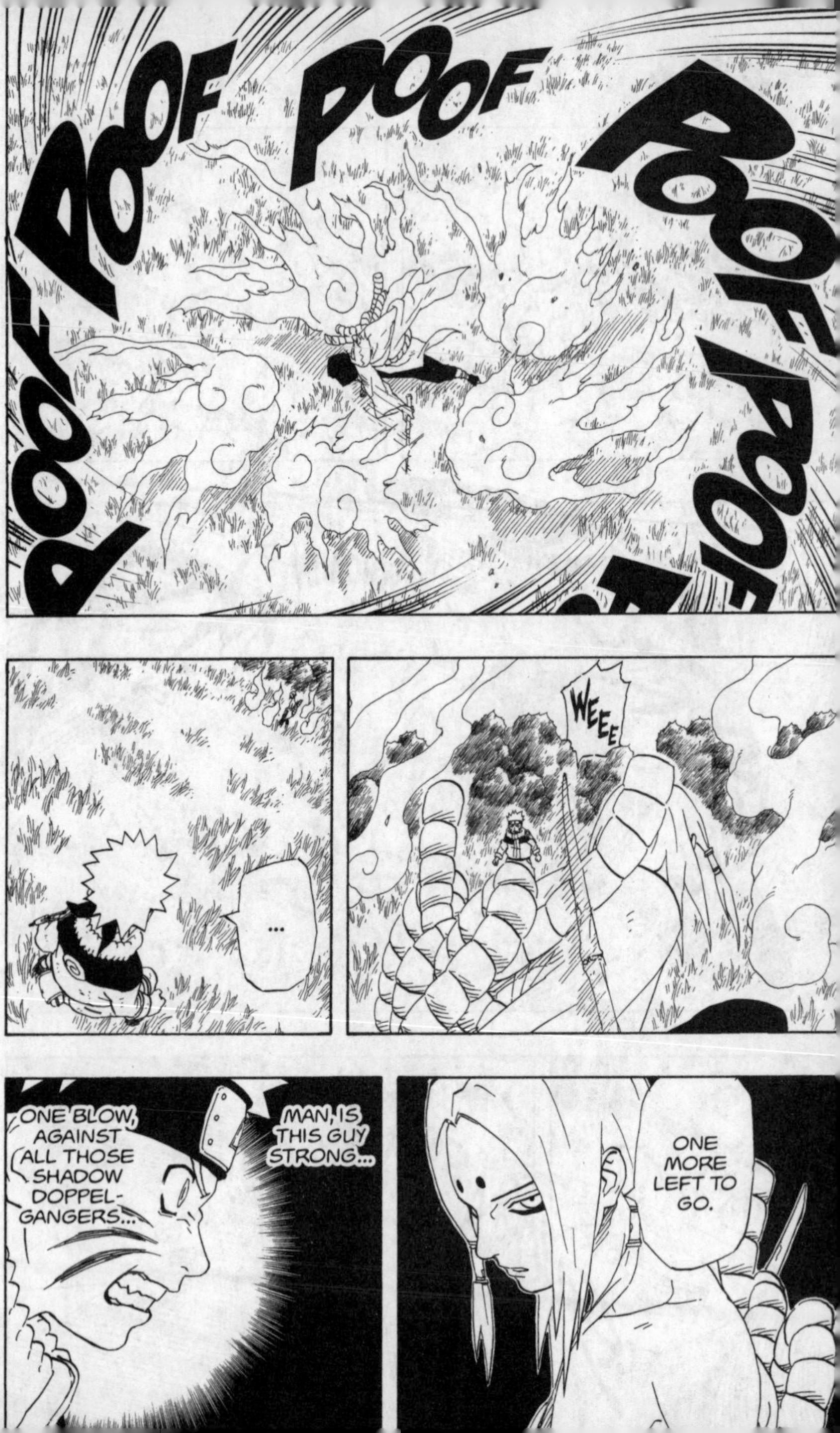

POOF POOF POOF POOF POOF

SSSSS
WE'VE WAITED TOO LONG... BUT THE TIME IS NIGH.
THIS IS OUR FIRST STEP TOWARD... LORD OROCHIMARU'S DESIGN.
...!!
SHRIP
BOMF

HUF
HUF
ZWURR
HUF
HUF
WUR

...?!

...
SASUKE...

...

SASUKE! WHAT ARE YOU DOIN' HERE?!
COME ON! LET'S GO!

HEH... HEH HEH...
?!

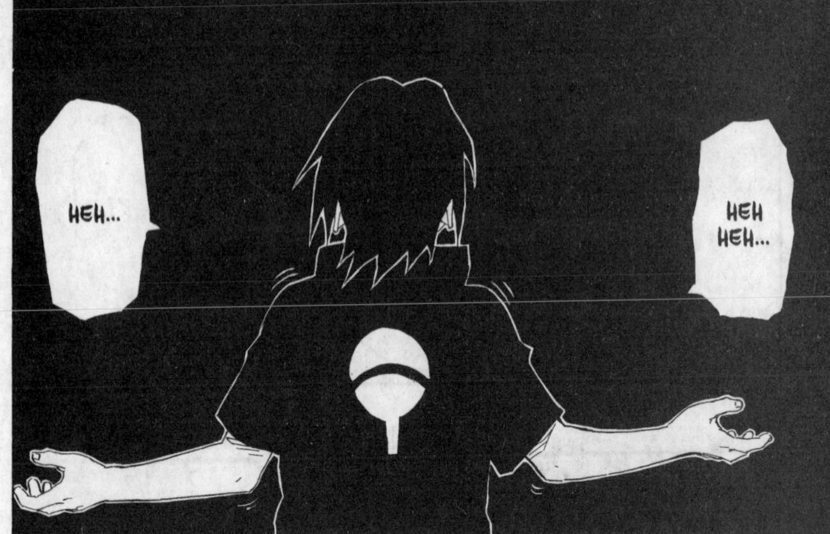
HEH
HEH...
HEH...

...

...

HEY...
SASUKE
...

I KNOW
YOU CAN
HEAR
ME!!

READ
THIS
WAY

SASUKE! WAIT!!

WSSH
WSSH

FORGET IT...
WSST
JOLT
?!

...IN DEATH.

KONOHA SENPÛ! KONOHA HURRICANE!!!

SKF

FIP
WHO...?

KONOHA'S HANDSOME BLUE BEAST IS BACK...
THE NAME'S ROCK LEE!

READ
THIS
WAY

...

BUSHY
BROWS
...!

HOW'S
IT
YOU'RE...
I
THOUGHT
...
NARUTO!
I'LL
HANDLE IT!
JUST GET
TO
SASUKE!

KWAH-
!!

LEAVE
THIS
GUY TO
ME!

HE'S...
NOT AS
EASY AS
THE
OTHERS.

NARUTO
TM

Number 210: Lee's Secret!!

HOOOOO

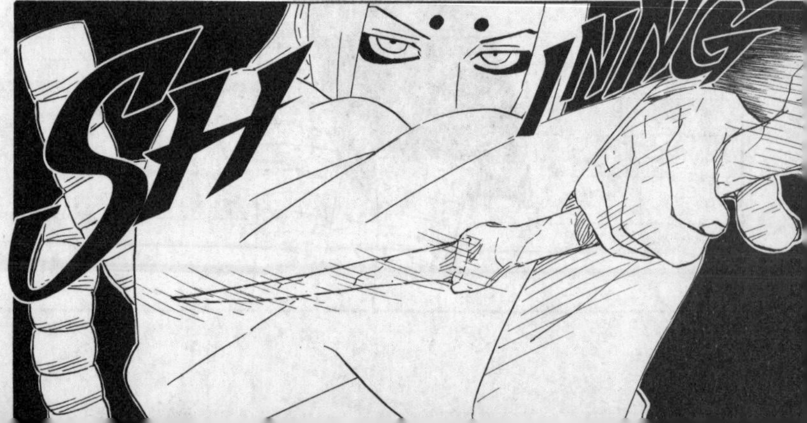

HE'S SUPER STRONG.

!
WIP
WHAT ARE YOU DOING?! GO! NOW!!

...

NARUTO...
REMEMBER, YOU PLAYED THE NICE GUY AND PROMISED SAKURA!

...

IT'S OKAY. I'LL BRING BACK SASUKE FOR SURE!
THAT'S MY PROMISE OF A LIFE-TIME!!

I'LL BEAT THIS GUY!
WUP
THAT'S MY PROMISE!!

FSSH

BUT MAN... IF IT WAS SASUKE INSIDE THAT CASKET...
AGAINST FOES LIKE THAT... A HANDFUL OF GENIN WON'T DO.
I MEAN, GRANTED, WE WERE COMING OFF A MISSION, AND OUT OF CHAKRA...
BUT LOOK WHAT HAPPENED TO US JÔNIN.
WE SHOULD THROW TOGETHER A TEAM OF JÔNIN AND SEND THEM IN AS BACKUP...

WE CAN'T DO THAT...
AFTER OROCHIMARU'S ATTACK, KONOHA HAS LOST ITS MANDATE AS A PRINCIPAL TERRITORY.
YOU KNOW THE SITUATION. ALL OUR JÔNIN AND CHÛNIN ARE BEING MOBILIZED TO NIP POTENTIAL DANGERS IN THE BUD AT HOME AND ABROAD...
EVEN IF THE SHARINGAN WERE TO FALL INTO OROCHIMARU'S HANDS...
RIGHT NOW OUR PRIORITY IS AVOIDING WAR WITH THE OTHER NATIONS.

READ THIS WAY

BUT... THIS SITUATION WITH OROCHIMARU...
IT'S NOT SOMETHING WE CAN KEEP PUTTING OFF.

HE'LL BE BACK AS SOON AS HE REGAINS HIS POWER...
I KNOW... I'M NOT AS STUPID AS I LOOK.

I'VE ALREADY TAKEN PRE-CAUTIONARY MEASURES.

FWIW
HUF
THIS WAY.
HUF
SHK

!
THOP

SHK
GUY?! WHAT HAPPENED TO YOU?
DID YOU SUCCEED?!
HUF
NO, I... I TOOK CARE OF IT, AND... RAN STRAIGHT BACK... IT WAS ALL I COULD DO!!
HUF
HUF
BUT NEVER MIND THAT!!
WHAT ABOUT LEE?! HOW IS HE?!! TELL ME!!
PAT
HIS SURGERY WAS A SUCCESS.
IF HE'S LIMITED TO JUTSU TRAINING, HE CAN START AS EARLY AS TOMORROW.
BUT IT WOULDN'T HURT TO TAKE IT EASY FOR A WHILE.

SKF
LADY TSUNADE!! WE'VE GOT A PROBLEM BACK HERE!! ROCK LEE IS MISSING!!

TAK TAK

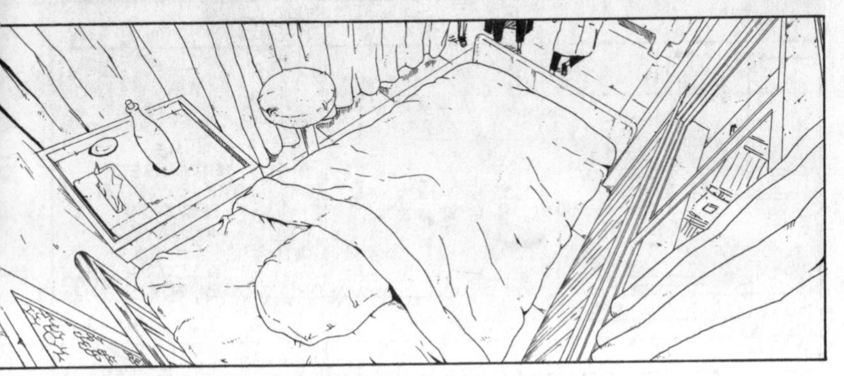

OH DEAR... IT MUST HAVE BEEN LAST NIGHT, WHEN I WAS TREATING GENMA AND RAIDO...
IT'S AMAZING. THIS WHOLE TIME YOU HARDLY LEFT HIS SIDE...
YET THE MOMENT WE TAKE OUR EYES OFF HIM, HE SLIPS AWAY.
...
LEE...

THAT FOOL...

HE'S GONE CHASING OFF AFTER THEM.

HAH...

SEE WHAT KIND OF A HURRY HE WAS IN...

IF HE DRINKS EVEN ONE DROP OF YOUR PRIVATE POTION...

...TERRIBLE THINGS WILL HAPPEN!

KONOHA DAISENPÛ! KONOHA GREAT HURRICANE!!
WUP
WUP

FSSH
FWOOM
SKFF
WIP

WIP
WOOSH

SHHK

YOUR AGILITY SURPRISES ME... AND YOUR STYLE IS SINGULAR...

IT'S AMAZING... I CAN'T LAND A SINGLE KICK...

WSST

READ THIS WAY

NGUP

...

GULP

BLEH...
THIS IS THE WORST ONE YET....

FWIW
...?

?!

READ THIS WAY

WHAT THE...
FWIW
HIC

YOU SEE... BACK WHEN LEE ACHIEVED THE REVERSE LOTUS, I BROUGHT HIM TO A RESTAURANT TO CELEBRATE.
AT ONE POINT, TAKING IT FOR WATER, LEE ACCIDENTALLY DOWNED A CUP OF SOMEONE ELSE'S PRIVATE POTION. AND THEN... THINGS GOT OUT OF HAND.
OUT OF HAND, YOU SAY?

WHEN HE CAME TO...

FWIW
THE PLACE WAS A DISASTER...

A DISAS-TER?
WHAT DO YOU MEAN?
FWIW

WHEN LEE DRANK THE POTION...
SLUMP

WHADDAYA LOOKIN' AT, YA JERK!?!

SHF

FWIW

...OF THE **POTION PUNCH!!**

NARUTO
TM

Number 211: Unorthodox...!!

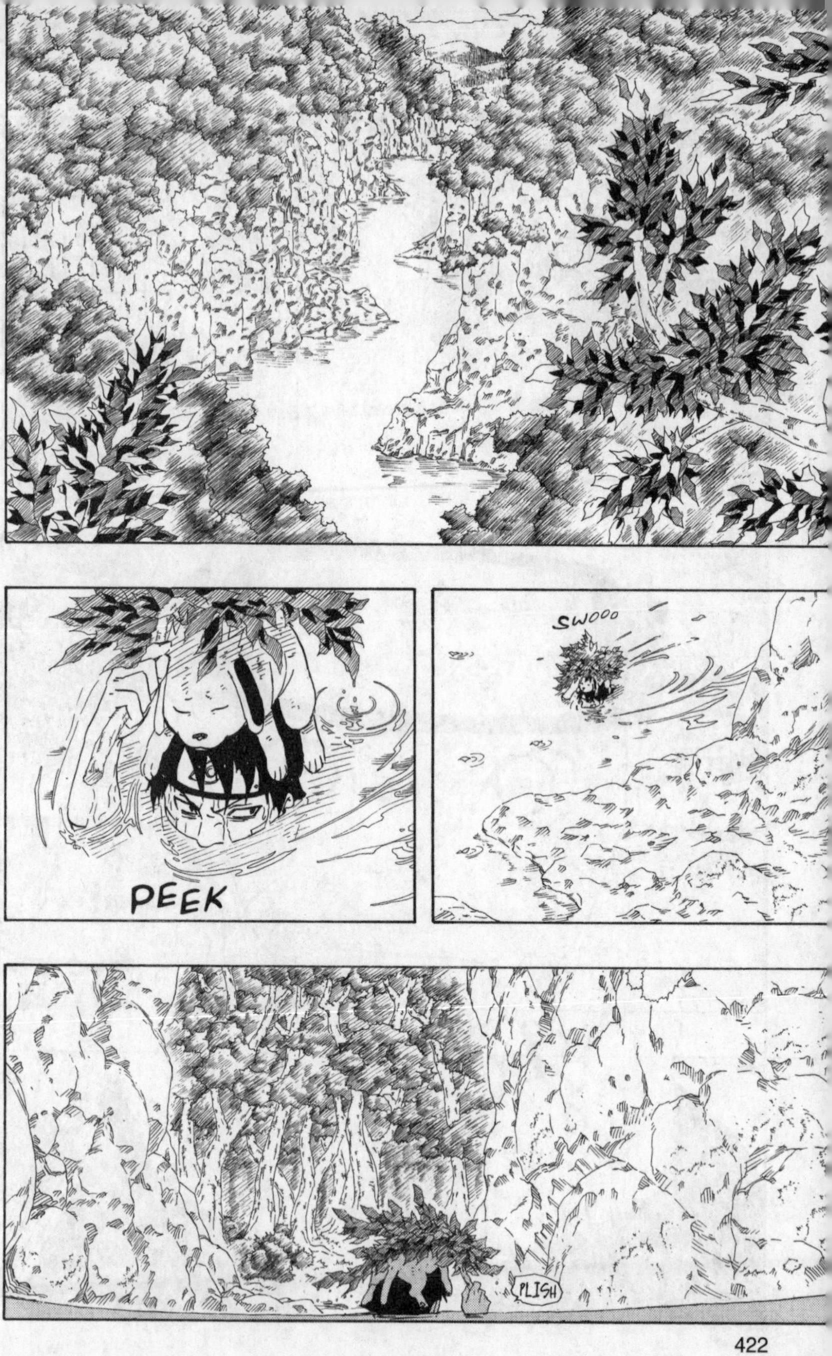

PEEK

SWOOO

PLISH

READ
THIS
WAY

FUP
SPISH

FLOOSH
HUF
HUF
HUF

HUF
HUF
UGH...
THIS WOUND... GUESS I NEED TO KEEP IT DRY...

HUF
HUF
HUF
TEP
TEP

PISH

FWIW
FWIW

FWIW

UNH... *HIC*
FWIW

PRIVATE POTION?
IT'S MADE THE BOY LOOPY!

SHAA
HYEER I COM-MAH!!

HYAH!
FWOOSH
FOOM
ACHAH!!
WIP
WSSH
!

DAM
TUK
WSSH
!!
SNAG
SKSSH

READ THIS WAY
FSSH
FWEE
!
TWAKAK
SKSSH
HE'S TOO HARD TO PREDICT...
MORE-OVER, TOO FAST!!
SHK

WOOSH

TAK TAK TAK TAK

SHF

WSH WSH WSH WSH WSH WSH WSH WSH
SHOOM SHOOM SHOOM SHOOM SHOOM

WHISH

FOOSH
TOUCHÉ!!

PAM
PAK
FASH
PAK
SKISH
!
SWIP
PEFF

FWOSH
!!
SWIP
FSSH
WIP

PAK

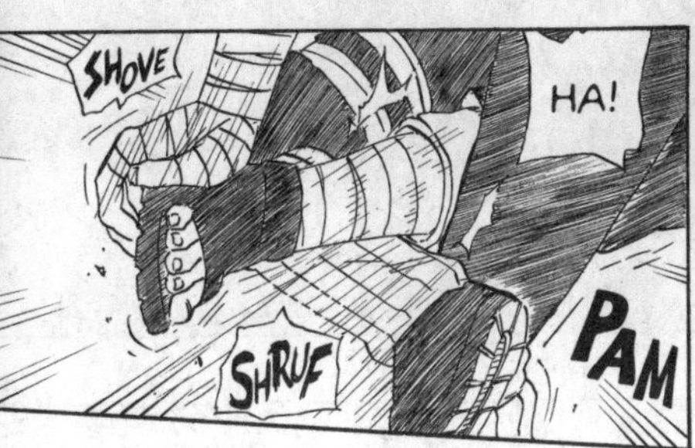
HA!
SHOVE
PAM
SHRUF

!
GWUM

URK!
FLUMP
HWAAAA...

SKRSSSH

FWIW

HIC

WUP

I CAN'T READ HIS MOVES.
HE HIT ME... THAT TAIJUTSU IS SOMETHING ELSE.

READ
THIS
WAY

I'M LEFT WITH NO CHOICE...
ZWUR
KRAK
SNAP

SLUFF
ZWURR
KRAK KRAK

KRAK KRAK KRAK
CRUNCH

?!

GWUR
GWUR

SLURR
SHLIK

SLURGE

MY ABILITIES STEM FROM MY BONES...

YOU WERE WARNED BY YOUR DOPPEL-GANGER FRIEND, NO?

DAM
SHK
DAM
SHOOM
SHK
SWAKK

?!
SLISH

THIS IS MY KEKKEI GENKAI.

UNORTH-ODOX, AREN'T I?

NARUTO
TM

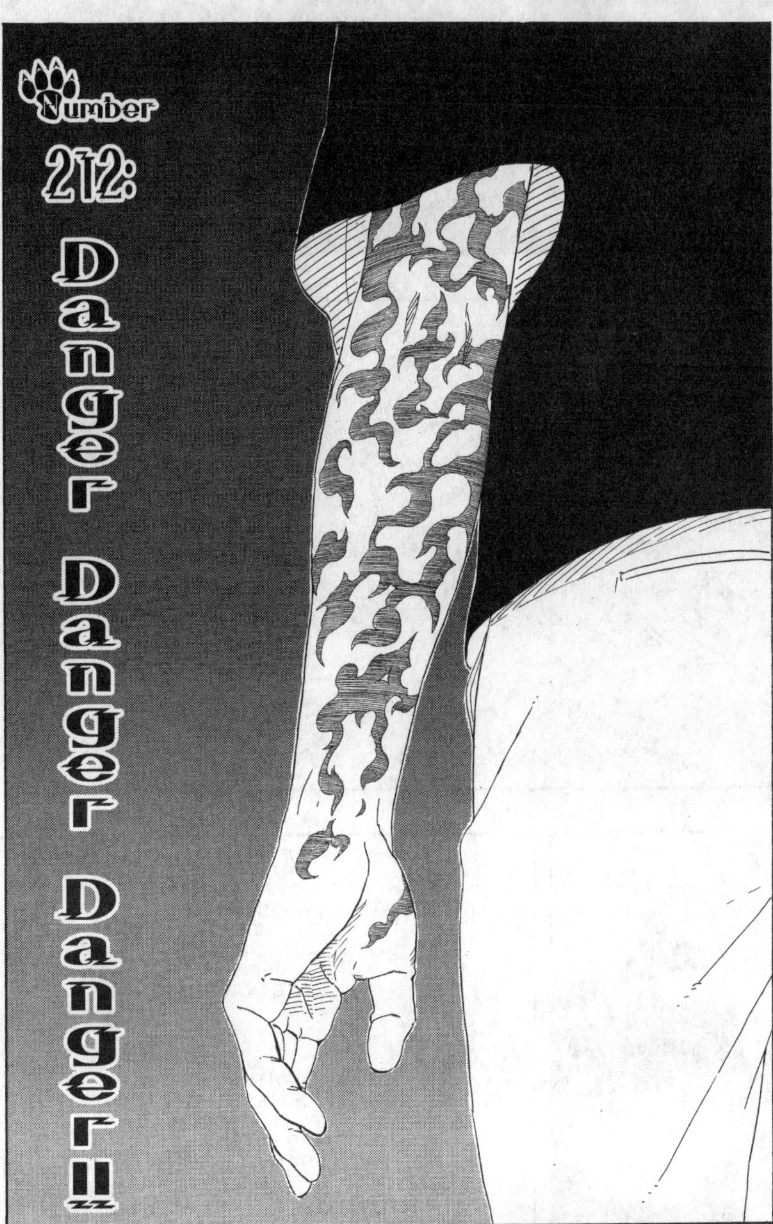
Number
212:
Danger Danger Danger!!

...!

LOOKS LIKE YOU'VE PULLED YOURSELF TOGETHER.

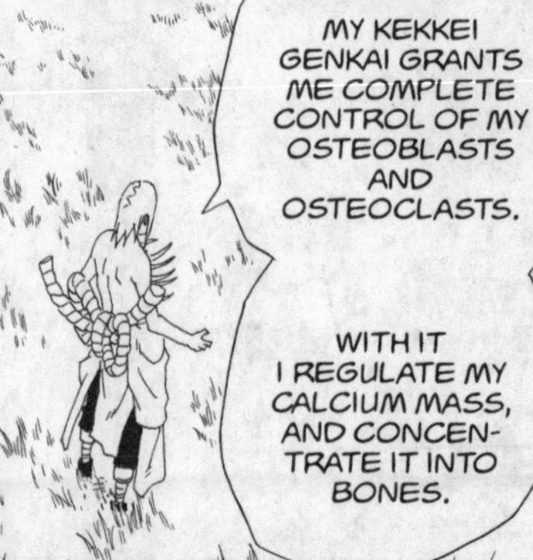
MY KEKKEI GENKAI GRANTS ME COMPLETE CONTROL OF MY OSTEOBLASTS AND OSTEOCLASTS.
WITH IT I REGULATE MY CALCIUM MASS, AND CONCENTRATE IT INTO BONES.

SHF
...?
KEKKEI GENKAI?!

READ
THIS
WAY

THE HUMAN BODY IS COMPOSED OF JUST OVER TWO HUNDRED BONES.
PWUP
AND YET FOR ME THAT NUMBER IS NOT FIXED...

SHLIK

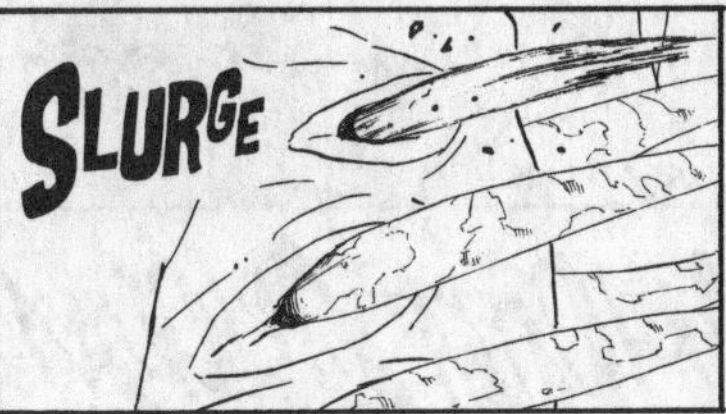
SLURGE

HMPH...
SHFF

TUP

SKIFF
KARAMATSU NO MAI! LARCH DANCE!
PUP
PUP
PUP
PUP
!
KASHOOM SHOOM SHOOM

READ
THIS
WAY

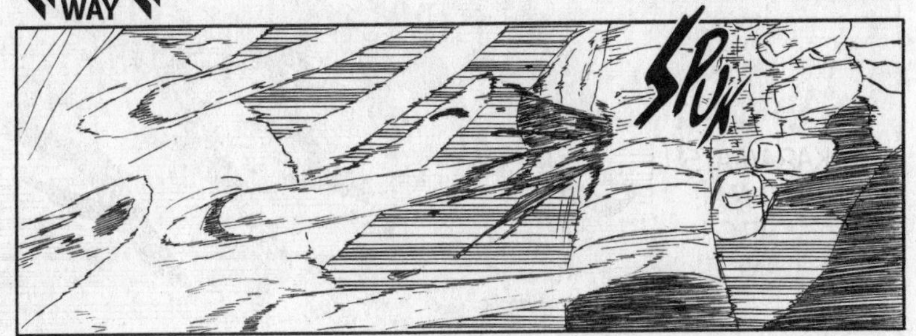
SPOK

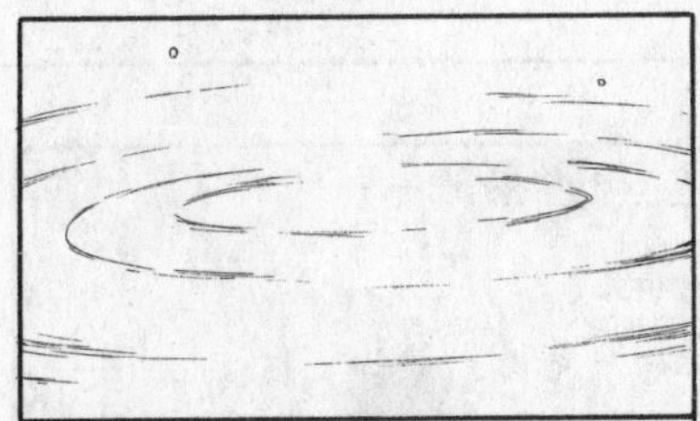

PISH

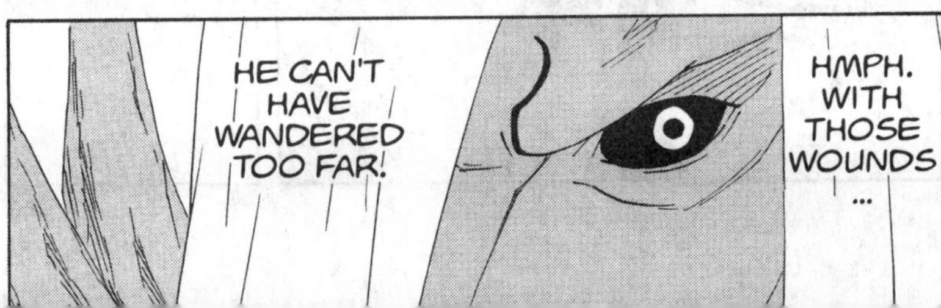
HMPH. WITH THOSE WOUNDS ...
HE CAN'T HAVE WANDERED TOO FAR.

THAT'S IT... I CAN'T MOVE ANOTHER INCH...
HUF
HUF

!!
SNUFF

TEP

OH NO...
HE'S CAUGHT UP ALREADY?!

AND...

READ THIS WAY

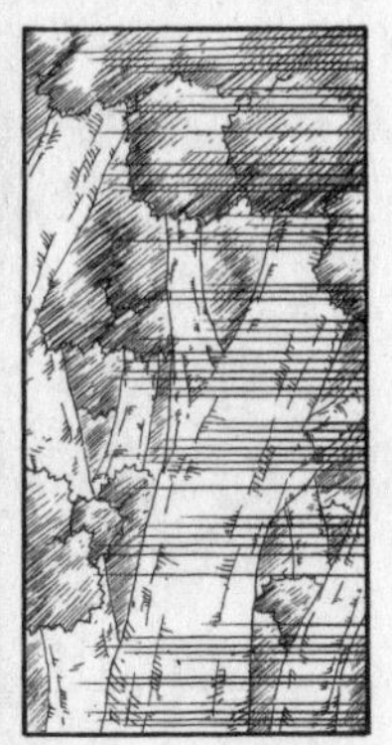

GRRG...

URRK...
RATS... THIS KEEPS UP, I'LL RUN CLEAN OUT OF CHAKRA...

ZWURK

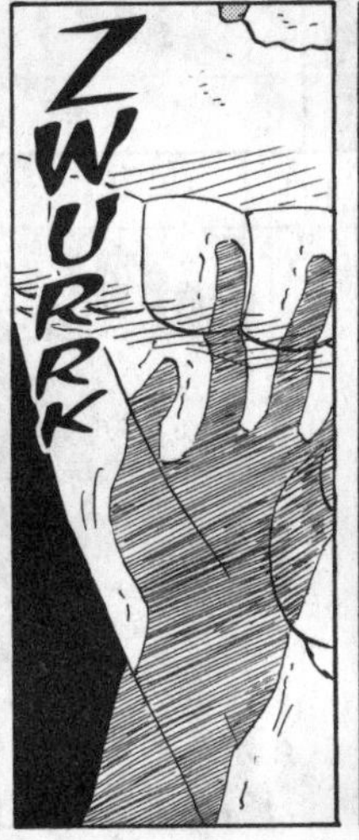
ZWURRK

OKAY, CALM DOWN.
NEED SOME KINDA STRATEGY HERE...
THINK, SHIKAMARU. THINK! THERE'S GOTTA BE SOME WAY...

HOOOOO

...
FOR SOME REASON... I DON'T FEEL SO GOOD...

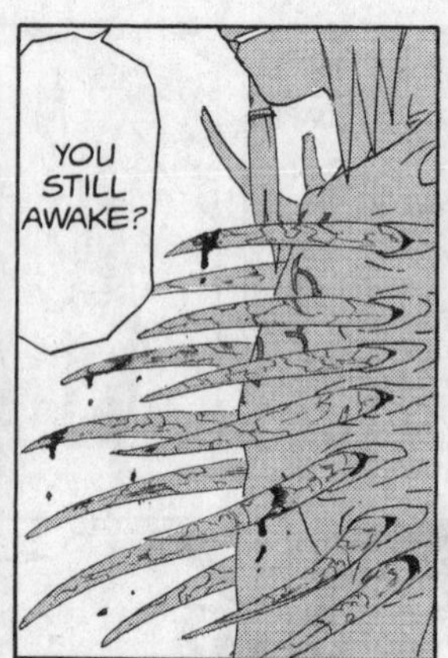
YOU STILL AWAKE?

HUF
HUF

WOBBLE
WELL, ANYWAY... THIS IS WHERE THE REAL FIGHT BEGINS!

READ THIS WAY

RIGHT NOW MY JOB IS TO HOLD HIM AS LONG AS I CAN.
SO I GUESS I SHOULD AVOID ANY MOVES BIG ENOUGH TO... WELL, KILL ME...

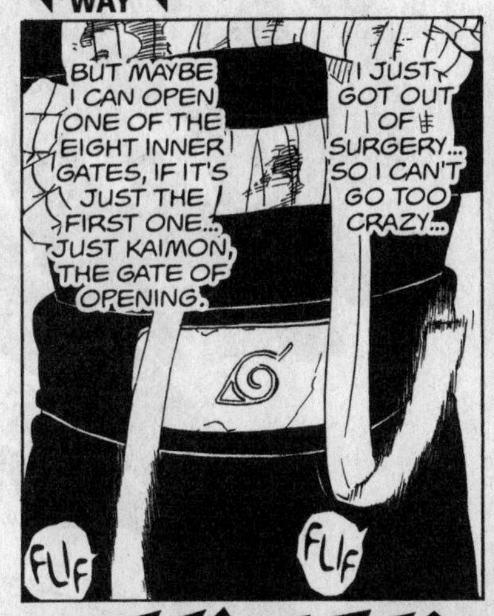
I JUST GOT OUT OF SURGERY... SO I CAN'T GO TOO CRAZY...
BUT MAYBE I CAN OPEN ONE OF THE EIGHT INNER GATES, IF IT'S JUST THE FIRST ONE... JUST KAIMON, THE GATE OF OPENING.
FLIF
FLIF

...

TAK TAK TAK TAK

FOR-WARD LOTUS!!

SPAK

?!!

CLAMP
URK!
HIS BONES ABSORBED THE IMPACT OF MY KICK?!

IMPRES-SIVE SPEED...
BUT IT STOPS HERE.

READ THIS WAY

POP
SHNNG

?!!

TEP
TEP

TEP

TEP
TEP

...

TEP
TEP

GRUNT!

TEP

READ THIS WAY

...
I'M NEARLY DRAINED...

THERE'S NO ONE COMING FOR ME. IT'S NOT LIKE THAT TIME WITH MASTER ASUMA...

JUST A LITTLE MORE... SCUMBAG!

COME ON... WHERE'S THE GOOD IN HOPING FOR A MIRACLE?
GET AHOLD OF YOURSELF!

...
SNIFF

HIS SCENT'S FADING...
PHEW. I'M... I'M SAFE.

WHO'S SAFE?

?!!

!

WAIT. MY JACKET?!

I KNEW IT... HEH HEH.
IT'S HARD TO DETECT YOUR OWN SCENT, ISN'T IT. IT'S ALL TOO FAMILIAR.
SO THAT'S HOW YOU ERASED YOUR SCENT, HUH?
LITTLE WONDER I COULDN'T PLACE YOU.
I'M IMPRESSED. YOU DO KNOW HOW ODOR WORKS.

READ THIS WAY

SHF
SNIK
AND THEN... THERE'S THE WAY YOU SPLIT UP TO HUNT. THAT DID A NUMBER ON US.
AW, RATS.

I'M STANDING BEFORE YOU. DON'T YOU THINK NOW IS A GOOD TIME TO BEG FOR YOUR LIFE?
HUH?!
SHFF

WIPE THAT SMIRK OFF YOUR FACE!
WSSH
THOK

CRUD... I CAN'T THINK OF A SINGLE WAY OUT OF THIS.
THAT'S IT, THEN. I'M DONE FOR.
GRR

SHRUFF
TWIK

NOW DIE!!
FOOSH

GAH!
?!!
GWEEN
?!!
SKF
GASP
!!

READ THIS WAY

TEP
ALLIES OF KONOHA.
THE SAND...

KLANG
... NINJA.

NARUTO
TM

Number 213: Debt...!!

Number 213:
Debt...!!

NARUTO
-ナルト-

SHK
SHK

SAND?!
AM I STILL LOOPY?
SHK
SHK

SHK
GAARA OF THE SAND...

GAARA.
SO YOU ARE HE.
KRAK
KRAK

FSSH
FSSH
TESHI-SENDAN! DIGITAL SHRAPNEL!!
SHOOM SHOOM

POFF
POFF
POFF
POFF
POFF
POFF

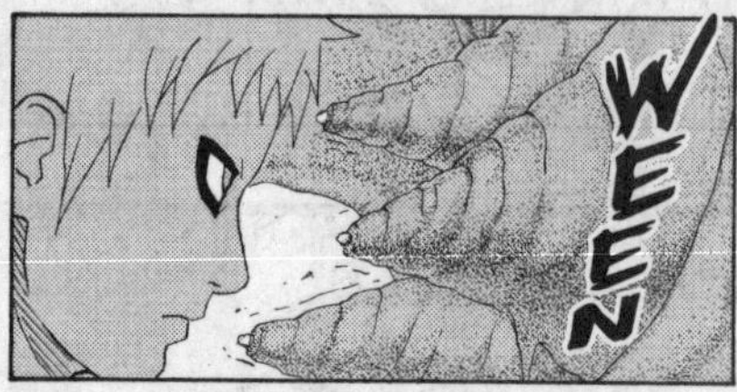

READ THIS WAY

DID HE JUST FIRE THE BONES FROM HIS FINGERTIPS?!

YOU'RE IMPA-TIENT.

...

WHEN LAST WE FOUGHT...
YOU WERE FASTER AND SHARPER THAN THIS.
!

...

THANKS FOR REMINDING ME.
WUP

NOT THAT I HOLD A GRUDGE...
BUT YOU REALLY DID A NUMBER ON ME.

...

I SEE...
SSS

...

ANYWAY. WHY ARE YOU HERE?

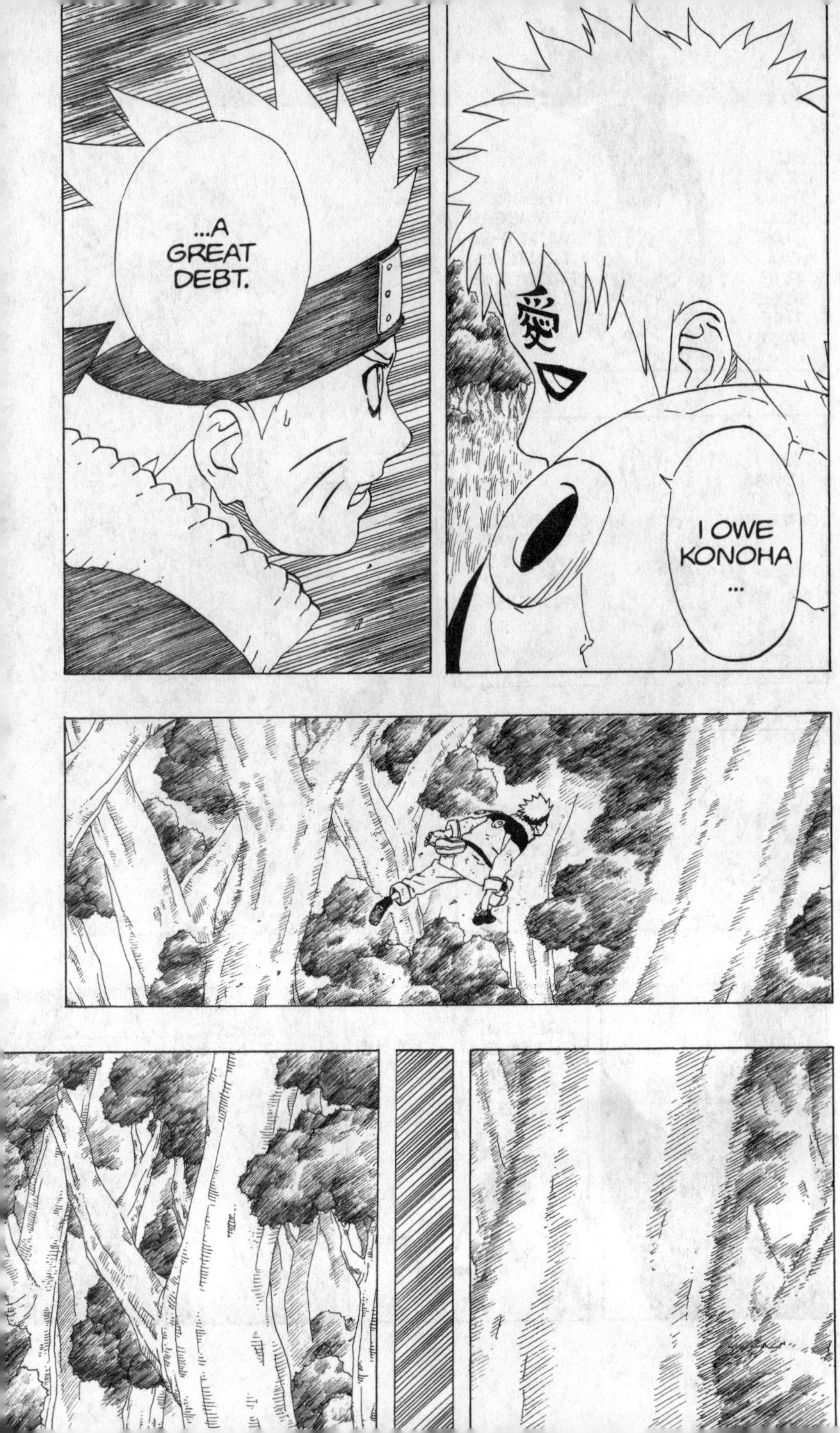

I OWE KONOHA ...

...A GREAT DEBT.

I HEARD WE MADE UP WITH THE TRAITORS FROM THE LAND OF SAND.
BUT I DIDN'T THINK YOU GUYS WOULD FLIP SIDES THIS FAST.

IT'S NOT LIKE WE WANTED TO RAID KONOHA.
IT WAS JUST ORDERS.

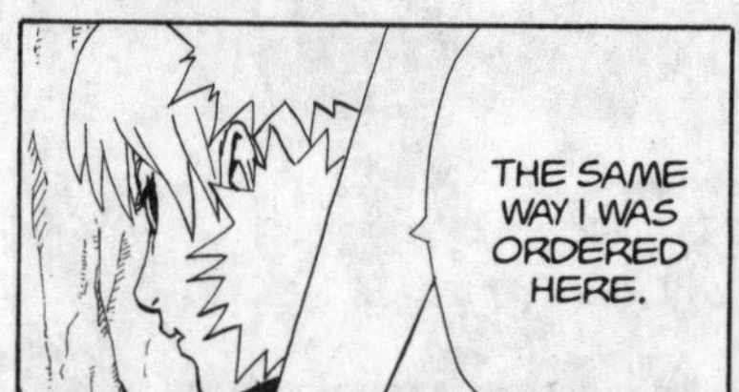
THE SAME WAY I WAS ORDERED HERE.

AHA... SO THE FIFTH HOKAGE SENT FOR HELP.
!
THANK GOODNESS.

BY THE WAY...
ARE YOU GETTING DUMBER BY THE MINUTE?

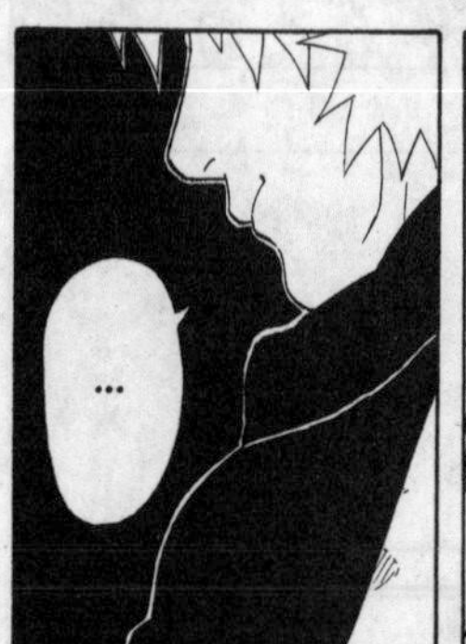
...

SO YOU WANNA PULL OUT AGAIN?
I CAN TAKE CARE OF HER, YOU KNOW.

SORRY, BUT... I CAN'T LET YOU.
A MAN CAN'T HAVE A WOMAN DEFENDING HIM.

HMPH. STILL TALKING ABOUT MEN THIS, WOMEN THAT.
LOOK, YOU FOOL, YOU DON'T HAVE TO POSE FOR ME. I CAN SEE RIGHT THROUGH YOU!

SO NOW YOU'RE WITH KONOHA?!
YOU GUYS SURE KEEP BUSY, SWITCHING SIDES ALL THE TIME!
SHF

THAT FLUTE, IT'S HOW SHE WIELDS GENJUTSU.
DUH!

DAI-KAMAITACHI NO JUTSU! CYCLONE SCYTHE TECHNIQUE!!
SHWEEE

READ THIS WAY

!!

VWUU

SLISH

IT'S NOT JUST BLASTING AWAY THE FLUTE SOUNDS... IT'S ALSO PHYSICALLY DAMAGING THE OPPONENT.

OFFENSE AND DEFENSE IN ONE MOVE.

SHE DOES HAVE SOME IMPRESSIVE JUTSU.

...

AS WE PLANNED, UKON...
...
...YOU BETTER HAVE CAUGHT HIM.

!!
SHOOM
FSSH

KRRT

READ THIS WAY

A GOLEM, HUH.
SHF

HEY, WEREN'T THERE THREE OF YOU?
THE OTHERS WENT AHEAD.
YOU GUYS NEED ALL THE HELP YOU CAN GET.

YOU MORON! THESE CREEPS AREN'T JUST YOUR AVERAGE...

!
TWIK

BEHIND YOU!!
!
FWOOP

SPAK

READ THIS WAY

PLAP
MMPF

SAKON, I'M LEAVING THEM IN YOUR HANDS.
FINISH THIS!

THAT POSITION...
!!

WATCH OUT! HE'S GONNA ENTER YOUR BODY AND FUSE WITH YOU!!

TOO LATE NOW...

SHUP

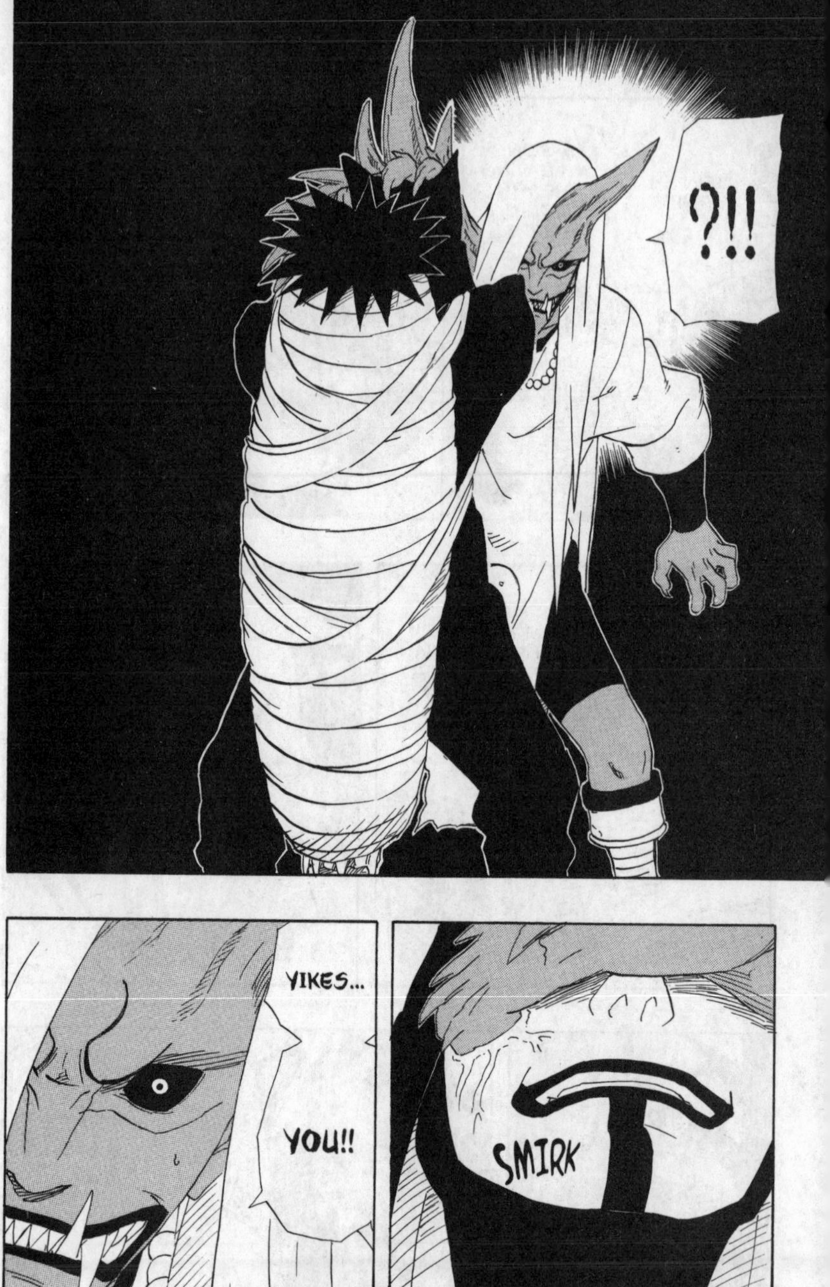

?!!

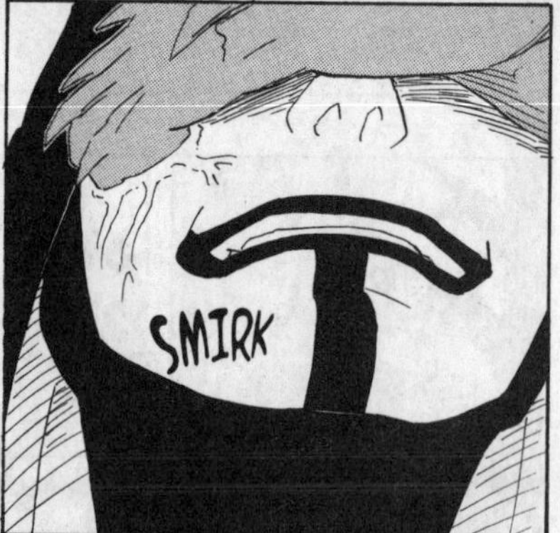
SMIRK

YIKES...
YOU!!

READ THIS WAY

?!

TAK

SAKON?! WHAT IS IT?!

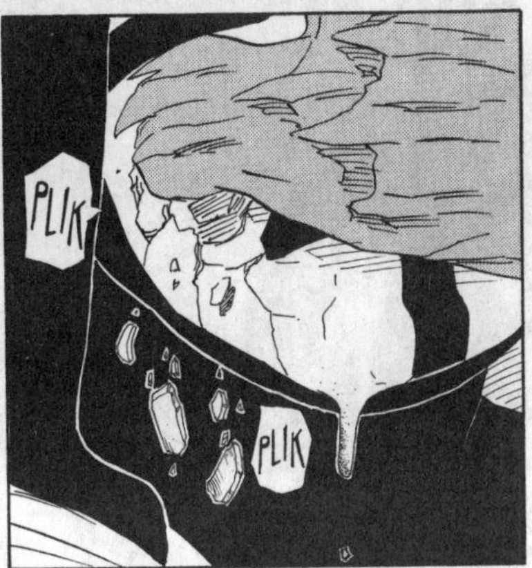
PLIK
PLIK

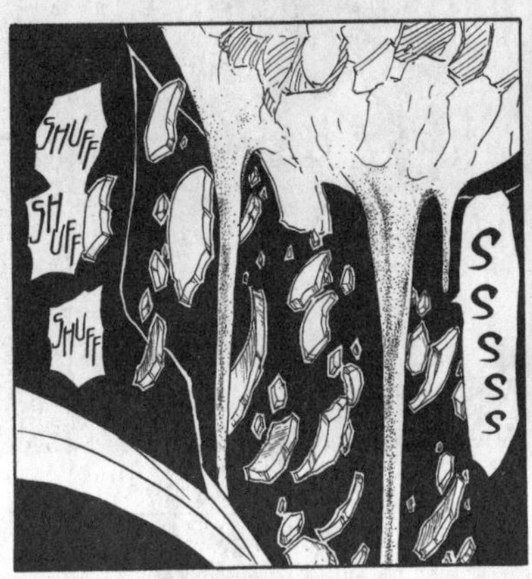
SSSSS
SHUFF
SHUFF
SHUFF

?!

?!

?!!

!!

THIS JUTSU OF YOURS... GUESS IT DOESN'T WORK ON A DOLL.
SHRIP

THIS ONE'S A DOLL TOO?!

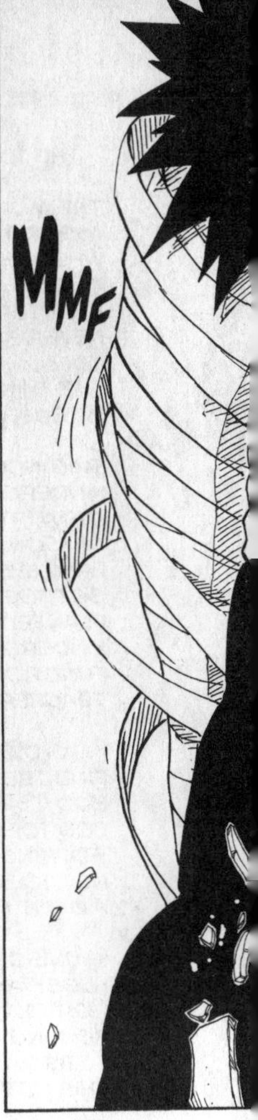
MMF

FWUP
LET ME TELL YOU SOMETHING. SAND NINJA AREN'T SO EASILY BRUSHED ASIDE AS LEAF.

WOMP
IF YOU STRAY TOO CLOSE TO MY KUROARI, THE ANT...

SKLORSH
GWAH!!
YOU'RE IN A BIND.

?!

HE WAS A TERRIBLE ENEMY...
BUT NOW THAT HE'S WITH ME, I SURE AS HECK CAN COUNT ON HIM.

THE WORLD OF KISHIMOTO MASASHI
PERSONAL HISTORY:
THE TOO-EMBARRASSING-TO-WRITE-ABOUT STORY, PART 3

THE MORE I ADD TO THIS PERSONAL HISTORY, THE MORE MISERY I RELIVE FROM MY EMBARRASSING PAST. I ASK MYSELF WHETHER I ONLY DREDGE UP ALL THESE STUPID MEMORIES OUT OF A COMPULSION TO FILL IN THE PAGES BETWEEN CHAPTERS. YET STILL I PERSIST. WELL, AT LEAST YOU CAN NEVER SAY I HELD BACK ON YOU AS AN ENTERTAINER.

THE THINGS I'M ABOUT TO DISCLOSE MAY GET A LITTLE INTENSE FOR SOME READERS. STILL, HERE WE GO.

THIS INCIDENT IS WEDGED IN MY BRAIN... IT WAS BACK IN KINDERGARTEN, THE DAY OF THE "POTATO DIGGING TOURNAMENT." THAT AUTUMN, THAT DAY, IN THE MIDST OF HARVESTING SEASON, JUST FOR THAT EVENT, OUR SCHOOL INVITED OUR FAMILIES TO JOIN US. KIDS, PARENTS, TEACHERS, ALL OF US GOT TOGETHER TO HARVEST THE SWEET POTATOES WE'D PLANTED AT A NEARBY FARM. IN THE COUNTRYSIDE, YOU SEE, KINDERGARTENS HOLD THESE HEARTWARMING COMMUNITY FUNCTIONS, INTENDED TO BRING KIDS, PARENTS, AND TEACHERS CLOSER TOGETHER.

I WAS DIGGING AWAY IN HIGH SPIRITS, TELLING MYSELF "I'LL FIND THE BIGGEST POTATO OF ALL, AND SURPRISE EVERYBODY!" AND THEN THERE IT WAS, A MONOLITH AMONGST POTATOES. IN MY DELIGHT, I STARTED DIGGING LIKE A STARVING MAN. MIND YOU, FOR ALL MY HASTE I WAS CAREFUL NOT TO BREAK THE ROOT. AND THEN THERE I WAS, CLUTCHING A GIANT POTATO.

IN UNISON, EVERYBODY SCREAMED: "WOW!!" AND "THAT'S HUGE!" AND SO ON. I WAS IN ANOTHER WORLD. SO THEN... I DON'T KNOW WHY I DID THIS, BUT I STARTED RUNNING AND ROLLING AROUND THE FIELD, GRASPING MY PRECIOUS POTATO. THEN THE THOUGHT HIT ME: "I GOTTA SHOW MOM THIS POTATO!" SO I GLANCED AROUND FOR HER AND REALIZED SHE WASN'T THERE. SHE WAS ACTUALLY DOWN AT MY TWIN BROTHER'S PLOT. SEE, THE FARM WAS TERRACED, AND HIS PLOT WAS IN A FIELD BELOW. SO I PELTED STRAIGHT TOWARD HER, SPRINTING FROM FIELD TO FIELD, HOPPING DOWN THE TERRACES AND EVERYTHING.

AND THAT'S WHEN IT HAPPENED. I WAS IN SUCH A HURRY I WASN'T LOOKING, BUT IN THE LOWER FIELD, IN THE FIVE SQUARE METER AREA WHERE I WAS DUE TO LAND, WAS A HEAPING PILE OF A TYPICAL RURAL ARTIFACT...

AS YOU MAY HAVE SURMISED, IT WAS, YES, A MOUNTAIN OF **COW MANURE**!

-- TO BE CONTINUED --

Number
214:
Retreat...!!

WHUMP
KRIK
WOMP
SHAA
KNK

READ THIS WAY

OWW...
SHRAK
I LET MY GUARD DOWN.
SLURGE
HERE, LEMME REST A BIT.
SLURR
SLURRR
YOU'RE PATHETIC.

WHAT'S WITH THEM?
THAT'S THEIR POWER.

HE MAY HAVE CAUGHT YOU OFF GUARD...
ZWURR
BUT STILL, YOU CONCEDE DEFEAT TO SOME STUPID PUPPET?!

...
ZWUR

LOOK... HE'S NOT THAT STRONG, HE'S NOT THAT FAST...
THAT TOY'S NOT ENOUGH TO TAKE US DOWN.

...

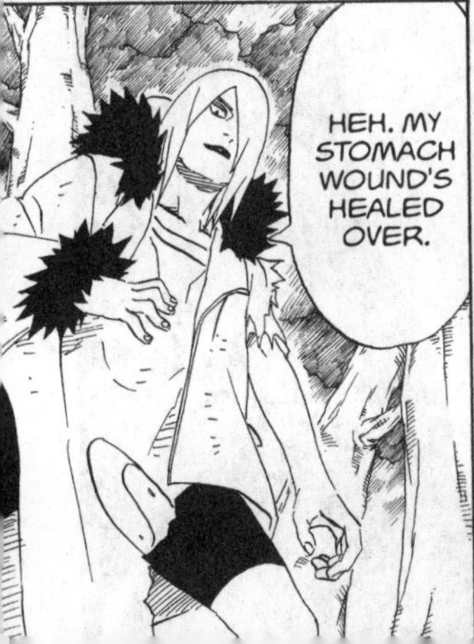
HEH. MY STOMACH WOUND'S HEALED OVER.

I AM RUNNING LOW ON CHAKRA...
BUT I'VE GOT ENOUGH TO SHRED THESE TWO.

LOOKS LIKE HIS WOUNDS HAVE HEALED.
HOW FAST HE RECOVERS...!

HMPH.

I'M NOT USUALLY THE ONE TO TAKE ON THE MAIN BODY.
IT'S FREAKIN' HARD TO MOVE IN THIS THING.
TAP TAP

YOU GUYS TAKE ME FOR A FOOL?
!

YOU CAN'T BEAT 'EM FIGHTING HEAD-ON!
WE SHOULD RETREAT FOR NOW...

SHAA
!!

SHKK
!

SHOOM
SHOOM
SHOOM

URK!!

BA
SHOOM
SHOOM
SHOOM
WHOA!!

THE ANT IS NOT AN OFFENSIVE PUPPET.
IT WAS ORIGINALLY DESIGNED FOR CAPTURING PREY.

I USUALLY USE THE ANT'S COUNTERPART, THE CROW, FOR THIS ATTACK.
TUG
?!

SPAKK

K'SHAK
K'SHAK
K'SHAK

YEEG!

I GIVE YOU...
...MY VERY OWN PUPPET SHOW!

LET ME OUTTA HERE!!
BAM

THE ART OF THE IRON MAIDEN!
WOMP

READ THIS WAY

FINIS.

READ
THIS
WAY

SHE'S RUN OFF...
WITH HER TAIL BETWEEN HER LEGS?

NO...
THAT'S NOT HER WAY. SHE'S AROUND.

?!
I JUST GOT HERE.
BRIEF ME...
UPDATE ME ON OUR TACTICAL SITUATION.

WELL... FIRST, HER BASIC APPROACH IS TO SPELLBIND HER ENEMIES WITH THE SOUND OF HER FLUTE...
THEN WHILE THEY'RE UNDER THE SPELL, SHE JUMPS THEM.
BASICALLY, SHE'S YOUR TYPICAL GENJUTSU-STYLE LONG-RANGE FIGHTER.

I'M GUESSING SHE SAW IMMEDIATELY HOW POORLY HER JUTSU MEASURED UP TO YOURS.
THAT, AND IT'S TWO AGAINST ONE. SHE WON'T SHOW HERSELF UNTIL SHE CASTS HER GENJUTSU ON US.

SOUND... HUH?
YEAH.
SEE, MOST GENJUTSU WORK ON THE FIVE SENSES.
THEY ACT UPON AND BEWITCH YOUR SIGHT, YOUR HEARING...
... YOUR SMELL, TASTE, AND TOUCH.

THE ONES BASED ON HEARING ARE THE MOST PROBLEMATIC.
NOT ONLY CAN SHE KEEP HER DISTANCE, BUT STAY AS CLOAKED AS SHE PLEASES.
WE'VE NO IDEA WHEN OR WHERE SHE'LL UNLOAD IT ON US.

BY THE TIME WE PINPOINT HER FROM THE SOUND...
SNAP
WE'RE ALREADY UNDER THE INFLUENCE OF HER GENJUTSU.
AWWG...
...

READ THIS WAY

WE'RE IN A HEAP OF TROUBLE, IF YOU ASK ME.
FACING SOMEONE LIKE HER IS FOOLISH WITHOUT THE SUPPORT OF GUYS LIKE KIBA OR NEJI... SOMEONE WITH KEEN DETECTION.
THROB THROB

IF WE STAY HERE, SOONER OR LATER WE'LL BE CORNERED.
WE SHOULD RETREAT FOR NOW, AND...
DID ANYONE ASK YOU FOR ADVICE?!
I ASKED YOU THE SITUATION. THAT'S ALL.

...?!

CHIP
DON'T UNDER-ESTIMATE ME.

IF SHE THINKS SHE'S SAFE...
CAMPED OUT JUST INSIDE THE RANGE OF HEARING...
SHE'S IN FOR A DOOZY.
SKLITCH

KUCHIYOSE! SUMMONING!
FWOOSH

KIRIKIRI-MAI! BLADE DANCE!
SLASH!!

SHF

SUSH

ALL RIGHT, FAR ENOUGH. LET THE GENJUTSU BEGIN...

WHAT?

!

CHOK

CHOK

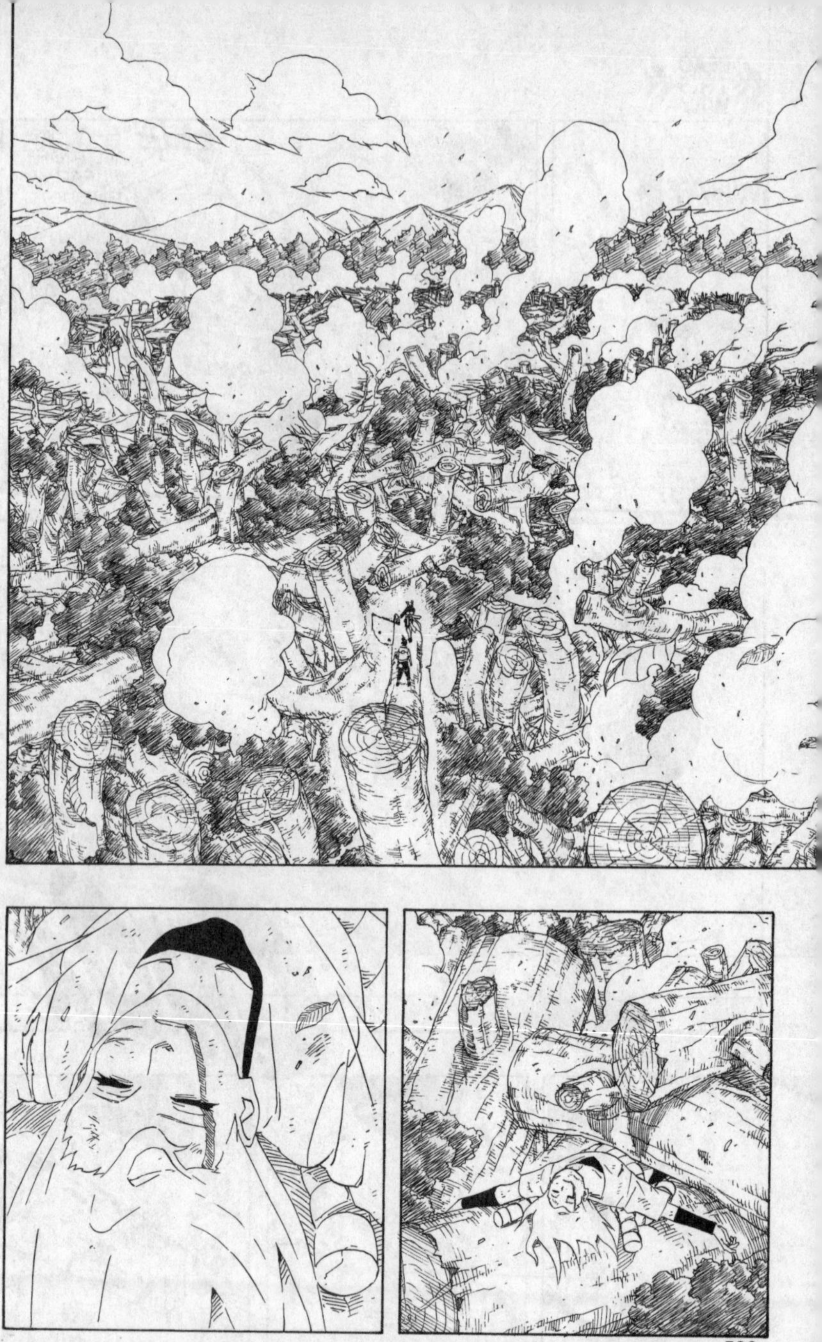

SEE?
ALL OVER.
...

SUBTLE AS A RHINO...
AND SCARIER THAN MY MOM...

TEE HEE
WHAT D'YA THINK?

...

BUT, WELL... I GUESS THIS TIME I GOTTA BE GRATEFUL.

THE WORLD OF KISHIMOTO MASASHI
PERSONAL HISTORY:
THE TOO-EMBARRASSING-TO-WRITE-ABOUT STORY, PART 4

THE IMAGE OF THAT SCENE IS ACID-ETCHED INTO MY MIND. I REMEMBER MY THOUGHTS, HOVERING THERE IN MIDAIR. WHAT WOULD HAPPEN IF I LOST MY BALANCE? OH NO. DON'T LET ME FALL DOWN. THAT'S IT, FORGET THE LEGS. IF I JUST LAND WITH MY UPPER BODY STRAIGHT, LIKE A GYMNAST...

ANYWAY, NEVER MIND THE POTATO. I TOSSED IT ASIDE. **SQUELCH**. IT HIT THE MOUND FIRST. HEARING THAT SOUND GAVE ME THE RESOLVE I NEEDED. **SQUISH SMUSSH!** BOTH MY LEGS, PLANTED IN THE DUNG! IT WAS DEEPER THAN I HAD ENVISIONED. BUT ACTUALLY, THAT WAS A GODSEND. CEMENTED KNEE-DEEP, I MANAGED TO MAINTAIN MY BALANCE.

INSTEAD OF SURPRISING EVERYBODY WITH MY PRIZE POTATO, I WOUND UP STIRRING THEM IN A DIFFERENT WAY.

AND THEN CAME THE MISERY. I CALLED TO A NEARBY CLASSMATE FOR HELP. HE RAN TO THE NEAREST TEACHER, SCREAMING FULL BLAST: "MASASHI'S BURIED IN POO!" I'LL NEVER FORGET WHAT HAPPENED NEXT... THE TEACHER REFUSED TO HELP ME. I GUESS SHE WAS AVERSE TO RURAL ARTIFACTS. TO MY RELIEF AND HER CREDIT, MY MOTHER THEN CAME TO THE RESCUE, LIFTING ME OUT OF MY PREDICAMENT WITHOUT HESITATION. IN THAT MOMENT I LEARNED AWE FOR THE LOVE OF A MOTHER.

TO THIS DAY WHEN A YAM CROSSES MY PATH, IT BRINGS ME BACK TO THAT EVENT. AND NOW THE MORAL (IN TWO PARTS): NO GOOD EVER COMES FROM BEING CAUGHT UP WITH THINGS; AND WHEN IT COMES TO IT, MOTHERS ARE BRAVE!

Number 215: Gaara of the Sand

SHF

...

DRUP

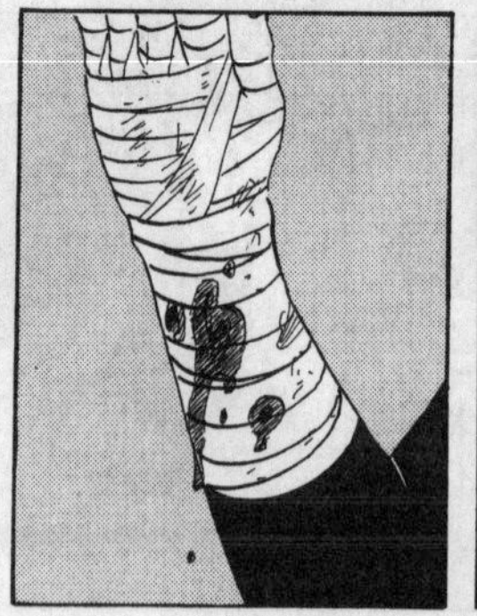

I'LL HANDLE THIS.
!

...
ARGH!!
FLOMP
SWUP

WIP
OH C'MON, LET GO!
TUG TUG

!!
UNH
THROB

SHK
SHK
YOU'RE IN NO SHAPE TO FIGHT.

SSS
!
SHK
SHK
I'LL HANDLE THIS.

GAARA OF THE SAND...
SO AS THE NAME SUGGESTS, YOU ARE OF THE SAND.

HE ATTACKS WITH HIS BONES!
LIKE YOU SAW, HE FIRES THEM OR JUTS THEM OUT OF HIS BODY.
IT'S AS AMAZING AS IT IS DISTURBING!!

SSS

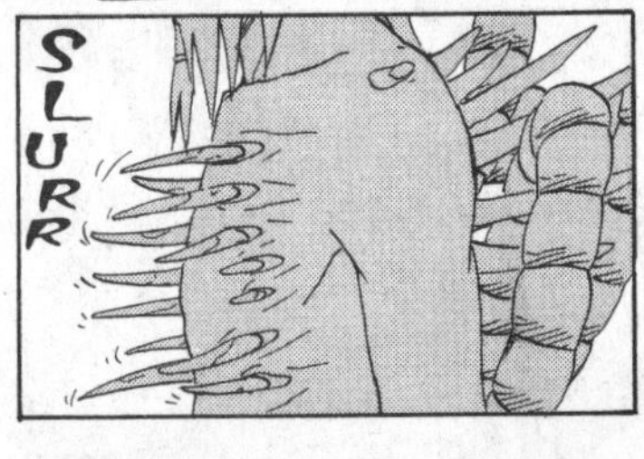
SLURR

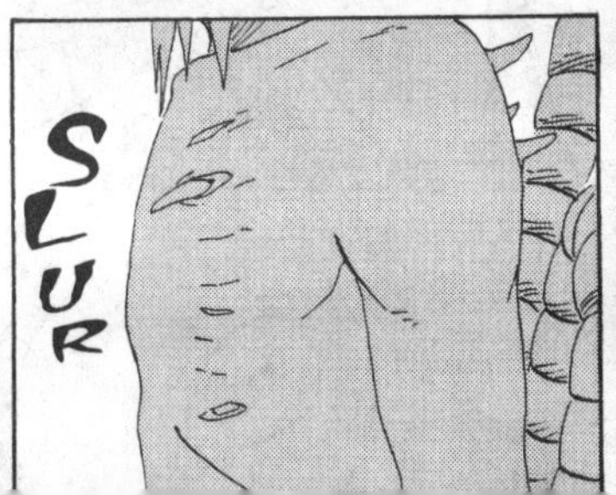
SLUR

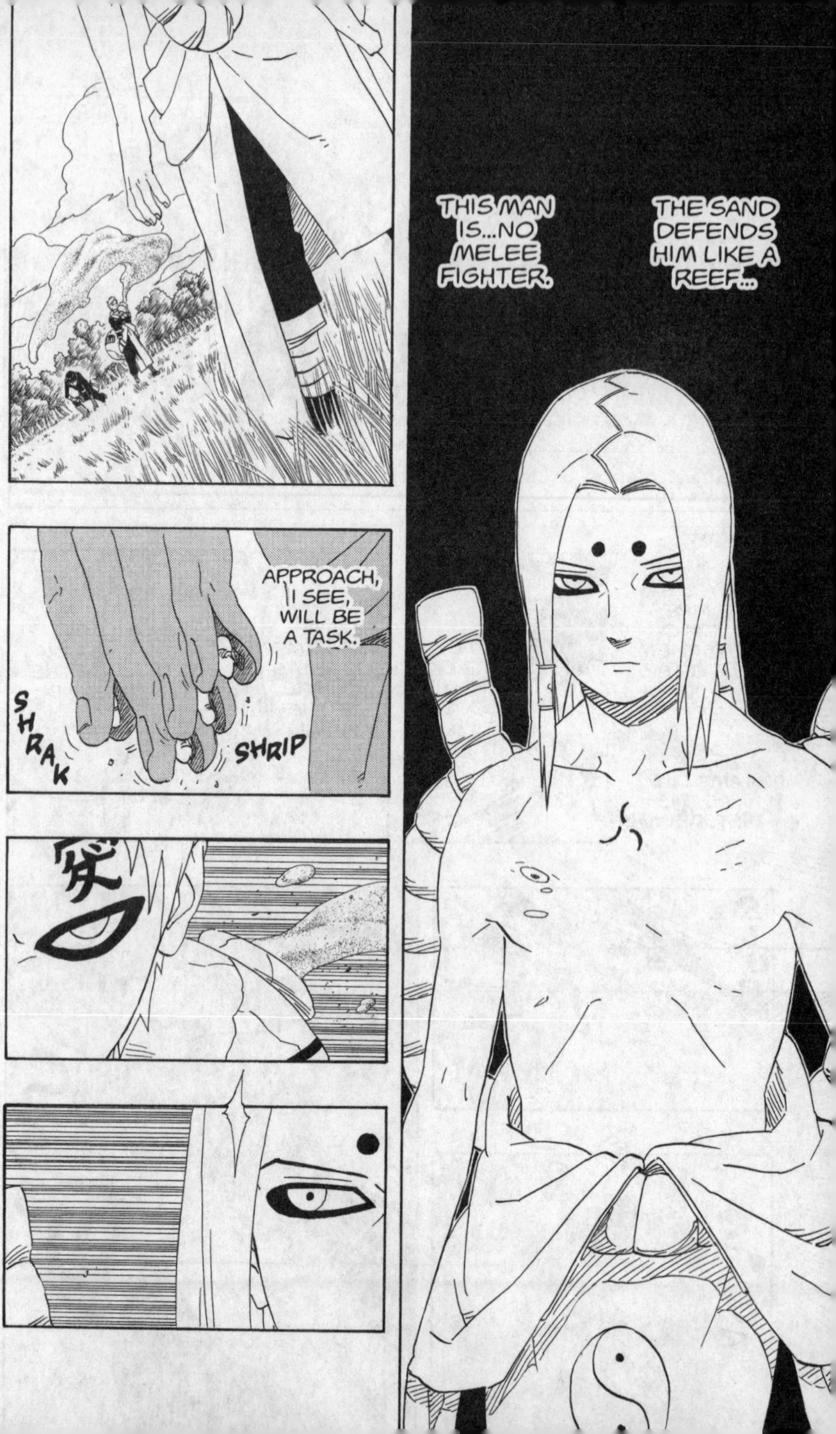

THE SAND DEFENDS HIM LIKE A REEF...
THIS MAN IS...NO MELEE FIGHTER.

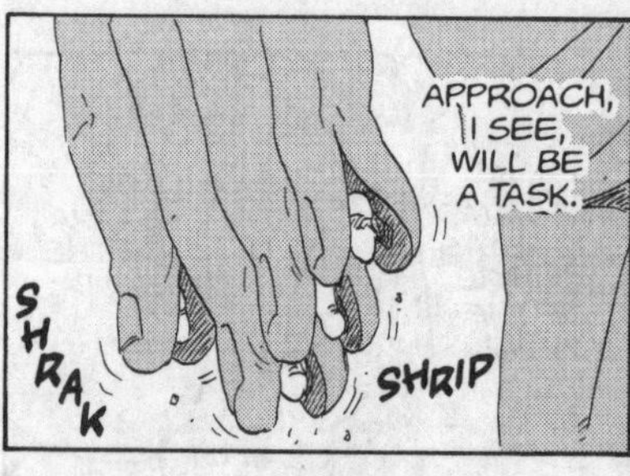
APPROACH, I SEE, WILL BE A TASK.
SHRAK
SHRIP

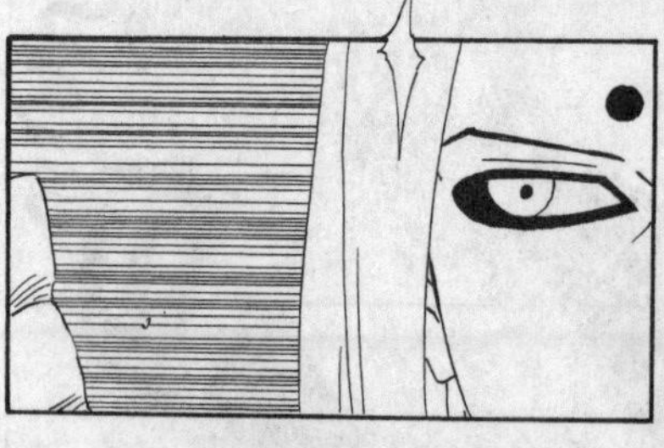

READ THIS WAY
TUP
FWOOSH
FWOOM
!

KRAK

HE'S A MASTER.
THERE'S NO WASTE TO HIS MOVEMENT.
!!

!

FSSH

TUP

WOOP
SHOOM

WOOM
SH
TAK
TAK
TAK

?!
SHISH
SHISH
SO LONG AS I HAVE SAND...
I CAN DO ANYTHING.
SHF
...!

PAK PAK PAK PAK PAK PAK PAK
!!

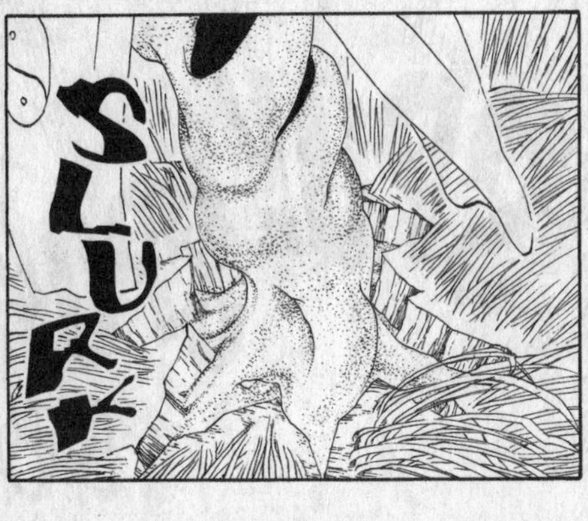
SLURP

TELL ME AGAIN WHO'S STUPID.
MAKING SAND FROM SOIL IS NO ART.

OF COURSE! HE CAN GRIND THE ROCKS AND MINERALS IN THE SOIL INTO SAND, USING HIS OWN.
HE'S NOT CALLED GAARA OF THE SAND FOR NOTHING. NOW THAT'S TALENT!!

SSSSS
YOU GOT HIM!
NOT JUST YET.

SABAKU-SÔSÔ! IMPLODING SAND FUNERAL!!
RIK
SPUK SPUK
SPUK
SPUK

READ THIS WAY

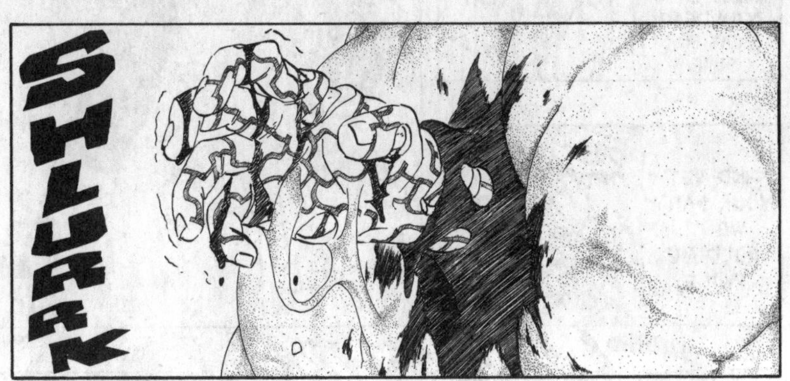

MORE BONES, HUH? HE'S A REAL FREAK, ISN'T HE...
HE'S CERTAINLY A NUISANCE.

THAT PRES-SURE WAS A FEAT.

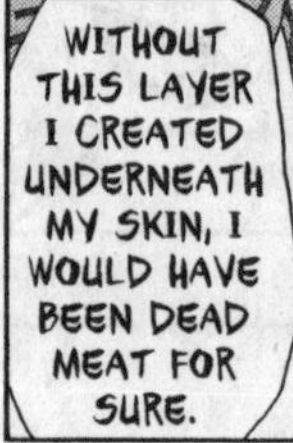
WITHOUT THIS LAYER I CREATED UNDERNEATH MY SKIN, I WOULD HAVE BEEN DEAD MEAT FOR SURE.

I UNDERES-TIMATED YOU...

AND YET YOUR SAND WON'T HOLD ME TWICE.

SHRK SHRK
SHRK
SHRK SHRK
TUMP

FOOF

SHA

WHOOSH
!!

GAH!!
SWASH
HSSS
SWSS
SWORSH

SWASSH

YOU... YOU DID IT...
NOT YET.
SHF

BAFF

SABAKU TAISÔ! TOTAL SAND FUNERAL!!
SHAKUNK
WHOA...!

...

WOW... WHAT A GUY...
HE'S EVEN STRONGER THAN WHEN I FOUGHT HIM...

WON'T HE EVER GIVE UP?
HUH?!

...?!

SLURK
SLURK

Number 216: Halberd and Shield...!!

SLURK

SLURK

...
WHAT IS THAT?!

FWOSH

SHOOSH

READ THIS WAY
SW UK
PFAF
SABAKUKYÛ! THE COFFIN OF CRUSHING SAND!
RIK
TUMP
SLURR
SKUSH
KRUP
MMF
SKASHOOSH
SPAP
THOP
TAK TAK

SHA

ZWOO
WHAT IS THAT FORM?!
?!!
愛
BAFF
SHUNK
PFOOF

SKASSH

!!

SsSss
BLOOF

IS THIS ALL THERE IS TO YOUR SO-CALLED TOTAL DEFENSE?

WHAT A JOKE.

...!
RRG...

...!

PLIK
PLIK

I SEE...
SO YOU COAT YOURSELF WITH SAND...
!
FSSH
HE'S NOT YOUR ONLY OPPONENT!
I'M HERE TOO!!
KAPOW
!
!
KWAH
PFOOF!!

SPOONG
WHOA!!

...

BOFF
UGH!

THIS SAND'S A NUISANCE...
YOU'RE THE FIRST TO GO... GAARA!

THROB
MY BODY'S STILL... I'LL ONLY GET IN THE WAY...
URG...

READ THIS WAY

SHRUK

SPUP

SLUR

...!

!

SLURR

SLURRGE
TESSENKA NO MAI! IRON FLOWER DANCE!!

DID HE JUST PULL OUT HIS... SPINE?!
VINE!
SHAA
PFOOF
SNAP
KRAK
KRAK
POFF
POFF
POFF
SKRIK

...

FLOWER!

SLURR

KRAK RAK
SLURR
KRAK
MY BONES HAVE CALCIFIED AS FAR AS THEY'LL GO.
THEY'LL PIERCE THROUGH YOUR BODY ALONG WITH THE SAND SHIELD.

KOOM

TOTAL SAND DEFENSE! SHUKAKU'S SHIELD!

KABUTO...
HOW MUCH LONGER WILL KIMIMARO LAST?

HE SHOULD BE FINE FOR A WHILE YET.

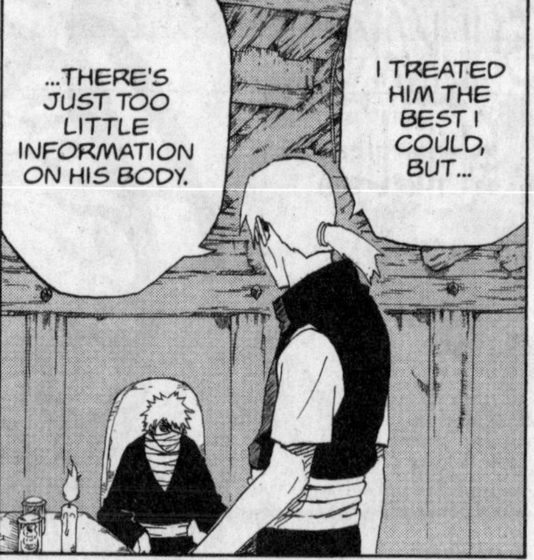
I TREATED HIM THE BEST I COULD, BUT...
...THERE'S JUST TOO LITTLE INFORMATION ON HIS BODY.

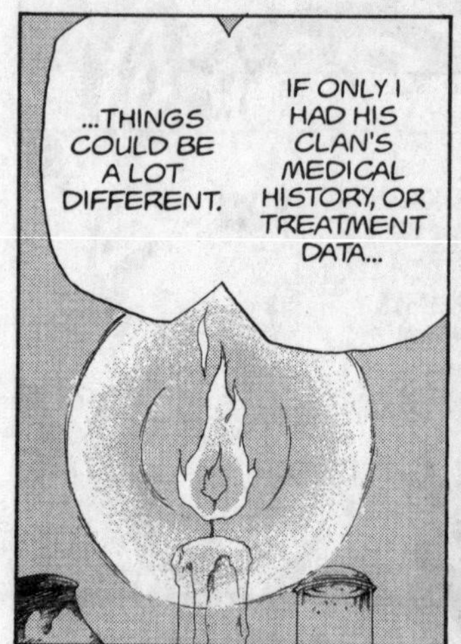
IF ONLY I HAD HIS CLAN'S MEDICAL HISTORY, OR TREATMENT DATA...
...THINGS COULD BE A LOT DIFFERENT.

READ
THIS
WAY

THE ONLY THING I COULD DIG UP WAS AN ACCOUNT OF HOW HE FOUND HIMSELF THE LAST OF THE KAGUYA CLAN.
IT'S JUST THE LAST STOP IN A BLOODY HISTORY.

...

THE WHOLE FOOLISH CLAN WAS WIPED OUT WHEN IT CHALLENGED...
...THE GREAT NATION OF KIRIGAKURE, ON THEIR OWN.

THEN YOU RESCUED ONLY THE YOUNGEST AND MOST PROMISING OF THE LOT.
THE LAST OF THE CLAN.

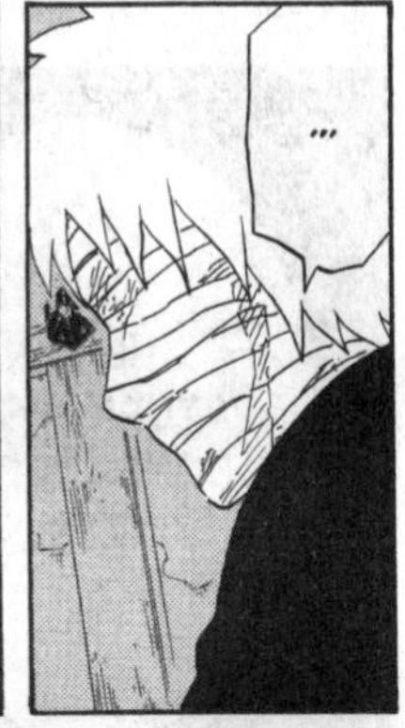
...

THE KAGUYA CLAN WAS A CLUTCH OF RABBLE, KNOWING ONLY THE THIRST FOR WAR.
BY WHAT I SAW OF THEM, THE BATTLEFIELD WAS THE ONLY PLACE THEY COULD FIND THEIR PEACE.

BUT THE ERA OF BLOOD-THIRSTY BEAST HERDS HAS LONG PASSED.
THE TIMES HAVE CHANGED.

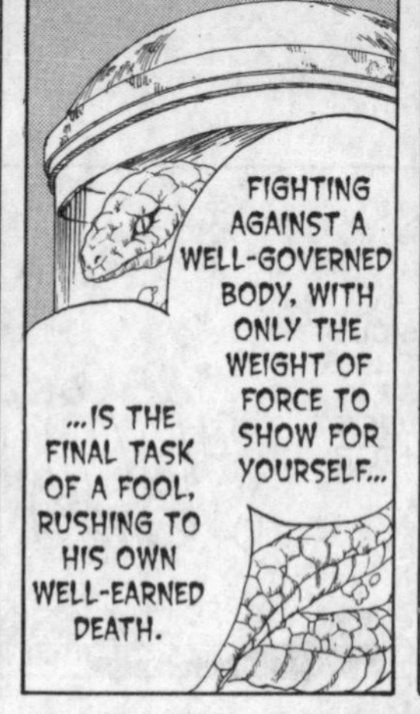
FIGHTING AGAINST A WELL-GOVERNED BODY, WITH ONLY THE WEIGHT OF FORCE TO SHOW FOR YOURSELF...
...IS THE FINAL TASK OF A FOOL, RUSHING TO HIS OWN WELL-EARNED DEATH.

AND YET...
...YOU THOUGHT IT A WASTE TO LET HIM DIE.

...

HMPH... WHO COULD RESIST HIS RARE KEKKEI GENKAI?
THOSE STRONG, FIRM BONES...
A DEFENSIVE SKILL TO FEND PHYSICAL BLOWS OF ANY FORM...

HIS OFFENSE IS EXCELLENT...
...HE CAN TURN HIS BONES INTO PIKES.

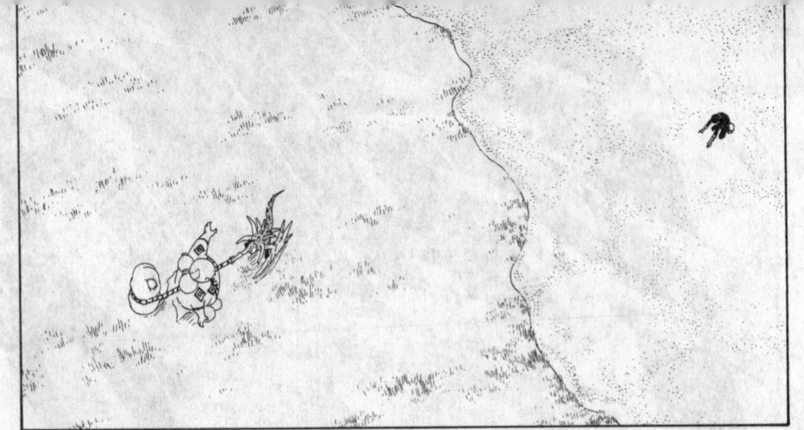

HIS SAND SHIELD TRULY IS THE PERFECT DEFENSE... IT TAKES NO MORE THAN ONE FIGHT TO SEE THAT...
...AND WITH THAT UNUSUAL FORM IT'S TAKEN... YES! HE'LL BE FINE! NOTHING COULD POSSIBLY PENETRATE THAT...

!

SHOOOM

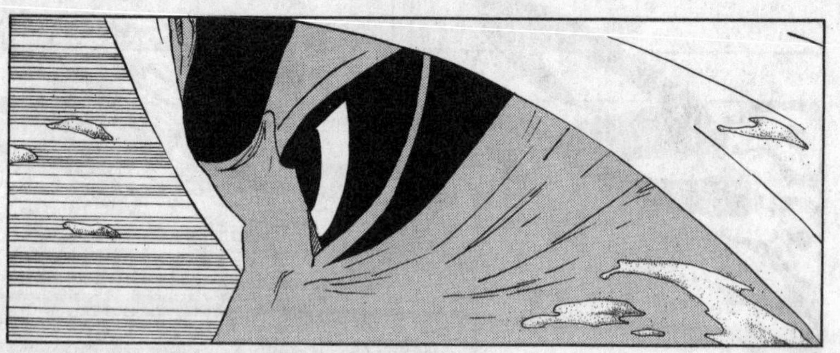

MEET KISHIMOTO MASASHI'S ASSISTANTS PART 8

ANOTHER YOUNG ASSISTANT HAS JOINED THE NARUTO STAFF. LATELY I'M BEGINNING TO FEEL THE AGE DIFFERENCE WITH MY ASSISTANTS. I GUESS I'M AN OLD MAN NOW.

ASSISTANT NO. 8: ITAKURA YÛICHI

PROFILE

- THE YOUNGEST ASSISTANT IN OUR WORKPLACE; THEREFORE, UNABLE TO KEEP UP WITH THE OTHERS' *GUNDAM* CHAT.
- LAUGHS IN A HIGHLY AFFECTED WAY, SIMILAR TO THAT OF MUROMACHI-ERA NOH THEATRE.
- VERY KNOWLEDGEABLE ABOUT *TRANSFORMERS: MYSTERY OF CONVOY*, FOR THE FAMICOM.
- CONVERSATION WITH OUR NO. 1 ASSISTANT, MR. TAKAHASHI, IS STILL AWKWARD. (DOESN'T HAVE THE HANG OF IT YET.)
- EATS VERY LITTLE.
- LOOKS LIKE HE WANTS US TO HURRY UP AND HOLD HIM A WELCOMING PARTY.
- IS A SWEET AND KINDHEARTED BOY.

Number 217: For The Most Precious

KRAK
KRAK
RAK

READ THIS WAY

...!!

VERY SOLID...

I PULLED TOGETHER THE DENSEST MINERALS IN THE SOIL...
...USED MY CHAKRA TO APPLY PRESSURE, AND KNEADED THEM INTO THE SAND.

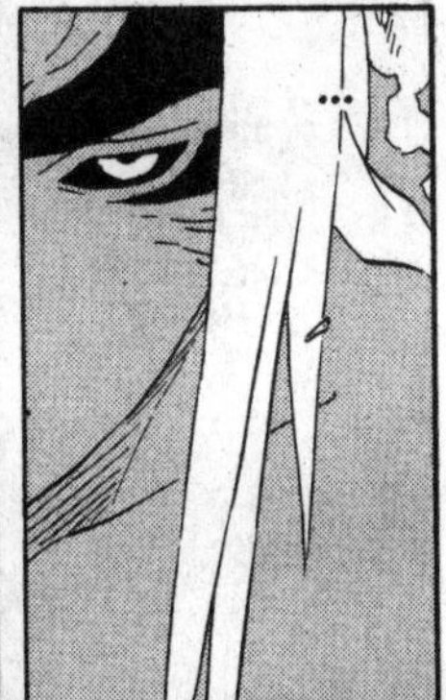
...

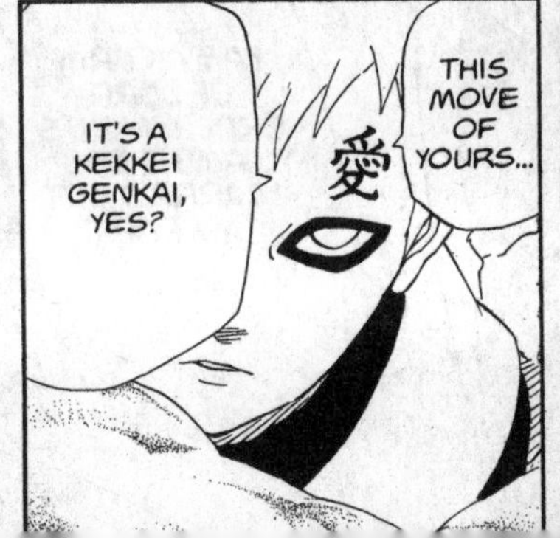
THIS MOVE OF YOURS...
IT'S A KEKKEI GENKAI, YES?

IT IS OF THE KAGUYA CLAN...
...A POWER I ALONE POSSESS.

...

SO YOU'RE THE LAST OF THE KAGUYA...
THAT MEANS TODAY THE CLAN PERISHES.

INDEED IT MAY BE SO...
...MY BODY IS RAVAGED WITH ILLNESS... MY DAYS ON EARTH...
...ARE NUM-BERED.

AND YET...I WILL NOT BE EXTIN-GUISHED.
FOR I AM NOT ALONE.

I AM AN ARM OF LORD OROCHIMARU'S AMBITION. I CARRIED OUT MY PART.
FOR THAT, I SHALL REMAIN FOREVER IN HIS HEART.

READ
THIS
WAY

...

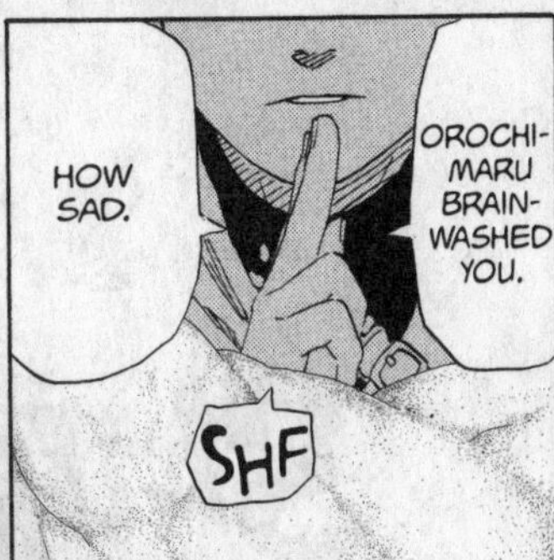
OROCHIMARU BRAINWASHED YOU.
HOW SAD.
SHF

!

SLURK

FWIP
I'VE DONE TOO MANY BIG MOVES... CHAKRA IS GETTING PRECIOUS.
THIS IS IT.

...!!
SSS
SLURGE

SLURSHHH

HOW MUCH CHAKRA IS HE USING...
...?!

SPLURP

SPLUP
YOU ARE INDEED FORMIDA-BLE...

READ THIS WAY

I'M SUCKING YOU DOWN AND BURYING YOU TWO HUNDRED METERS DOWN.
WITH THAT SAND PRESSURE ON EVERY INCH OF YOUR BODY, YOU WON'T BE ABLE TO MOVE A FINGER.

...
SPLURRP

...

YOU DID IT...
THIS TIME, YOU... REALLY DID IT.

...

SAWARABI NO MAI!
BRACKEN DANCE!

PA SPAK SPAK SPAK
!!
THOK THOK THOK THOK
THAK THAK
!

READ THIS WAY

SHOULDN'T HE BE HERE BY NOW?

DRIP

I'M GETTING IMPATIENT.
A WATCHED KETTLE NEVER BOILS.

KABUTO... DO NOT PATRONIZE ME.
I'M SORRY...
IT'S JUST THAT... LORD OROCHIMARU, YOU KNOW.
IT DOESN'T MATTER WHO STANDS IN HIS WAY...
THERE'S NOBODY WHO COULD OVERCOME KIMIMARO.

YOU... YOU SAVED ME.

I NEVER IMAGINED YOU COULD DO SOMETHING LIKE THIS.

THIS IS THE SAME SAND I'M ALWAYS THROWING AROUND...

IT'S JUST IN HOW YOU USE IT.

FWUP FWUP

HUF

FWUP

HUF

I'M NOT BRAIN-WASHED...

KRAK KAK

HE'S THE ONLY ONE WHO TRULY UNDERSTANDS.

SLUR

!!

...!

...?!
WHA...

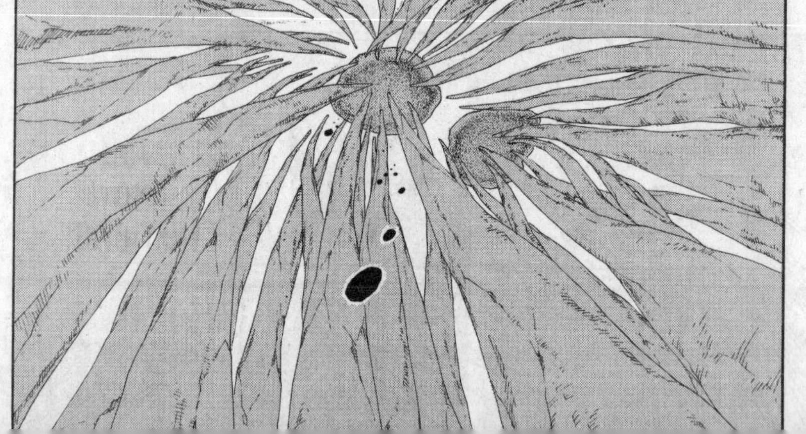

READ
THIS
WAY

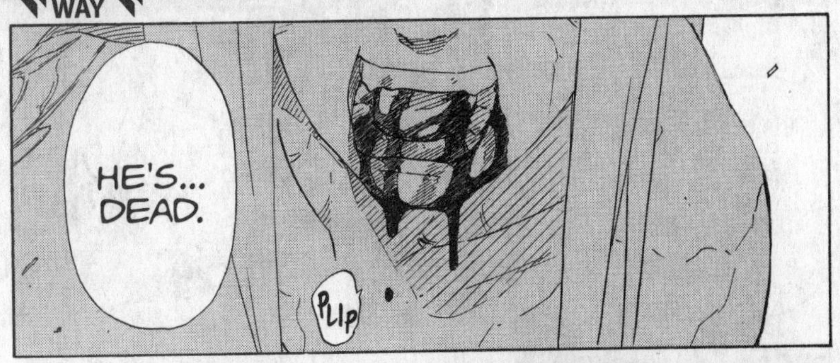
HE'S... DEAD.
PLIP

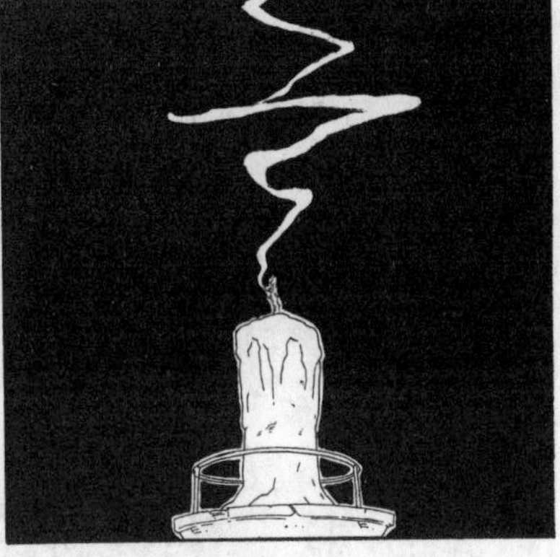

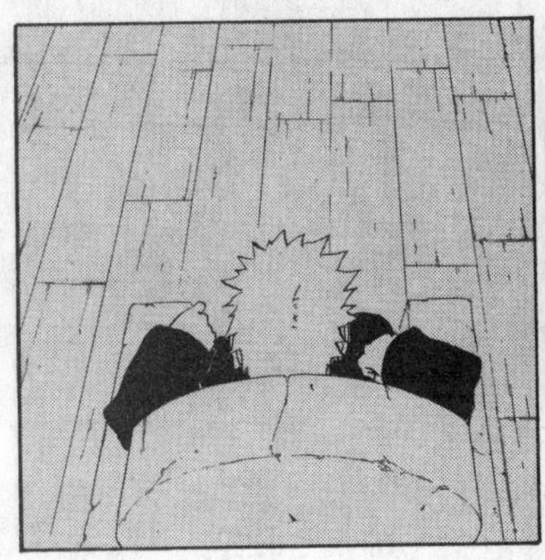

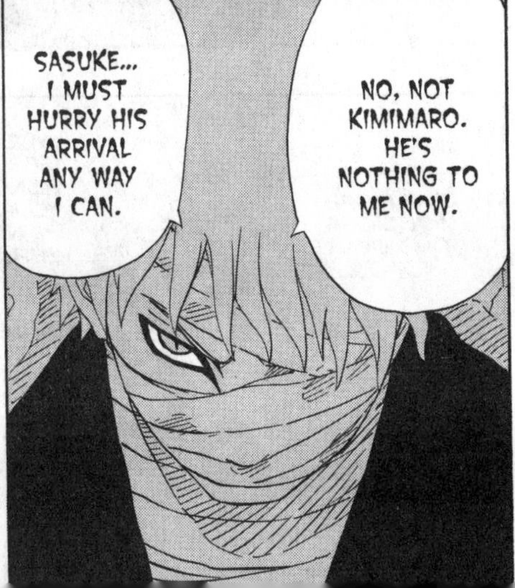
NO, NOT KIMIMARO. HE'S NOTHING TO ME NOW.
SASUKE... I MUST HURRY HIS ARRIVAL ANY WAY I CAN.

HE WILL FIND ME. OR I WILL FIND HIM FIRST!

HE HAD ME...
THAT'S NOT TRUE.

MY MASTER ALWAYS USED TO SAY...
...A BIG PART OF SKILL IS LUCK.
YOU MEAN THAT MEDDLE-SOME TRAINER?

HE WASN'T MEDDLING!
HE JUST KNEW I WASN'T STRONG ENOUGH, WAS ALL!
DON'T TALK ABOUT MY MASTER THAT WAY!!

YOU'RE THE SAME, THEN.
THE MORE PRECIOUS YOUR IDOL IS TO YOU...
WHEN YOU FEEL THE HONOR OF YOUR IDOL UNDER SCRUTINY...
YOU BECOME ENRAGED... AS IF IT WERE YOUR OWN HONOR BEING QUESTIONED.

READ THIS WAY

...!

I WILL NOT BE EXTIN-GUISHED ...
FOR I AM NOT ALONE. FOR THAT, I SHALL REMAIN FOR-EVER IN HIS HEART.

HE'S THE ONLY ONE WHO TRULY UNDER-STANDS.
KRAK KAK
SLUR

YOU KNOW NOTHING!!

...THE HARDER YOU FIGHT FOR HIM.

HE ALSO...
...REMINDS ME OF UZUMAKI NARUTO.

?!
STILL...
JUST BECAUSE SOMEONE'S PRECIOUS DOESN'T MEAN HE IS GOOD.
I CAN'T SEE HOW ANYONE COULD THINK SOMEONE BAD WAS SO PRECIOUS.

I DIS-AGREE.
EVEN IF YOU KNOW HE'S EVIL...
...YOU JUST CAN'T OVERCOME YOUR OWN SOLITUDE.
...

SHK
TUP
TUP
TUP

SWASSH

SASUKE!!

HUF
HUF
SHHK
PLIP

HUF
HUF

SWOOSH

IN THE NEXT VOLUME...

BONDS

As the battle between Naruto and Sasuke grows even more heated, Sasuke delves deep into the past to recall how his brother Itachi became such a feared ninja. Unwilling to do what Itachi instructs he must do in order to obtain the power of the Mangekyo, Sasuke flees the site of battle. Naruto reluctantly agrees to give up chasing Sasuke and begins training under Jiraiya.

NARUTO 3-IN-1 EDITION VOLUME 9 AVAILABLE NOW!

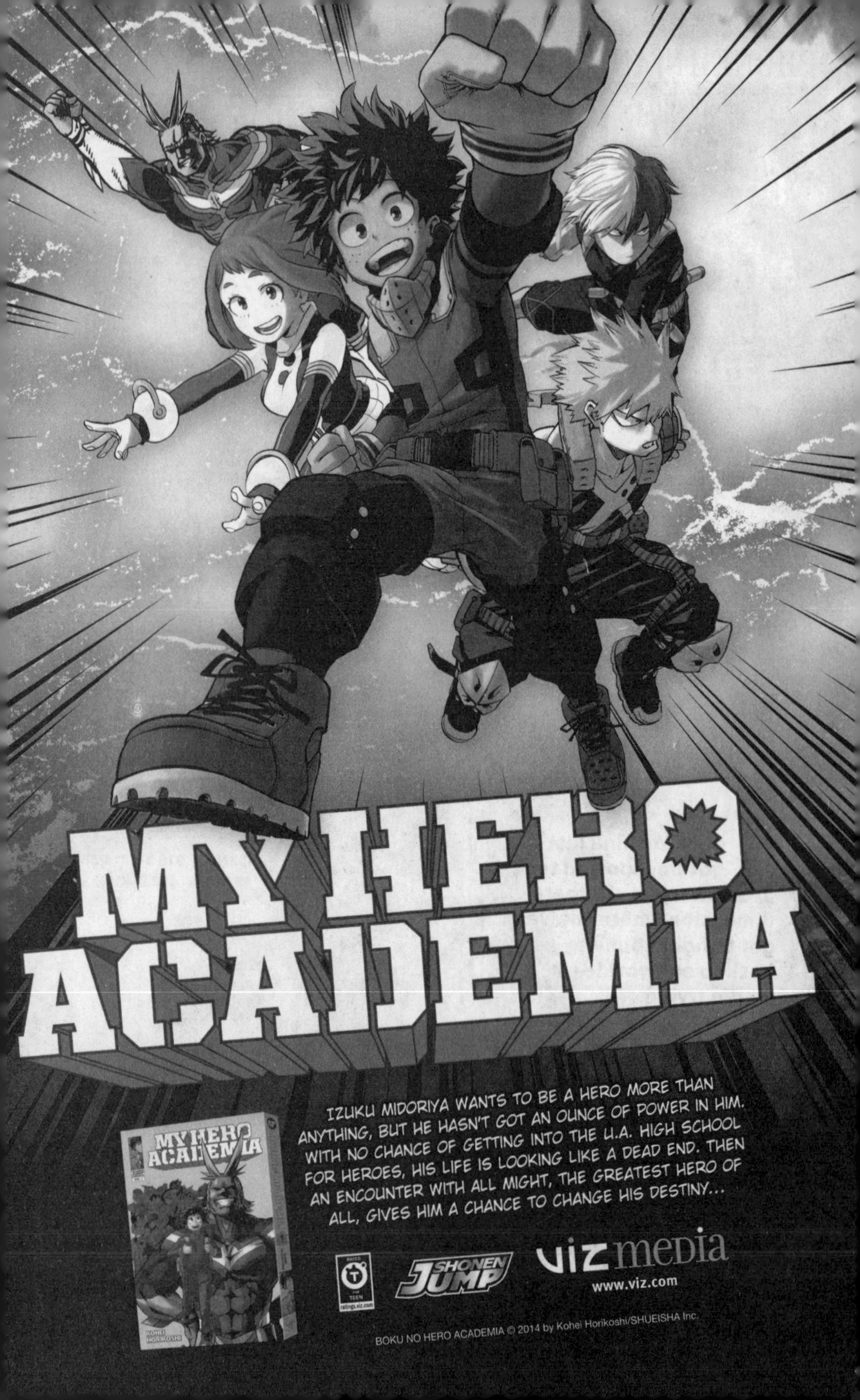

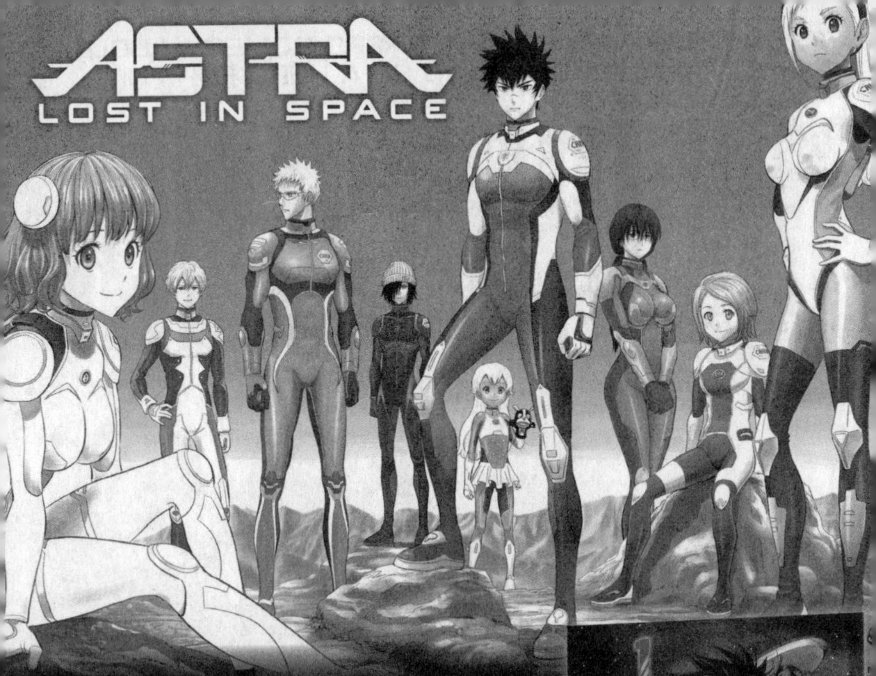

ASTRA
LOST IN SPACE

CAN EIGHT TEENAGERS FIND THEIR WAY HOME FROM 5,000 LIGHT-YEARS AWAY?

It's the year 2063, and interstellar space travel has become the norm. Eight students from Caird High School and one child set out on a routine planet camp excursion. While there, the students are mysteriously transported 5,000 light-years away to the middle of nowhere! Will they ever make it back home?!

Ruby, Weiss, Blake and Yang are students at Beacon Academy, learning to protect the world of Remnant from the fearsome Grimm!
RWBY
MANGA BY Shirow Miwa
BASED ON THE ROOSTER TEETH SERIES
CREATED BY Monty Oum
RATED T TEEN
VIZ
viz.com
RWBY © 2017 Rooster Teeth Productions, LLC
© 2015 by Shirow Miwa/SHUEISHA Inc.